P9-DDU-537

the
BACKWASH SQUEEZE
& Other Improbable Feats

the
BACKWASH SQUEEZE
& Other Improbable Feats

A Newcomer's Journey into the
WORLD of BRIDGE

EDWARD McPHERSON

HarperCollins*Publishers*

THE BACKWASH SQUEEZE AND OTHER IMPROBABLE FEATS. Copyright © 2007 by Edward McPherson. All rights reserved. Printed in the United States of America. No part of this book may be used or reproduced in any manner whatsoever without written permission except in the case of brief quotations embodied in critical articles and reviews. For information, address Harper-Collins Publishers, 10 East 53rd Street, New York, NY 10022.

HarperCollins books may be purchased for educational, business, or sales promotional use. For information, please write: Special Markets Department, HarperCollins Publishers, 10 East 53rd Street, New York, NY 10022.

FIRST EDITION

Designed by Laura Lindgren

Library of Congress Cataloging-in-Publication Data is available upon request.

ISBN: 978-0-06-112764-9
ISBN-10: 0-06-112764-7

07 08 09 10 11   NMSG/RRD   10 9 8 7 6 5 4 3 2 1

For Heather

CONTENTS

ACKNOWLEDGMENTS

Above all, I must thank Heather for her love, guidance, and editorial insights, never mind her generous willingness to share the first year of our marriage with the dastardly Bridge Baron.

Similarly, my parents, sister, and grandparents all provided unyielding support.

I am indebted to my wise and patient agent, Emma Parry, as well as to Christy Fletcher, Kate Scherler, and the rest of the Fletcher & Parry crew. I also owe a great deal to my keen editor, John Williams, Jill Schwartzman, Jonathan Burnham, and the dedicated people at HarperCollins. As always, Walter Donohue and Esther Margolis were their usual magnanimous selves.

Last but clearly not least, I am grateful to Tina, a fun and forgiving bridge partner—and a great friend.

And while I hate acknowledgments that read like a high school yearbook, this book benefited from the help of many wonderful people, all of whom gave their time, expertise, food, and drink freely—often for no particular fondness for me, but for their deep love of the game. For that my thanks go to: Bud and Sherry Larson, Taylor Hamra, Adeline Hamra, Hampton and Rachel Richards, Jesús Arias, Jeff Hearn, Jeff Bayone, Tommy Ng, Irma Schulman, Lisanne Clapp, Michael Polowan, The Girls, Bob Yellis, Josephine Stayman, Choire Sicha, Julio Espada, Joshua Goldfarb, Sharon Osberg, Warren Buffett, Gail Greenberg, Maclear Jacoby Jr., Bob Hamman, Bart Bramley, Justin Lall, Chuck and Marti Malcolm, Marlene and Bill Wass, Judy Nolan, Bruce Reeve,

Jay Bates, Darleen Boone, Rob Meckstroth, the Gatlinburg caddies, Greg Keidan, Bob and Lynn Blanchard, Hillary S. Pratte, Zia Mahmood, Andrew Robson, Susanna Gross, Neil Mendoza, Samantha Weinberg, Jean Hartman, Holly Giles, Jeff Meckstroth, Harriette Buckman, Dick Anderson, Linda Granell, and Ruth Francis.

The Introduction I Am Not Qualified to Write: A Brief Bridge Tutorial

This introduction is to provide a brief—and wildly superficial—primer on bridge. If you are familiar with the game, feel free to skip it. Seriously. If you are new to bridge, you might want to skip it anyway and consult back as needed. There is nothing as discouraging and dull as having someone explain a game to you—especially one as brawling and exciting as bridge. It's a bit like trying to understand the thrill of flying a jet by leafing through a text on aerodynamics. This book won't teach you to play bridge, but maybe it will let you hear the roar of the exhaust. The game can only be picked up at the table; if you want to learn, get thee to a bridge club.

Bridge is a game of deep complexity and infinite mystery. Almost all bridge players, from the rankest of beginners to the greatest of pros, say part of the addiction is the game's inspiring—and maddening—refusal to be mastered. Bridge addicts typically regard other games as mere competitive sitting. One high-level player, who like many bridge buffs cut his teeth playing chess, told me, "Bridge is different than chess, where you can read a book and learn the first thirty moves—the queen's gambit, pawn-to-king-four, whatever—and get up to a certain level. Same thing for Scrabble; you study it and you recognize positions. Bridge is a game where you learn by experience, and experience takes many, many years. You might become a good chess player by the age of twelve, but you're not going to be a good bridge player." In bridge, you also are dependent on a partner. For this, and other reasons I will discuss later, computers can play high-level chess but not bridge. It is a different breed of animal.

So in a sense we are all equally beginners at bridge, though I guess, as the paraphrase goes, some players are more equal than others. When I started this project, I knew next to nothing. Thus this is not a book of great hands or dazzling plays, though in the course of my roughly yearlong investigation I have been an unwitting (and often unaware) witness to both. Pearls before swine, you might say. A note to all of my instructors: please hold your laughter until the end.

Basically, the game has two components: first comes *the auction,* then comes *the play.* I am going to put the horse in front of the cart and start with a short word about the play. Players compete in teams of two, sitting opposite their partner. For easy reference, each person is designated by one of the cardinal points: *North, South, East*, and *West.* As in the games Hearts and Spades (which might be more familiar to some readers), players collect tricks, or sets of four cards (one from each player). Once a card is put down (or led), players must follow suit in a clockwise fashion, the highest card winning the trick. If you cannot follow suit—i.e., hearts are led and you don't have any hearts—you can discard anything you want. If during the auction a suit was designated to be *trump,* you may trump (or *ruff*) the trick by playing a card from that suit. If no one else plays a higher trump, the trick is yours.

Now let's back up. After all fifty-two cards are dealt, the dealer commences what is called the auction, when players compete for the right to name a trump suit (spades, hearts, diamonds, or clubs) or play without any suit being trump (called *no-trump*). What makes the process an auction is that players are bidding on the number of tricks their side will take given a certain suit as trump. In essence, they are trying to predict what they hope will happen during the play. So a bid consists of a number and a suit—e.g., "one club." As there are thirteen tricks in every hand (fifty-two cards divided by four), the lowest legal bid a player can make is for his side to take seven tricks, or one more than the opponents. For that reason—and to simplify matters—a bid of "one club" does not commit your side to making one measly trick with clubs as trump, but seven of them. A bid of "two clubs," then, would promise to take eight tricks. A bid of "three no-trump" would be for nine tricks (without a trump suit). And so it goes up to the seven level—when you are bidding to take all thirteen tricks.

To facilitate the auction, the suits are arbitrarily ranked in ascending order from clubs to diamonds to hearts to spades—with "no-trump" highest of all. (Rather than memorize this, you can always remember the suits go in alphabetical order from lowest to highest.) Thus the bid "one heart" is higher than the bid "one club" but lower than "one no-trump." As with any auction, a new bid must exceed the previous one. That means over a bid of "one no-trump," the cheapest call that can be made is "two clubs"—followed by "two diamonds," "two hearts," "two spades," "two no-trump," "three clubs," "three diamonds," and so on. Of course players are under no obligation to bid incrementally up the line like that. After their partner's bid of "one heart," they may jump (or skip) to "three hearts." If a player does not wish to bid, he may *pass.* If all four players pass from the get-go, the hand is redealt.

After the first round of bidding, once three players have passed in a row, the auction is over, the last bid having named both the trump suit (or no-trump, as the case may be) and the minimum number of tricks the winners of the auction must take to avoid a penalty. The final bid is called the *contract.* One side is now on offense (i.e., trying to make the contract) and one side is on defense (trying to stop, or *set,* them).

Now it is time to play the hand as I previously described, although I originally oversimplified things a bit. In bridge, only three people ever play at one time. Whoever first named the trump suit (or lack thereof, if the contract is in "no-trump") is called the *declarer*. He gets to play both his and his partner's hand, which will be laid out on the table for all to see once the opening lead is made. In an uncharitable fashion, the exposed hand—and the person it belonged to, who is now generally out of the action—is called the *dummy*.

Okay, let's walk through a simple example. The cards are dealt. The player who dealt—let's call him North—gets to bid first. He opens the auction with a bid of "one spade." His left-hand opponent, East, bids "two clubs." His partner, South, jumps to "four spades," which is too rich for West's blood, who passes. After North and East also pass, the auction ends. The contract is set at four spades, meaning North and South must make ten tricks with spades as trump. Note that even though South was the one who made the final bid ("four spades"), his partner, North, is the declarer *since he was the first to mention spades* (with his "one-spade" bid). South is the dummy. After the person on the declarer's left makes the opening lead (in this case East), South lays out his hand (arranged by suits) on the table. After thinking for a while, North picks the card he wants to play from South's hand. Then West plays. Then North plays from his own hand—and the first trick is over. Whoever played the highest card won it, and now that person leads into the second trick.

Once all thirteen tricks have been played, and the contract has either been made or set, the score is recorded. Bridge scoring is complicated and differs slightly depending on how you are playing. Basically, you get points for making your contract—and for every trick above and beyond that—while your opponents get points for every trick they set you. Thus if you bid four spades and take eleven tricks, you get points for making your contract (ten tricks) plus extra for the *overtrick*. But if you make only nine tricks, your opponents get points for setting you by one trick (called an *undertrick*).

There are two more bids left to discuss. If your opponents doubt you can make your contract, they can bid a *double* at the end of the auction, which increases both the rewards and the penalties for either making or going down in the contract, thus raising the stakes on the hand. If you are extremely confident that the opponents have doubled unwisely, you can then *redouble*, which ups the ante even more.

And now a vague word on scoring. Basically, in bridge the goal is to score a *game*, or one hundred points. Each trick you take is worth a certain amount, but only those tricks you have contracted for count toward making your game. Because hearts and spades are the two higher suits—and score better—they are called the *major suits*. Clubs and diamonds are called the *minor suits*. The two major suits score the same, as do the two minors. No-trump outscores them all (thus one no-trump scores more than one heart or one spade, which scores more than one club or one diamond). A seven-level contract, one that would promise to take all thirteen tricks, is called a *grand slam*. Taking all but one trick is called a *small slam* (or sometimes simply a *slam*). There are scoring bonuses for both.

The two kinds of bridge I will be discussing are *rubber bridge* and *duplicate bridge*. A *rubber of bridge* is simply the best of three games, with a game being the usual accumulation of one hundred points. After a side has won two games, the rubber is over. Some contracts can score a game in a single hand; other times it takes a few deals. When a side wins a game, they get a bonus. That bonus—and any points for making overtricks or for setting the opponents in their contracts—is tallied separately from the amount needed to reach one hundred.

After one side has won a game—and thus needs only one more to end the rubber—they are said to be *vulnerable*. In general, that means the rewards and penalties for making or missing tricks are increased. For example, an undertrick that normally would be worth fifty points is worth one hundred points if your opponents are vulnerable. If both sides have won a game, then both are considered vulnerable. While vulnerability strictly only effects the scoring—the play of the game remains unchanged—whether or not your side is vulnerable usually tempers your strategy. Most players bid more cautiously when they're vulnerable, and take more risks when they are not.

When someone wins two games, the rubber is over and all the points are added up. I should point out that rubber bridge is often—but not always—played for stakes, and some people use the term broadly to mean bridge played for money.

Duplicate bridge is the more formal tournament version of the game. It is designed to allow a number of pairs to compete against each other by factoring out the luck of the deal. In a duplicate game, all tables play the same cards under the same conditions, which allows scores to be compared. It no longer matters what cards you get, but what you do with them. In duplicate bridge, each hand is scored separately, with no points carried forward. Whether your side is vulnerable is artificially assigned and rotates around the table.

But enough about scoring, because you need to marshal all your wits to focus on the *bidding*. Perhaps now is a good time for a nap and a cup of coffee. What follows will be brief and hopefully painless, but no doubt will demonstrate why bridge cannot—despite the enthusiastic entreaties of my cheerfully clueless friends—be taught in a night.

In the bidding, players use a highly detailed prearranged code to communicate to each other the strength and shape of their hand, a process by which they hopefully will land in a sound contract. When you are learning bridge, everyone tells you it is best to consider bidding as a foreign language, an idiom with its own grammar and syntax that will confuse the hell out of you the first time you hear it. This is true. Beginner bidding is not unlike ordering food in a strange land; you think you've settled on pizza (clubs), but instead you get squid (spades). To make matters worse, there are many languages, or systems, that you can bid in. In other words, a bid of "one no-trump" might mean something different to a British person than it would to an American, because there are plenty of complete bidding systems that people with more time and brainpower than I have devised over the years. The French have a system known as *la Majeure Cinquième*, the Poles have their *Polish Club*, and the British play something called *Acol*. These are just a few of the systems out there. Somewhere, someone is always dreaming up a new one—not all of them good. In the United States, the most basic system is known as *Standard American*, and that's mainly what I will be using in this book.

During the auction, players try to describe their hand to their partner. Unfortunately, they can't blurt out, "I have good cards and lots of spades." They have to relay that information in bridge language, with a bid. But how to quantitatively evaluate the strength of a hand? One method (popularized by a man named Charles Goren) relies on attributing *points* to your cards. An ace is worth four points, a king three, a queen two, and a jack one. Adding up the points in your hand gives you a numerical representation of how good it is. For example, if you hold two aces, a king, and a jack, you have twelve so-called *high-card points*. As there is one ace, king, queen, and jack in each of the four suits, there are forty points in a deck.

As the auction progresses, and players respond to their partners' bids, they often reevaluate their hands based on the distribution of their cards—that is, how many spades they have, how many hearts they have, and so on. Depending on how the auction goes, you might be able to give yourself extra points for having only one, two—or even no—cards in a suit (called a *singleton*, a *doubleton*, or a *void*). You may give yourself points for having a very long advantageous suit. This is an important part of the game, as not everything is aces, kings, queens, and jacks. The distribution of the suits can be quite powerful. To use a simplistic example, if the bridge gods smile on me and one day I am dealt all thirteen cards in a suit from the ace to the two (at the Do-Not-Pass-Go-But-Move-Directly-to-Las-Vegas odds of one in 158,753,389,900), even though I have only ten high-card points (an ace, a king, a queen, and a jack), I will take all thirteen tricks—provided my suit is trump.

The first clue that someone has a good hand is that they are able to *open the auction*—or make the first bid rather than "pass." What that bid is depends on the strength of that hand and the distribution of the suits. For example, in so-called Standard American bidding, an opening bid of one no-trump "announces" that you have between fifteen to seventeen points and a fairly evenly distributed (or *balanced*) hand—meaning that your shortest suit has at least two cards in it, and that you have at most only one such short suit. It is a very descriptive bid. Other opening bids are more nebulous. An opening bid of a major suit—either one heart or one spade—says you have at least twelve points and at least five cards in that suit. An opening bid of a minor suit—either one club or one diamond—signifies you have at least twelve points and at least three cards in that suit.

Once someone has opened the auction, it is up to his partner to respond. Usually, with less than six points in his hand, a player passes; with six points or more, he responds. What the player bids might say something about whether he likes the suit his partner opened and/or how many points he has. For example, if your partner opens one heart and you respond two hearts, you are offering lukewarm support, saying that while you have at least three hearts, you have only between six to nine points. If instead of bidding hearts you bid a new suit—for example, one spade—you are saying you have at least six points (but maybe more) and at least four spades.

Of course these are only oversimplified examples. In practice, bidding is an imperfect science. Players fudge their point counts all the time, opening and responding "light" or "heavy." Beyond that, many people wouldn't even agree with my basic parameters; for example, I say you need at least twelve points to open the bidding with a major or a minor suit, but some Standard Americans think you need thirteen. And of course auctions are rarely so one-sided. The opponents have an annoying tendency to get in the way, bidding their suits and pushing the auction out of your range. When an opponent bids immediately after you—for example, you open one heart and your left-hand opponent bids one spade—it is called an *overcall.* When both sides are bidding, making overcalls and interfering in other ways, life gets complicated and the game gets interesting. In general, you need to know your side has a fair amount of points to keep bidding at the higher levels.

So far, the bids I have described would be considered *natural.* That means when you bid a heart, you are actually saying something about hearts. But as systems get more sophisticated, many bids become *artificial,* and they complicate matters. To their overall arsenal, a partnership can add a number of special agreements called *conventions.* Basically, a convention is a pre-arranged understanding between partners that a certain bid (or play) in a particular situation has a meaning beyond what might be obvious to the opponents.

For example, starting the auction off with *an opening bid of two clubs* does not mean what it sounds like—that you have a lot of clubs. Instead, it means you have a whopping hand with at least twenty-two high-card points. This is the definition of a two-club opening. It is purely a convention, or agreement, between partners. I would call it a code, but secrets are not allowed at the bridge table, or at least in terms of what bids mean. If you are using an unusual convention, you must explain it to your opponents. You can lie *with* your bid (which is sometimes called a *psych* or *psychic bid*)—e.g., bid one no-trump without the requisite number of points (fifteen to seventeen)—but you can't lie *about* your bid (e.g., tell your opponents that in your system one no-trump means you have exactly nineteen points and the jack of clubs). The auction is supposed to be transparent.

The artificial two-club opening is straightforward. Other conventions are slightly more involved. For example, after you open one no-trump, your partner can "ask" you if you have a four-card or longer major suit (either four-plus hearts or spades) by bidding two clubs. The bid says nothing about clubs. (And, given the earlier example, you will note it is different to *respond* with a bid of two clubs than it is to *open* with a bid of two clubs.) You answer your partner's question by essentially bidding a major (if you have one) or by bidding two diamonds (another artificial bid, saying you don't). This very common convention is called *Stayman*, after Samuel Stayman, who, in a curious bit of bridge history, is not the man who invented it but the one who first reported it, in 1945 (he was partners with the presumably perturbed man who invented it). It is also worth noting that a British version arose independently even earlier, but its publication was delayed by World War II.

Anyone can make up a convention, and lots of people do. Some become quite complex. To clear up confusion, tournament players are required to carry *convention cards* that summarize their agreements, and they must alert their opponents when their bids have an unusual meaning. Complicated conventions give the game depth, but at the same time the endless possible number of artificial bids puts a tax on the tournament player. Listening in on a modern competitive bridge table can seem like eavesdropping at the Tower of Babel, with everyone speaking their own language while struggling to decipher their opponents'. We beginners have a hard enough time remembering our own conventions, let alone trying to interpret someone else's . . .

the
BACKWASH
SQUEEZE
& Other Improbable Feats

CHAPTER ONE

A Clean, Well-Caffeinated Place

New York, New York, April 2005
"If you're stupid, you can't play good bridge," says the man at the front of the class. I would settle for decent bridge, but I keep my mouth shut. The guy is a six-foot-four 190-pounder, who seems to bear a spiritual kinship and distant resemblance to Groucho Marx, complete with mustache and hundred-mile-an-hour New York yawp. He promises he has much to teach us, before launching into a long riff about card games, intuition, and the film *Pirates of the Caribbean,* which he claims to have seen about ninety-two times. He talks with his hands, which are grabby and communicative and have absentmindedly picked a rubber band off a deck of cards and now stretch it to mesmeric effect. We are on the fourteenth floor of a building in midtown Manhattan. There are twelve of us in the room; we sit four to a table, our rapt attention on this man, Jeff Bayone, who is our counselor, our confidant, and—above all else—our bridge teacher.

"I am your mother," Jeff insists, stealing a line from his book, *It's Bridge, Baby,* copies of which he has already passed out—and signed—without our having to ask. He looks nothing like my mom, a Texas blonde named Sally, but what do I know? We are all newcomers to the game. For $149, we have signed up for six two-and-a-half-hour lessons, two practice sessions, and a copy of Jeff's book. He has taught more than three thousand students. He is the co-owner of the Manhattan Bridge Club, and, as it says on the back cover, "bridge teacher to the stars."

We are not stars. But contrary to common preconceptions about bridge, we are not batty old ladies or nerdy chain-smoking neurotics, either. We are everything in between. There is a harried yuppie couple who refused to hold the elevator, an older woman with a diamond brooch and a shopping bag from Zabar's, a mousy forty-something mom, a young gum-chewing Greenwich Village teacher, a well-tanned English gent just back from a cruise, and a balding Turkish man who favors crisp blue button-downs. The woman on my right, a chatty Cathy in her fifties with a close-cropped coif, seems a little starstruck—she takes one look at my copy of *It's Bridge, Baby* and points out that Jeff is the author of the book he just signed. I nod and she beams. She had to find this class through the Yellow Pages because an Internet search for "New York" and "bridge" mainly turned up architectural sites (and doubtless got her on a watch list). She has dragged along her silent-but-smiley friend, with whom it soon becomes clear she is living, though she seems reluctant to admit it to strangers.

She is excited; we are all excited—not to mention a little scared and intimidated. For bridge is no walk in the park. You use the same fifty-two cards that you use to play poker, War, and Go Fish, but the game is closer to brain surgery than rummy. It starts simply enough. There are four players, two teams of two. For each team, the goal is to bid on and then win a certain number of "tricks." This is where beginners fall off the deep end. During the bidding, which happens before the card play begins, partners employ sophisticated systems that function as specific codes. Through a combination of bids ("one spade," "three hearts," etc.), they exchange detailed information about their hands—what they have, what they don't have, their high cards, their longest suit, and so on—all the while trying to bid the "correct" number of tricks they think they can win, given a certain trump suit. The more intricate the system, the greater the precision, but even the most complex conventions are overwhelmed by staggering odds. There are fifteen legal words—"one," "two," "three," "four," "five," "six," "seven," "clubs," "diamonds," "hearts," "spades," "no-trump," "pass," "double," "redouble"—that can form exactly thirty-eight bids, which must be used to discuss the 635,013,559,600 possible hands a player might be dealt. Thus partners work and work to refine their private language, all before a single card is played.

The play of the hand is brisk, cunning, and mentally taxing. For starters, you are expected to count all fifty-two cards. (As one professional bridge player later explained to me: "Keeping track of fifty-two? That's easy. You should be able to do that right away. It's a given, really.") There are stratagems galore, a host of offenses, defenses, feints, fake outs, and finesses. In his memoir, *The Bridge Bum,* world champion Alan Sontag quotes the writer Marshal Smith, who declared a bridge player should possess "'the conceit of a peacock, night habits of an owl, rapacity of a crocodile, sly inscrutability of a snake, memory of an elephant, boldness of a lion, endurance of a bulldog, and killer instincts of a wolf'"—a list to which I might add, given the Herculean amounts of coffee consumed around the table, the bladder of a whale.

I am in Jeff's class for a simple reason—I want to write a book about bridge. And let it be said up front: I set out to write this book for money. When I conceived of this plan, I was poor, having spent the previous year cobbling together freelance gigs; I was getting married; I needed a new computer. I had written a biography of Buster Keaton, which was enjoyed by my mother and dozens of others, and after a desultory month or two of halfheartedly shopping the first chapters of an unfinished novel—apparently nobody wanted to pay up front for a hazily conceived, disappointingly autobiographical story from a would-be first-time novelist—I was ready to leave behind my personal obsessions (which ran along the lines of old movies, subway tunnels, and chorizo) and really sell out. I would pick a topic so commercial, so calculatingly crass, that it would guarantee me oodles of cash—from here on out it would be fine dining, exotic trips, and maybe one of those posh gold-plated iPods or a washer-dryer.

So I picked bridge.

You may laugh, gentle reader, but there are a lot of bridge clubs and bridge players, not to mention people who buy random books, or at least pick them up in bookstores—you're obviously one—and the idea somehow seemed to make sense. Of course I was wrong about bridge in many other respects, too—starting with its cultural cache. Telling my friends I was "off to the club" didn't actually make me sound part of some secret old-boy network or hip downtown scene. In fact, when I told one friend what I was doing, he turned to my fiancée and said, "Well, is that the death of eroticism or what?" Not exactly, as I would find out—bridge is hardly a game for drowsy old biddies. The competitive hotheads I would meet exhibited the antisocial aggression of rugby players. The game was nothing like I expected. It was both better and worse than I had imagined—friendly yet fierce, traumatic yet comforting. Learning to play was intimidating, terrifying, and addictive.

I guess the problem was that I started out knowing nothing about bridge. I don't come from much of a card family; my grandmother played bridge, but in our house Stratego or Sorry! was more our thing. As a kid, I recall bridge being something that cluttered the cartoon pages of the paper, incomprehensible adult stuff, à la *Apartment 3G*, that got in the way of *Blondie, Marmaduke,* and *Marvin.* Then, after college, bridge was something that cluttered the elevators of my strange old New York apartment building, a rundown residential hotel whose penthouse had been the home of the Manhattan Bridge Club for decades. At that time, I was essentially a shut-in, writing a book, but occasionally I ventured to the roof to see the sun or watch fireworks. That top floor was a mystery: packed with card tables, stale snacks, and inscrutable eccentrics. Week in and week out players crowded the elevators, slowing things down as they held the doors for latecomers, chattering on the way up about the heat, the cold, their luck, their health, their cards—they were a fervent bunch.

Now, a few years later, after both the club and I have been booted from the building, I am looking them up again. And despite the fact that I can't properly shuffle a pack of cards (for years I have been using a makeshift no-thumbs method that gets the job done but certainly isn't pretty) and the fact that the last math-science class I ever took (in college) was called "Physics for Poets," I have decided to learn the world's deepest, most difficult card game.

One morning I catch Jeff outside of class, and he invites me to step into his office, right off the main room of the club and adjacent to the coffee machine, which he watches like a hawk. There, he immediately tries to talk me out of writing a book on bridge. He has a better idea—"Why don't you do a book about something people actually want to know about, like poker?" His position is clear: first-person bridge journalism is a fool's errand, with no hope of an audience ("No one gives a shit about bridge"), even among the faithful ("Bridge players couldn't care less about other bridge players. A bridge player is a doer, not an observer!"). The future is Texas Hold'em Poker, as seen on TV. He bangs on things (the desk, the computer) to make his points. He mentions a few bridge giants who have crossed over to poker. When I point out that he himself wrote a book on bridge, Jeff changes the subject—he demands to know if I have a title in mind. I tell him I don't. He launches into a complaint about his. *"It's Bridge, Baby?* What the hell is that? The editor said we'd go after the kids. Who cares? They don't! I don't want the kids—I want the fifty-five-year-olds! I wanted to call the book *Bridge at My Mother's Knee.* But you know, they paid me, so I just shut the hell up and said, 'Thanks.'"

Jeff has owned part of the Manhattan Bridge Club since 1976.

It is the oldest public bridge club in the city. Over the years, the club has flitted about the Upper West Side. In 2004, it moved into its current digs in the Fisk Building, a historic block-long office tower below Columbus Circle. With LCD screens in the elevators and generic corporate-suite interiors, the swank new space is nothing like the former clubhouse in my old apartment building. The new club is bright and open, with a reception area, glass-enclosed classrooms, and wraparound windows overlooking the canyons of midtown.

At the time of my first lesson, the club boasted some 2,000 regular players, 250 of whom played more than once a week. (In more than a year, these numbers will grow to 3,000 and 400, respectively.) The room is open every day with games from noon until night except on Saturdays, when there is no evening game. The club provides the snacks. In the corner stretches an ample but decidedly motley around-the-clock spread: chips, dips, pita, nuts, cookies, candy, and crudités. Nearby is a large, overworked coffee machine, the continuous operation of which seems a concern of everyone in the room. An empty pot produces panic; coffee is the club's lifeblood—hot, strong, and brutally burnt—and for the newcomer, fetching a cup can be more harrowing than at a crowded SoHo Starbucks. Fill, sweeten, lighten, and get the hell out of the way.

This morning, running the club is giving Jeff the usual headaches. The front door of the bridge club has been taken off its hinges for repairs; now the screws are missing. A shipment of coffee has come in but it is all decaf. The manager of a smaller, East Side outpost of the club shows up to complain that the two clubs' schedules are competing with each other; he also wants to see if Jeff has a line on a cheap fruit plate. There was a verbal altercation at last night's duplicate game. Two maintenance crews are MIA. An older woman drops into Jeff's office, late to work, looking for his advice on a bet (she has come from the OTB). Between interruptions, Jeff pushes the poker idea—hard.

Again and again he emphasizes what a harsh mistress bridge is. He paints a bleak picture. Out of all the beginners he manages to lure into the club, less than 5 percent will go on to play in the club's duplicate matches. (Duplicate bridge is the tournament form of the game, where pairs play the same hands.) Bridge is dying; the kids prefer poker. When asked, in various forms, about the future, Jeff eventually loses his patience: "There is no young generation playing bridge! IT. DOES. NOT. EXIST."

Indeed, many players are older than the game itself, which turned eighty in the fall of 2005. On average, American bridge champions live well into their seventies. Top tournaments have been won by players in their eighties, which raises an interesting question: is bridge an old person's game—or are bridge players living longer?

Bridge seems unique among games in the way it stretches the synapses. Playing bridge has been found to significantly reduce the risk of Alzheimer's and dementia; it is a recommended mental exercise for patients who have suffered head trauma. A 1999 study from the University of California–Berkeley found that playing bridge actually strengthens the immune system.

Still, running the club wears Jeff down. "You ask if this is all I do? It kills me. I get home and I say, I didn't do anything all day." And so he brought in a co-owner in 2004 to help—interestingly enough—develop new players. Indeed, Jeff's tough talk belies a severe and abiding love of the game. When asked about his status as a "teacher to the stars," Jeff spits, "Bullshit. I never taught no stars." It's just more publicity wrangling from his publisher. He then adds, "It's Hold'em poker the stars play—probably because they're nitwits."

And so his true colors come through in fits and flashes, and another way to view Jeff's poker fixation is that it is simply his most recent shrewd strategy to keep the club afloat. In the Fisk Building, the club's rent is $15,000 a month; poker is another means to make the space pay for itself. Jeff will rent out the club for private events—charity poker nights or corporate parties—

for which he provides the food, dealers, and know-how. He also has begun hosting weekend poker games; the club is usually less crowded anyway, as many of the serious bridge players are off competing in tournaments.

Thus pushing poker is a way of fighting for bridge, which explains some of Jeff's more compelling contradictions. He doesn't care about young people, yet he works to recruit new players, who are lowering the average age at the club. He claims to be a misanthrope ("I don't like bridge players in general"), yet he surrounds himself with them day and night ("I never leave these four walls"). He is a bitter man who clings hard to the game and his club, a gambler who knows the odds but relishes a fight.

Jeff indeed learned bridge at his mother's knee. He got his first chance to play sitting in for his aunt Flo—but he didn't stick with it. He was a serious chess player first, and a semiprofessional gambler for fifteen years, and despite a rigorously analytical mind—which won him the math award at New York's prestigious Stuyvesant High—he still seems a little distrustful of bridge, if not overawed by the game. He says, "I thought I was a hell of a player after five years. After ten, I realized how little I knew at five. And at twenty, I realized I knew nothing at all." And so he stopped playing as much, perhaps overwhelmed by the subtleties. Despite his early success (he won the national Non-Life Master Pairs in Las Vegas), he lost his taste for competition—it got too old, he had been doing it for too long. These days, Jeff won't play in tournaments. The reason he gives: "I don't like three hours of batting your head against people." Looking back on his career, Jeff admits, "I never got to the highest levels. Maybe I wasn't talented, maybe I wasn't driven." Or maybe he lays some of the blame on the game, a fifty-two-card conundrum that once seemed solvable but still might turn out just to be a joke—on him. Summing up a life of devoted disappointment, he says, "We have people quit every night. Sometimes they come back."

When they do, Jeff will be there with snacks, coffee, and a seat at the table. It is a fellowship he enjoys in spite of himself, and, between protests, Jeff will wax poetic and passionate. He directs his greatest fury at what he believes is the fundamental misconception about bridge—that it is just an antiquated pastime for little old ladies. He points out, "The reason old people play so much is that sixty years ago—in the heyday of bridge, when it was bigger than baseball, when these people were young men and women in their prime—they were fascinated by the game, and they are still held by it." It is a sport neither for the immature nor the infirm of mind. "You want a bridge player to be about fifty-five. You want your biological clock to be wound down, so you can sit at the table and enjoy the thinking, the learning, the company. Not that it's a slow game—it takes lightning judgment and quick processing—but you have to want to think, to see all of the cards."

As a small crowd begins to collect outside his office—awaiting an audience with the chief to voice their various concerns—Jeff works himself up for a final jab at poker and those nitwits who play it. "You know, it takes thirty minutes to teach Texas Hold'em, and in an hour you can be as good as fifty percent of the people playing the game. That would take years of study in bridge. Bridge is as complicated as rocket science. You need a dozen lessons—at two hours apiece—just to learn how to play!" He shakes his head and waves in the crowd. Interview over. On my way out the front door, still off its hinges, I hear a final shout from the back of the club: "Just think about poker!"

Without a doubt, poker is the elephant in the bridge club. Part of my enthusiasm for bridge might have to do with a perverse irritation with my friends who play poker—to say nothing of the starry-eyed, fast-money fools on TV shelling out $10,000 buy-ins at the World Series of Poker, all in the vain hope of becoming the next Cinderella story. (And speaking of Cinderella, since when is the ultimate sign of sport a championship *dia-*

mond bracelet?) For years, this country has been in the throes of a well-documented poker craze. There is a glut of TV shows (*Celebrity Poker Showdown, World Poker Tour, Poker After Dark*), magazines (*Card Player, All In, Bluff*), and merchandise (poker tables, poker chips, poker video games, poker fantasy camps, even poker vitamins). In 2006, players spent more than $527 million worldwide buying in to live tournaments in casinos. On the Internet, the numbers were even wilder until Congress passed a bill in October 2006 that cracked down on illegal online gambling. In 2005, the traffic on one popular poker Web site, partypoker.com, averaged out to thirty-two hands of poker played—or $1,454 bet—every second, totaling $45 billion that year. In response to the 2006 legislation—which banned U.S. banks from processing online gambling transactions—partypoker.com no longer accepts bets from U.S. residents, though many sites still do. In 2006, "poker" was the most popular search term on lycos.com.

Lost in the shuffle is bridge. If Ben Affleck is the doofy, affable poster boy of poker, then the face of bridge would be someone like Norma Desmond—proud, difficult, iconic, eccentric, infinitely more interesting, and hungry for a comeback.

Over the years, the game has produced an impressive array of bridge buffs. General Dwight D. Eisenhower was a nut for the game. Winston Churchill played devotedly—but badly—with his signature wit and panache. (He was known to spout such charming but grandiloquent hogwash as, "The king cannot fall unworthily if it falls to the sword of the ace.") Other enthusiasts have included the Marx Brothers, George Burns, George S. Kaufman, Wilt Chamberlain, Deng Xiaoping, Mahatma Gandhi, and Charles Schulz. (In 1997, three years before Schulz died, Snoopy was named a Life Master, one of the game's greatest honors, by the American Contract Bridge League.) Hands have been played on Mount Everest, atop the Eiffel Tower, and at the South Pole—where, as one article pointed out, everyone sat north. Somerset Maugham, a dedicated player, found the game endlessly edifying: "I would have children taught bridge. It will be useful in the end. . . . When all else fails—sports, love, ambition—bridge remains a solace and an entertainment."

Indeed, the game can be a powerful distraction. Bridge has long been popular with POWs. During World War II, in a Japanese prison in West Java, the duplicate game organized by a cadre of Dutch officers ran to eight tables. Bridge was also a pastime for American prisoners in Vietnam; when John McCain lost to his best friend in camp, he didn't speak to him for days. Even today in Iraq, U.S. soldiers turn to bridge. There is a club sanctioned by the American Contract Bridge League that meets Sunday afternoons twenty miles outside Baghdad at Abu Ghraib prison.

The second-richest man in the world, investor Warren Buffett, has said, "Bridge is such a sensational game that I wouldn't mind being in jail if I had three cellmates who were decent players and who were willing to keep the game going twenty-four hours a day." In truth, the game has been a jailhouse favorite. During the 1950s, some 250 Alcatraz inmates would gather every weekend for hours of bridge; at night, alone in their cells, many were said to restage the matches from memory. In the 1970s, there was a weekly game in Leavenworth. One day a year visitors were allowed to play, and it would become the largest men's pair event in Kansas.

Thus in some ways, Buffett's quip is more telling than it appears. Bridge attracts a dedicated, calculating crowd; it is a game popular with both businessmen and serial killers. In the early 1990s, a Death Row foursome composed of the Freeway Killer, the Sunset-Strip Killer, the Scorecard Killer (who murdered two of his victims after a bridge game), and a man named Lawrence "Pliers" Bittaker met daily in Yard Four at San Quentin and played with makeshift cards. The men didn't talk much. When they did, it was often to pick on the weakest player, the Freeway Killer, who, because of a beef with both the Scorecard and the Sunset-Strip Killers, usually ended up playing with Pliers. The game fell apart in 1996 with the execution of the Free-way Killer.

Today, there are more than 25 million bridge players in the United States. A 2005 survey revealed that the country's bridge corps is middle aged, well educated, comfortably fixed, and hopelessly hooked. Fifty-three percent have at least a bachelor's degree (as opposed to 28 percent in the population at large). The average player's income was $61,500 a year, much higher than the national median of $43,300. The mean age was found to be fifty-one. Some 3.3 million people play at least once a week, and 5.1 million read a bridge column regularly. Perhaps more insightful, when stranded on a desert island, the majority of bridge players would choose the company of three random bridge-playing companions over the perhaps more reliable com-forts of Betty Crocker, Jacques Cousteau, and Dr. Phil. To me, only the last case is easy to understand.

In the United States, the game is governed by the American Contract Bridge League, established in 1937. The organization tracks the cumulative points won in competition, called "mas-ter points," for each of its 160,000 members playing in 3,300 clubs and at 1,200 tournaments in North America each year. By accumulating master points, players progress through the ranks to attain the status of Life Master, bridge's highest honor. The Memphis-based body sanctions 2.5 million tables in play annu-ally, plus some two hundred thousand tables online, spending an annual budget of $15 million. It publishes a monthly maga-zine, the *Bridge Bulletin*, which is mailed to all its members. The ACBL also oversees the North American Bridge Champion-ships, held three times a year. An eleven-day tournament, each NABC draws eight thousand players from around the world and provides lectures, child care, and a daily newspaper. Specta-tors (known as "kibitzers") can watch the big games—at table-side—for free. (That said, beware the too-casual kibitzer. Once at the Manhattan Bridge Club, a tubby guy with a Mohawk gave me the biggest stink eye I've ever seen, an unwaveringly homicidal glare that followed me until I, slightly spooked, left the room. My offense: while grazing the snack table, I had glanced over and, presumably, seen his cards. Perhaps he thought I was a stooge, ready to signal his suits and strengths with my carrots and dip; perhaps he thought I coveted his Megadeth T-shirt. Either way, a level of spirited paranoia seems par for the course.) Even more remarkable than the front-row spectating, however, is the fact that for less than $20 a session anyone can compete against champs and chumps alike. Few contests boast this kind of egalitarian goodwill—imagine toting your racquet to Wimbledon and being allowed to step on the court.

Back at the Manhattan Bridge Club, players walk through the door seeking the same thing—the company of like-minded obsessives. Bridge is a social sport that can overtake your life. At the club, no fewer than three couples in recent memory have met and married. One night before class, co-owner Jesús Arias tells me, "It's almost incestuous."

In fact, it was companionship that first drew Arias to the game. He was in the college chess club when he says it hit him: "Few females play chess." So he switched to bridge, and in fourteen years he has accumulated nearly five thousand master points, more than sixteen times the requirement to become a Life Master. In his clipped, machine-gun-like patter, he explains, "I play in everything—I'm a game junkie." He plays bridge eight times a week. He bought a stake in the club when Jeff was looking to raise extra cash to make the move from the Upper West Side.

Arias, who wears a Knicks cap and makes even more bad jokes than Jeff, is known to all by the nickname "Zeus." He is affable and approachable, something of a bridge bon vivant. Tonight Zeus sits at a front table eating Chinese takeout and greeting all comers. Between mouthfuls of chicken wings and fried rice, he answers questions and heckles walk-ins, distributing air kisses to all. His cell phone bleeps constantly. He tells me he gets a "natural high" from competing, but clearly he's a people person. He especially enjoys playing in tournaments, where he says, "the best attendance is often at the bar after the game."

Occasionally Zeus takes over our beginner class. He is a natural teacher, easygoing and patient. More often, we get short, wiry Irma, who wears her glasses atop her head like a contrary librarian and drops her "r"s like a peppy Long Island grandma ("Now who's the declaaaarah?"). A player from the old school, she shushes us when we chatter and refuses to play online. ("It's a tactile game," she says.) Usually the instructors are assisted by Lisanne, their enthusiastic amanuensis; though she has only been playing for four years, Lisanne is a self-professed "zealot," with the bright eyes and feverish clichés of the newly converted. ("I'm really into the game's deeper beauties.") She is smart and somewhat sphinxlike, the kind of person who, after watching a hand, turns to a player and asks out of the blue, "Are you from New England?" It turns out her question has something to do with her theory that Yankees tend to store tricks for the winter. She might be joking, but I can't tell. She says I have a hidden talent for bridge, though I imagine she tells that to all the players.

As we newbies sit in the glass-enclosed classroom, the club heavyweights lumber by and stare in at us as if we're zoo animals; we gaze blankly back, like the sad, confused menagerie that we are. Outside, in the big room, some seventy people are murmuring over their cards. It is a mixed crowd. There is a smattering of yarmulkes, baseball hats, and garden-variety bonnets; a young guy in leather sits across from a blue-hair in a seasonally themed sweater.

The club abounds with characters. One of the more dignified is Tse Mei, a woman of a certain age with a dry wit and British accent. An architect, she is protective of the new facility, which she helped design. While we sit before class, she eyes Zeus's plate of rice warily, and scoots a Coke can away from the table's edge. To my eyes, the club is gleaming, spotless; she thinks it is already getting messy. She has been playing for six years, which is long enough for her to offer me a word of warning when no one is listening: "Bridge players are mean." Then she adds, with a forlorn glance at something in the carpet that perhaps only she can see, "And sloppy."

A bearded man wanders in looking for a book he left in the room a week ago. Jeff imagines he's out of luck. At the club some abandoned articles have a better chance of recovery than others. Books and umbrellas invariably disappear, he says, "but you could leave a coat in here for weeks."

While I'm sitting with Zeus, a white-haired Austrian in a leather vest and wraparound shades known only as "H.G." stops over to say hi. The word on him is that he runs a computer company and comes to town only a few weeks a year, when he has meetings all day and plays bridge all night. H.G. is hoarse, but he manages to put in his two cents: "You'll never learn bridge. At best, once in a while you'll bump into a beautiful girl."

Almost on cue, Barbara—a fifty-something in glasses, a green suit, and a perm—bounces over to announce, "I play with a child." For this privilege, she brags, "I pay him big bucks—five hundred dollars for every two sessions." The child in question is actually a twenty-year-old Canadian professional player she met through a friend. Barbara coos like a girl with a crush. "I love, love, love Daniel. He is just wonderful!" In fact, it seems he might just be too wonderful. "He is getting too good; he has too many master points—he keeps pushing us up into too high a bracket." She sighs. "Soon I am going to have to dump him." The point is more or less moot, however, because she has almost accumulated enough master points to reach the Life Master rank—which is the very reason she hired a partner to begin with.

By day, Barbara is the president of a foundation that awards grants to college students (she seems a little perturbed that her Canadian whiz kid is toying with the idea of putting off college for another year); by night, she plays bridge in clubs and online, often until two in the morning. She learned the game young, though she once set it aside for twenty-five years. Today it consumes her. At any lull in the conversation, she will pull from her purse a small dog-eared book on bridge—which has grown thick with hand-scrawled notes, meticulous marginalia, and computer printouts paper-clipped to the pages—and go over bidding scenarios with Zeus. She carries a thick stack of convention cards, one for each of her partners, to help her keep track of the various systems she might play. Thumbing through them reminds her how much she will miss her Daniel. She admits, "You know, I like the young ones. The older people around bridge are weird." To this, Zeus counters: "There's something weird about the youngsters, too. What does it say about them that they like to spend the bulk of their time with people three times their age?" Once Barbara is gone, Zeus points out that the average age of an ACBL member hovers around sixty-eight.

After class, one of my fellow students stops me on the way out. She is a perky schoolteacher who clearly outplayed me at the table. She asks what I do. When I say I'm a writer, she says, "So, why are you here—are you writing a book?" I am too stunned to reply. She continues, "That's okay. I figured you out by your notebook. Just make me a character!" Done. She taught me two lessons that night. Not only am I a lackluster bridge player, I am an even worse spy.

Michael Polowan is a man of easygoing contradictions. His scruffy beard and shock of dark unkempt hair seem at odds with the natty blazer he wears over a striped Oxford buttoned to the top. He is mild-mannered and polite, but arrives ten minutes late. It is about a month after my first bridge lesson with Jeff, who passed on Polowan's number. For our first meeting, I had offered to take Michael to lunch. I was imagining something along the lines of a diner. He picks a swank French bistro near his apartment on the Upper West Side. These bridge players are no dummies, and, as it says on his business card, Polowan is an international bridge professional.

Polowan is forty-seven. His look—call it either bohemian bond trader or pocket-protector Picasso—is in keeping with his philosophy of the game. When asked why he plays bridge, he responds, "Not many things make you think creatively and analytically." Polowan learned the rules young, at the age of nine or ten, when he became curious about the odd column that ran opposite chess in the *New York Times.* His father bought him a bridge book. Polowan played his first hand in high school on Long Island. When he dropped out of graduate school, where he was pursuing a doctorate in clinical psychology, he drifted into bridge; it was a stopgap while he figured out what to do next. He had won a number of regional tournaments and had had a few decent results at national events when he was invited to a tournament in Iceland through a friend who knew the organizers. A Dutch tournament followed, and for more than twenty years Polowan has been playing bridge full time.

Within a certain insular world, he is a celebrity. Some five or six times in his life, he has been stopped on the street and asked for his autograph. Still, he never has used his relative anonymity for dark purposes. He refuses to hustle; when playing in private games for stakes, Polowan always makes sure his opponents know who he is. In general, he does not enjoy playing rubber bridge for money. Last year he turned down an invitation to play in the big game at New York's private Regency Whist Club, where the stakes run a dollar a point. Polowan says he mainly enjoys the bidding, the theory, and the partnership play—all of which he finds less emphasized in rubber bridge.

His professional routine is somewhat atypical. He competes in all of the major U.S. tournaments, where he might get paid to play with a client or be part of a team, but he forgoes playing in the regionals, a grueling circuit that some professionals travel for up to forty weeks a year. By comparison, Polowan is on the road only some eighty days a year. He teaches occasionally, but only to wealthy individuals who can pay for his time. He does not particularly enjoy the one-on-one lessons, saying, "What can I get from playing bad bridge, other than some cash?" Still, ambitious amateurs seek him out by word of mouth. He does not advertise. He admits, "I've never been good at the self-promotional aspect of being a professional—meeting strangers and convincing them to throw lots of money at me."

Jeff holds Polowan in high regard; he is obviously pleased to consider him a member of the Manhattan Bridge Club, where the pro occasionally conducts his one-on-one lessons. Polowan is popular at the club; he is treated with great respect. One night I mentioned to a woman how nervous it made me to play with him looking over my shoulder. With ecstatic eyes she turned and said, "It's like having God watching over you!"

To Polowan, the difference between a pro and a club player lies in the "understanding of the game." He says, "To be a professional requires a disciplined mind, the ability to think inductively and deductively, competitive toughness, and some degree of intangible talent that cannot be described." Lest he sound too mystical, Polowan points out that he does not believe in "card sense," that preternatural tableside intuition that many players swear by. "It just doesn't exist," he says. "What 'card sense' really is is a mental process on a nonverbal level. There is nothing mystical or magical about it; you're just picking up on cues and remembering when you've seen similar cues before—when your opponents stop to think, the rhythm of the play. In some way, players always tattle on their hand." To give an example, he points out that a quick discard from your opponent of a suit not bid in auction is likely to be from a five-card or longer suit (because, according to him, such discards are considered "safe"), which in turn can help you inferentially count the cards.

In the course of a long lunch, this is the only nugget of bridge wisdom I manage to catch, and as Polowan heads down deeper and deeper rabbit holes of logic and inference, I see why he has a reputation as a formidable theorist. The word around the club is that Polowan could be a high-paid trainer, a coach of sorts to the big-time teams, but instead he chooses to play. When asked about this, he says, "If your goal in life is to maximize your income, you don't play bridge." Pressed further, he admits, "Playing in high-level games is fun. Sitting there watching others play is frustrating."

Another way Polowan is unusual is that he's a loner. Most pros have a partner; many of the top players also have a dedicated sponsor. Polowan has neither. For the past four years, he has played a fair amount with Richard Pavlicek, who lives in Florida; the pair competed together in a prestigious event called the Vanderbilt Knockout at the 2005 spring national championships in Pittsburgh, where their team lost in the round of sixteen to the eventual winners of the event. (The two were on a team that won the title in 1995.) He also plays with a New Yorker named Chris Willenken.

A sponsor is usually a well-heeled but weaker player who hires a team of professionals. At the 2005 nationals in Pittsburgh, reportedly about one in four teams competing for the Vanderbilt Cup had a sponsor. The tournament itself pays no prize money, but it is long on prestige. Some sponsors play as much as possible (i.e., until their team falls behind); others enjoy watching from the bench. Either way, the sponsors are there to bask in the somewhat reflected glory. The hired guns can earn between $20,000 to $25,000, plus bonuses, for their appearance, with the sponsor usually handling travel expenses and entry fees.

The most famous—and hands-on—sponsor was multimillionaire Ira G. Corn Jr., of Dallas, who put together an all-professional team, known as the Aces, in the late 1960s. Corn himself didn't play, but he moved his teammates to Texas, where he paid them a salary and hired a retired U.S. Air Force lieutenant colonel to be their coach. Those days are gone, says Polowan, who points out that while today's sponsors typically play, none are as involved as Corn. He says, "Now, when you're hired for a tournament, how you prep is your business. Your only commitment is to show up."

Still, competing at an eleven-day national championship takes its toll. One study suggested that playing a four-and-a-half-hour session of tournament bridge is more strenuous than performing two to eight hours of demanding surgery. It is an exercise in nerves, passion, intellect, and even superstition. Some players refrain from eating in order to keep blood flowing to the brain, not the stomach; others cut out carbs; some drink, others don't. That said, the hours bridge players keep are almost quaintly collegiate. According to Polowan, the trend at large tournaments is for the major events to start "early," or, say, around one o'clock in the afternoon; the evening session usually begins between seven and eight. Once play is over for the day, Polowan repairs to the hotel bar. (He admits, "There are some people who disappear right into their room, but I'm not one.") There the players talk and talk, sometimes about hands, sometimes not, into the small hours. By three o'clock, Polowan is in bed; at eleven, he rolls down for breakfast. After an eleven-day tournament, he goes home and sleeps a lot.

In general, Polowan thinks international bridge has grown more professional and homogenized since the days when players chomped cigars and got rowdy at the table. He claims there are fewer "characters" in the game, though I would argue there remain plenty of odd ducks—they're just birds of a different feather. He says, "If you look at match records from the sixties and seventies, the bidding is unbelievably dreadful. There was more scope for people with less discipline. There was more room for quirky individuals—the partnerships mattered less. It would be harder for such people to be successful in the game today." So then is the trend toward inward, cerebral competitors who play their cards evenly, quietly, like perfect poker-faced automatons? Is the game being idealized away from its colorful brawling backroom roots? Is bridge becoming boring?

Yes and no. Indeed the game is becoming more virtual, moving away from impassioned, face-to-face conflict and occurring more and more in the perfect distant recesses of the mind. In some ways, bridge has gone from social game to math problem. Compare accounts of high-stakes games in the 1960s, when table-side drinking and floozy hangers-on could prove to be reliable distractions, and today's tournament conditions—screened-off tables clustered about a silent smoke-free room—look downright monkish. And this is to say nothing of the runaway success of Internet bridge.

But, on the other hand, there are the players themselves, Polowan and his brethren, who include businessmen and bar-hoppers, playboys and programmers, plus a small but successful Objectivist bridge sect, whose members strive to live and play by Ayn Rand's fierce philosophy of unbending logic and indifferent self-interest. Taken in context, that postmatch trip to the bar seems well worth the trouble.

Polowan understands the conflict between personality and precision. Talking of tournaments, he says, "In late rounds, the game feels incredibly dramatic and heated—but not in any overt way. It's more internalized. Unlike most sports, there are not many opportunities for visceral, physical releases." In some ways, Polowan is a model of internalized physical releases. When he was young, Bob Hamman, for decades considered the best player in the world, told him: "You are there to win. Anything that does not contribute to that—get rid of." Polowan has been paring down ever since. Thus the care with which he eats his crab salad, scooped and scraped to the middle of the plate in neat, deliberate forkfuls, as he seems to order his sentences in his head before he speaks them. He says things like, "It's trivial," in that particular cadence familiar to high school mathletes everywhere. At lunch, he drinks four decaf iced coffees and carries his own Splenda.

But this is not to say Polowan is dull. Far from it. Like the flip side of Flaubert's famous formulation, "Be regular and orderly in your life like a bourgeois, so that you may be violent and original in your work," he is unstructured in his life so that he can be all the more orderly in his work. Because of his success at bridge, he has received various offers to work on Wall Street ("trading is also a game," he says); he has turned them all down.

Polowan, for his part, usually stays out late; he is rarely in bed before three. Asked what he does away from the bridge table, he says, "I watch TV, see friends, go to the theater." He reads a couple of books at a time. The day I met him he had just finished a critique of the Wilson administration and was simultaneously enjoying a biography of George Washington and a book on modern militarism. He occasionally glances at the *New York Times* bridge column, which he calls "relatively newsy," but usually he has already heard about the hand online.

Polowan doesn't regularly check his e-mail, though he's often on his cell phone. He has numerous friends, here and abroad, many of whom he has met through bridge. His phone rings during lunch. It's a woman, a downtown lawyer with whom he was on a date the previous night. They were out until two in the morning, hanging out at Cafe Lalo and other Upper West Side haunts. Unlike many pros, Michael has never dated a bridge player; this woman, he says, "just thinks bridge is this strange thing that I do."

CHAPTER TWO

The Miseducation of a Bridge Player

On the first night of class, Jeff had told us, "It'll take two to three lessons before you're comfortable at the table." At the time I resented the implication that I somehow wasn't house-broken, but he was right. The mechanics of bridge—juggling thirteen cards and a plate or two of snacks—take some time to master. Never mind the game itself. With so much on my mind, I found my saving grace to be a handy little device called the "bidding box."

In informal bridge games, players simply speak their bids. At the club, we use bidding boxes. Small upright containers that stand a few inches high, bidding boxes hold a color-coded array of plastic cards printed with every conceivable bid, from one club to seven no-trump (as well as pass, double, and redouble). To make a bid, a player simply selects the desired card from his box and lays it flat on the table. As the auction progresses, bids pile up in front of each player, providing a visual history of the bidding. Bidding boxes usually are used in more rigorous play, like duplicate or tournament games. Not only do they provide an extra measure of clarity to the auction (no one can claim to have misheard a bid) and allow for very large games (a packed room can bid in absolute silence), but they prevent players from unintentionally (or even deliberately) passing on illegal infor-mation through the inflection of their voices. There is a world of difference between a loud, firm four-spades bid and the same four spades being squeaked out in a thin wavering tone. Most of all, for easily distracted dolts like me, they make it easy to remember what my partner bid—it's right there on the table.

Yet while I am growing more at ease with the trappings of the table, I continue to be astounded by the creatures in the club. Heidi, who is probably pushing eighty, paints her shoes with white polka dots to match her pants. When I compliment her on them, she says in her German accent, "I do that. I'm an artist." Heidi is my favorite among what I like to think of as the anarchists, a gang of cheerfully crabby beginners who always sit at the same table. They talk when they want to, get snacks mid-hand, take potty breaks willy-nilly, even leave class early. They seem to be in revolt against the complexity of the game. One of them, who wears big beaded Navajo earrings, refuses to let logic get in the way of her bids, which she makes based on what she calls her "good card sense." She also says she is an artist. She is not one of the teacher's pets.

Heidi usually brings along her sister for support. She is a good player, and her contribution mainly involves clucking over Heidi's cards and snapping at her when she mis-bids, misplays, or mangles the cards in the bidding box. Throughout the lesson, the sisters fight back and forth under their breath: "What you do?" "You crazy!" "You wrong!" "Shut up!" Heidi waggles her tongue out of her mouth when she plays, kind of like Michael Jordan. At the table, nothing can faze her—not even her own curious play. More than once, with a perfect poker face, she trumps a trick I, her partner, was winning—apparently all part of her master plan. I like Heidi because of the way she rolls her r's when she says, "Trrrrrrump."

At the Manhattan Bridge Club, you never know what to expect. One night at the coffeepot I overheard a man say, "I believe the young lady would like some coffee." I turned to see a woman in her sixties. As for her knight in shining armor, he was at least a decade older. It turns out the young lady also wanted real sugar, but there was none in sight—only the synthetic stuff.

Before I could offer my help, the man dropped to his knees and began rooting through the cupboard. And so I left these two to their coffeepot courting.

These are not the only members acting younger than their years. For a while I have enjoyed tracking the movements of one of Manhattan's oldest momma's boys, a man in his late forties who sometimes shows up with his mother. While we are settling down to class, he shouts across the room, "Two cushions or one, Mom?" She answers back, "Honey, do you want me to pay the fifteen dollars for you?" They then proceed to argue over the bidding.

As for our play—which at this point can only barely be called bridge—it might be pedestrian, but it's certainly intense. In 2004, an article in the *Washington Post* advised young D.C. singles to pick up bridge; it quoted a Londoner who described her bridge club as "an upmarket dating agency." I'm not so sure about that. Despite the "incestuous" bridge marriages Zeus mentioned, the glances I see being thrown around the club—and within the class—seem more cutthroat than coy. We gather around the watercooler like lions on safari, looking to cull the weakest wildebeest from the herd. Bridge is a game that is supposed to pit mind directly against mind, and I find myself growing surprisingly competitive.

My nemesis is named Molly. Molly is an aggressive dropout from the last beginner session who plays her cards sloppily and slowly, with a dramatic bend-and-hold maneuver—putting intense pressure on the card for a full second before releasing it (snap!) to the table, where it is finally revealed. Often she takes back her card (or her bid) after someone else has played; because we're nice, we let her. She doesn't listen to anyone; she's always late; she's usually rude. Her most obnoxious habit, however, is her incessant, deafening gum chomping.

Killing time one day before class, Heidi and I sit down against Molly and one of her cronies. With a little help from the peanut gallery, we bid up to what seems to me a rather outlandish five-diamond contract, meaning we are obligated to take all of the tricks but two. I am the declarer looking for eleven tricks with diamonds as trump. It's up to Molly and her pal to stop me.

When Heidi, the dummy, puts her cards on the table—upon the opening lead—I try to reason the way we have been learning to in class. I see between my two hands I have nine diamonds. Chances are that the remaining four diamonds are split between my opponents 3–1 (because an even number of cards tends to break oddly). I am missing the diamond ace and king, which means I will lose those two tricks for sure. I can't lose any more than that.

The actual play of the hand is a blur. My partner has left me with some lame spades, which I see no way of getting rid of, but somehow things keep going my way. My collection of tricks grows. With each victory for me, Molly's gum goes faster, beating a loud, wet war tattoo, which is the height of distraction to everyone but her.

It all comes down to the last trick, the outcome of which is a total mystery to me. I have lost the two tricks I knew I would, but somehow I have won the rest. I should have been counting the cards, but I have become so tangled in my strategies that I can't remember exactly what is left.

My fate hinges on clubs. I lead the eight, the last card in my hand. I know no one can trump it—I am sure all the diamonds are gone. Molly's partner pitches a heart, which is worthless. If Molly has a club higher than my eight, she will win. She chews for a long time. What's the choice? She only has one card! Down it comes: first the dramatic bend—I can see it is a club—then the snap . . . it's a four. I win! I immediately try to shrug off my glee. No big deal.

Irma, tonight's teacher, saunters over and asks how we did. She greets my success with a shocked, happy face. She asks, "Bythrowingawaytwospadelosersonthekingjackandruffingandrunningclubs?"—or at least that's the kind of nonsense I might have heard had her words not hit my ears like grown-up speech in a *Peanuts* movie: "Wuh-waa, wuh-waa, wuh-waaaaa . . ." I shrug gamely.

"Brilliant!" she says and goes to brag to Zeus, who had watched a few rounds. She explains, he responds, and I see her face fall.

She calls back to me, "No, you didn't. You just got lucky, kid." Molly smiles and gobbles a doughnut hole. Yet I remain unbowed. Tonight, this joker is king.

That said, every bridge story, no matter how bloody the battle, is in part a love story. Bridge is a partnership game. Not even the world's best can go it alone. You and your partner need to be in sync. You must like your partner, understand your partner, and—above all—trust your partner. As we swap seats in class, with varied results, this becomes apparent. As entertaining as Heidi might be, you can only have so many of your aces trumped before you start to lose patience.

And so I go in search of my bridge better half. Enter Tina, a quiet elderly woman with a neat coif of gray hair. At the first class, I pretty much pigeonholed her as the sweet grandmother type. Then, weeks later, I overhear the table behind me discussing her short new haircut. The perky young schoolteacher says to her—in that pleasant but ultimately patronizing voice we often inflict on the elderly—"Tina, I love your new 'do!" It is a throwaway comment, just pleasantries before class. Tina tells her with a perfect deadpan, "I look like Caesar." Conversation over.

I begin trying to play more with Tina. She is often the first to class, and if I come early, I can get a seat at her table. Whereas many of our classmates are loud and bossy, she is polite and unassuming, though her wry asides continue. When Irma gushes, "You guys are doing terrific," Tina mutters under her breath, "We're terrific people." No one really hears her—they're all busy beating their chests—but we strike up a friendship. As a rule, she is reluctant to talk about herself, but in time I learn Tina is a voracious reader and a dedicated newshound, always up on the latest book review or political coup. She is constantly watching foreign films—she belongs to both the Spanish society and the French society—but she's not a snob about it. When I ask her about an Argentine movie she went to, the most I get out of her is, "It had the funniest little dog." The Saturdays she doesn't come to the club, she is usually seeing some off-off Broadway show in the East Village, where she subscribes to several of the theaters. Tina is a political gal. She listens to something called "Peace and Justice Community Radio," because she says mainstream public radio is "too moderate" for her. When I sit down at the table with a can of Coke, she sighs. After a few weeks she can no longer take it, and Tina politely asks if I'm aware of the evils the Coca-Cola Company perpetrates in Latin America. She is full of dark humor. When one of our instructors promises we'll figure bridge out "given twenty-two years or so," Tina tells our table, "My time is near. I better get a move on." I laugh, though the others don't.

And so Tina and I begin the bridge-club dance of seduction, a clumsy process akin to middle school dating. Tina has been moonlighting at a midday intermediate class. It is a wildly popular session, one where it's best to bring a partner. I think Tina might be fishing for someone to accompany her, maybe even me, but I'm not sure. In seventh grade, I once gathered up the courage to ask a girl to "go with me"—the choice phrase at the time for "be my girlfriend"—and she devastated me with the uncomprehending reply, "Where?" I figured when I got engaged such moments were behind me. Today, Tina and I need Lisanne to step in and make the suggestion.

Lisanne says, "So do you guys want to be partners or what?"

Tina, taken a little aback: "I don't know. Do you?"

Me: "I guess. You?"

Tina: "Sure."

Me: "Okay." Then I get her number.

I call Tina on the eve of our date. The answering machine picks up, but when I begin leaving a message, pandemonium erupts. Tina gets on the line to tell me to hold on—she doesn't know how to turn off the machine. She tries to make it stop, but it begins beeping loudly and she doesn't want to do anything because she desperately needs to save a message that's on there. She punctuates her explanation with frantic sounds of helplessness ("Ooh, ooh!"), but eventually the tape runs its course and all is well. She apologizes for screening her calls, offering the cryptic explanation, "I'm trying to avoid these people." (Weeks later, and after a few more similar episodes, I will find out "these people" are financial advisors calling about an old account of hers. The company has been bought by a larger firm, and now both the old broker and the new broker are calling, trying to woo her business. She just wants them to go away.)

With the machine silenced, we agree to meet the next day. The class starts at noon, but from her past forays, Tina knows the drill. She has been taken under the wing of a more advanced threesome she refers to as "the Girls." Tina tells me, "The Girls get there by eleven thirty and set up their table. We'll start our own, but if you want to eat lunch, you have to be there by then."

The next day, at eleven twenty-five, I find the Manhattan Bridge Club in the middle of a feeding frenzy. There are about thirty-six people filling plates of food (cold-cut sandwiches, chicken salad, and the like) and settling into the classroom. This is my introduction to what I will call "Tommy's Lunch-n-Lecture." Tommy Ng is one of the club's star teachers. Everyone loves Tommy. For $20, intermediate students—mainly older women with lots of free time during the day—flock to his class for lunch, a brief tutorial, and an afternoon of prepared hands that tie in to the lesson. The women all know each other; some have been coming for years. As Tina suggested, the seating is fiercely territorial, and once again I feel like I'm back in middle school, surveying a cafeteria of cool cliques and alpha tables. As we're standing in line for a sandwich, Tina whispers, "Wherever we sit, don't tell them you're a beginner. Never let on! If someone asks how long you've been playing, just mumble something. Otherwise, we'll end up being picked on."

Because the room is packed, we have to sit with the Girls after all. Together, we make five, and they graciously tell Tommy they don't mind rotating one player in and out. I meet Ranko, a stylish Japanese septuagenarian who not only plays her cards skillfully, but, when she is dummy, lays them down perfectly straight on the table. You could plumb a line by her hand. Eru, perhaps the most advanced player, is in her eighties with a deep dark voice and a hearing aid. Kathy, the most bubbly, might be the youngest by a few years; she wears a T-shirt.

Tommy is a master of playing the hand. Today he is teaching us how to execute a "trump coup." In general, a coup is bridge-speak for a tricky play. There are a gazillion of them: the Dentist's Coup (a neat extraction from an opponent's hand), the Crocodile Coup (where you swallow up a partner's problematic high card), and the Scissors coup (cutting communication between the defenders). Today's coup involves the declarer bringing about a specific endplay, whereby leading from the "correct" hand in a late-round trick enables the declarer to make the contract. Essentially, the theme is being in the right place (either in your hand or in the dummy's) at the right time (at a specific trick). It is heady stuff.

Tommy's lecture is like a tent revival. His teaching style is a spirited call-and-response. He says, "We're stuck here because trumps have broken badly . . . Am I right or am I right?" and in unison we shout, "You're right!" We will sit at the table until four thirty, nearly five hours, and as the lessons progress through the fall, I will learn a lot from both Tommy and the Girls. For a while, Tina, the Girls, and I will become something of a regular fivesome. Tommy tries to teach us to imagine the cards that remain at the end of the hand, and how by engaging in what he calls "cat and mouse" games, we can make extra tricks out of seemingly thin air. For example, knowing when to purposefully lose a trick so the opponents are on lead and have to break a new, untouched suit sometimes can get you an extra trick.

From the Girls, I don't learn much about cards, but I learn a lot about Elderhostel, a nonprofit organization that runs trips for senior citizens. All the Girls, and even Tina, take them. Through Elderhostel, these women have toured the opera houses of Italy, biked from Berlin to Prague, and rambled through Russia. I become well versed in the pros (the company) and cons (the snoring) of having a randomly assigned roommate. Because of her insomnia, Tina has spent entire nights reading in a bathtub. These days she always ponies up the little extra to have her own room.

As I get to know these women, I realize we're not so different. The freelance writer-slash-shut-in has much in common with the ladies who lunch-n-lecture. We keep the same solitary schedules; we are all socially starved. They come to the club looking for the same thing—companionship, a better lunch than they have at home—that I do. I am now married, and I think my busy wife is glad I've found some new friends, spared as she now is from my midday calls to her office, when I am eager to share the plot of the *Simon and Simon* rerun I just watched or describe in detail how I made a really great sandwich. This is working out well for everyone.

Bridge has long been played for its social component. One place the bridge community is booming is on the Internet, which allows hermits of all stripes a seat at the table. They log on to experience the company of like-minded fans, though as in all cyber-communities, it is a shuttered sort of socializing.

One day before one of my first lessons, Zeus takes me over to his computer and logs on to Bridge Base Online (www.bridge base.com), a site where players can watch or play bridge for free. A championship match is taking place in Houston, and we check out the live Vugraph, which is essentially a digital broadcast of the game with the bidding, play, and all four hands represented in real time by brightly colored graphics. With a click, Zeus steers us to a table where some friends of his are playing. It is a hot table—515 of the 1,028 people online are watching it, too. Zeus points to the list of kibitzers, running his finger down the screen names and giving little verbal shout-outs—"We're one big family," he says. Indeed, he seems to know most of the onlookers by their Internet handles alone, and within seconds of logging on, his screen floods with instant messages. A guy from Israel

sends greetings while Zeus drops a flirty hello to a woman working the tournament ("Hi, sexy"). As people walk by, they peer
at the Vugraph. The news spreads around the club that Zeus's
friends—a team of New Yorkers—are kicking some butt.

Zeus is a professed computer nut; he says the Web game is
growing like crazy. A survey published by the ACBL in 2005
revealed that 4.1 million Americans play over the Internet—
more than 12 percent of them play daily. Zeus says, "There is a
never-ending appetite for information on bridge. Whatever we
post online, people want more." In many ways, Web-casting is
ideally suited for the game. The audience is not wide enough
to make traditional broadcasting feasible, but by building a fan
base one Vugraph at a time, players and organizers hope one
day to see their sport on prime time. In a few months from our
conversation, on the final day of the 2005 world championship,
more than eight thousand fans will log on to watch the games
live from Portugal, while another two thousand souls go about
their business playing bridge.

The Internet provides a truly global game. The Bridge Base
software runs in English, Spanish, French, Italian, German, Polish, Portuguese, Czech, Turkish, Romanian, Japanese, and Russian. The Web site's discussion boards read like a mini model
UN. There might be posts from a Norwegian kid looking for
someone to learn and play his amalgamated bidding system,
a German man in need of a multilingual teacher, or a woman
seeking two roommates for a tournament in Tenerife. Not every
comment is on topic, either. There are postings about the pope,
President Bush, and Talk Like a Pirate Day.

Bridge Base is not the only popular site. There is e-bridge and
OKbridge, the largest pay service, as well as many others—Microsoft, AOL, and Yahoo! all operate game sites that tend to draw
more players, though experts say the quality of play suffers. Some
services—Bridge Base, OKbridge, and a site called Swan Games—
even offer ACBL-sanctioned master points. The organization
sponsors some two hundred thousand online tables a year.

Early one random Wednesday morning, at around half past midnight, some one thousand players from across the globe are trolling the Yahoo! bridge site, chatting, playing, and flitting between tables. Fourteen "lounges" (six advanced, five intermediate, one beginner, and two social) are up and running, each filling up with a shifting mosaic of screen names. Clicking on a specific table reveals a foursome of little personalized icons, a menagerie of guys, girls, flora, and fauna of all kinds and colors sporting caps and ponytails and a variety of hairstyles—each avatar, one assumes, something of a labor of love.

The site is huge, free, and public, which lends a certain Wild West lawlessness to the place. Some players talk trash ("i saw ur image in ur profile u are soooooo old"), while others try to lure people to their Web cams or to look at "hot!!! pics!!!" Meanwhile, rambunctious killjoys (known as "trolls") infiltrate the beginner lounges and mess with the newbies by bidding outrageous contracts (opening seven no-trump) and making false claims.

In general, however, the beginners keep things civil, telling each other "glp" (good luck, partner), "wpp" (well played, partner), and "sp" (sorry, partner), depending on the situation. I even witness the following somewhat incredible exchange between an alien and a cat:

"sp. that was dumb."

"u did well . . . it's only a game."

"u r too kind but thanks. lets play again."

In the advanced lounge, the chatter is more matter-of-fact, mostly about the bidding. The play is fast and the tempers hot. While silently kibitzing an "expert" table, I watch one player blow up at his partner ("WHY DIDN'T U PLAY SNGLTON???") and "storm off" from the table, at which point I am unceremoniously booted out of the room.

Before shutting down, I check in with AOL, whose site is boasting some fifteen hundred players. Meanwhile, the Microsoft Network teems with two thousand. It is nearing one o'clock, and there are seemingly limitless chances to play. At this point in our tutelage, many of my classmates have wandered online and found themselves in a game over their head, where they are invariably treated rudely. Bridge players are not known to suffer fools in person, let alone online. Molly once had an entire threesome walk out on her after one hand (after cursing her out in French), though I'm not sure I can entirely blame them.

Boorish manners aside, the online games offer stiff competition to the brick-and-mortar bridge clubs. Somewhere, someone in the world is always up for a game; bridge now can be played twenty-four hours a day from Denver to Dubai in the comfort of your pajamas. One no longer has to block out three to four hours to play—online, there's no travel, no unwanted chitchat, or even sluggish shuffling of cards.

But in the end, most say the Internet will complement bridge, not conquer it. There is no such thing as a high-level or big-stakes online game because there is no way to guarantee match security. (You could kibitz and play at the same time through two different accounts—or simply phone up your partner and discuss your cards.) Ultimately, bridge is a social sport played in the flesh. Even a cerebral theory–junkie like Polowan—who is sometimes paid to play promotionally online—agrees. He says, "When it's online, it doesn't feel like bridge. It feels more like someone has written a hand down on a napkin for me."

While playing such hands might be unsatisfying for Polowan, for me, they're good practice. So that I'm not at the mercy of some punk kid in Peoria (or Poland, for that matter), I invest in one of the more popular computer bridge programs, Bridge Baron 15. For $59 plus tax and shipping, I get to be whisked off to a medieval castle to do battle against a baron whose accent sounds suspiciously like he's from my block in Brooklyn ("Thanks for playin' bridge wid me!").

I am instantly hooked. On the computer, I can take back mistakes and replay the hand until I get it right. Of course, in some ways this is terrible practice. I can go through an exceptional number of hands in a night, playing them more quickly than I ever would at the club because the stakes are so much lower. In the Baron's world, I am a maverick, a fearlessly self-ish but brilliant player free from all social constraints. With no partner to please (save a mere robot, or "bot"), I bid outrageous contracts—just to infuriate the Baron—and try to force them to work through prodigious use of the "take back play" button.

Even after I learn how to mute the program, Heather, my wife, comes to recognize the difference between the quiet sounds of industry issuing forth from the study (of me, say, writing late into the night) and the rhythmic clicks and clacks of another grudge match against the Baron. Occasionally, she'll remind me from the other room that I have work to do. But at this point it's too late. I have developed an unhealthy relationship with the Baron. I can no longer start my day nor end my night without truly trouncing him. No matter if I have all the good cards and the hand is one a monkey could make, I have to play and play until I thoroughly embarrass him. The problem is that after a while the victories begin to feel empty. No stolen contract or jerry-rigged coup is enough. Because by now I have come to a startling realization—the Baron isn't perfect.

These days it is pretty well documented that computers have vastly outstripped humans in the ability to play chess. Worse, it's not only the supercomputers like Deep Blue—which famously defeated world champion Gary Kasparov in 1997—that can whup us, but programs that run on a household PC. The machines are depending less on so-called "brute force" analysis than on stra-tegic heuristics that have led to startlingly creative, superhuman play—play that often confounds the programmers themselves. We are actually relearning the game we taught to computers. They have found resolutions to endgames long considered hope-less. They work on a horizon beyond human scope. Computers are teaching us better chess.

Thankfully, computers still stink at bridge. The calculations are more devilish. Not all the variables are known; cards are concealed—as are partners' motivations. Teaching computers to play defense is particularly tricky. While one powerful program named Deep Finesse can immediately analyze the chances of making a hand—thus rendering one of the favorite pastimes of bridge hobbyists effectively obsolete—computers cannot compete with the pros. I am not the only one who notices the Baron's occasional poor play. The ACBL magazine, the *Bridge Bulletin,* runs a regular feature titled "It's Your Call," in which experts are asked what they would bid on a number of hands. Answers typically vary, with some choices rated better than others. Each is assigned a score, and the person with the best total score wins the contest. Every month a computer program is included among the panelists, and most months it finishes toward the bottom.

For that reason, computers are left to play against themselves. Every year the top programs face off in the World Computer Bridge Championships. Bridge Baron won the inaugural event, in 1997, but the best he has finished recently has been runner-up. In 2005, the year I bought the program, the Baron—representing the United States—battled bots from the U.K., Netherlands, Germany, Japan, and France. In a stunning defeat, Jack, the four-time defending Dutch champion, was dethroned by WBridge5, a French program. Meanwhile, the Baron finished fifth (and will do so again in 2006), making me think perhaps I'm being too hard on him.

Over the course of the next few months, as I become more facile at bidding (picking up useful conventions, solidifying my understanding of the system), I learn some of the basic strategies of card play. The beauty of bridge is in the dummy. Once it hits the table, each player is no longer limited to his own meager hand. The horizons stretch open. Everyone can now see twenty-six cards—thirteen in his hand, thirteen in dummy—and that kind of information, plus whatever inferences can be made from the auction, is powerful fodder for thought. For example, after the first few tricks, most professional players can tell you—without peeking—the cards that are in each hand.

For the declarer, the one trying to make the contract (who is playing both his hand and his partner's), there are many tactics. Basically, once the dummy comes down and the declarer can see his twenty-six cards, he must formulate a plan. First, he analyzes the opening lead. What does it suggest? I will get into defense in a minute, but certain leads signal different things. (For many players, leading the queen, for example, promises that they also have the jack.) So the declarer can often get a clue about the cards held by the person on lead. Next, the declarer reviews the auction. Any bidding by the opponents supplies further information. Often he or she can guess about how many points the opposition has in their hands—which can further help the declarer locate the important missing high cards. Finally, he or she looks at how the two hands match up, and either counts how many tricks can be won outright (called "winners") or how many tricks it looks as if will be lost to the opponents (called, not surprisingly, "losers"). The wonderful thing about losers is that there are ways of getting rid of them. They can be trumped, discarded (or "sluffed," when the declarer can't follow suit), finessed (a way of winning a cheap trick by taking advantage of the position of the cards), or promoted (that is, turned into winners by continuing to lead a suit until all the outranking cards have been played).

These are just the basics. There are enough fancy ruses and so-called "bridge rules" to fill a library, such as the Rule of Seven and the Rule of Eleven (which dates to 1890 and derives from the English game whist, a predecessor to bridge), plus mysterious-sounding mnemonics like "eight ever, nine never." The old-fashioned way to learn bridge was simply to memorize as many as you could and then stick to them come hell or high water. Today teachers try to emphasize the logic behind the play and spend less time drilling dictums into students' heads.

And now a short word about defense, which is a science unto itself. Careful reasoning can guide certain plays—and bridge pros know the mathematical odds of certain layouts of cards—but often your partner can be infinitely more helpful than any dusty bridge law. During the hand, defenders can use their cards to signal their strengths to each other. There are times when you have a choice of what card to play and it won't affect the outcome of the trick. Given the situation, this is a chance to convey to your partner one of three things: your attitude (or how you feel about a certain suit), your count (or how many cards you hold in a suit), or your suit preference.

Of course you don't always have the cards necessary to signal what you want. Defense requires imagination, skill, and—above all else—working with your partner. At the beginning, Tina and I tend to defend with our heads down, ignoring signals—that is, when we even bother to give them—and we suffer the consequences of our myopic play.

At least we are beginning to sound like bridge players. Unable to walk the walk, we can at least try to talk the talk, which is in itself no mean feat. The game boasts a colorful vocabulary: Baby Blackwood, elopement, grand slam force, ruffing finesse, wish trick, psychic lead, phantom sacrifice, nuisance bid, Morton's Fork Coup, isolating the menace, kibitzer's make, kiss of death, Gum Wrapper Coup, and the winkle. In general, the more evocative the term the more fiendish the play. A more pedestrian nomenclature is reserved for the deck itself. The numbered cards (two through ten) are called the "spot cards" or "spots." The "face cards" are the king, queen, and jack; the "honor cards" (or "honors") are the face cards plus the ace and the ten—or the top five cards in a suit. Meanwhile, because it sits on the table, the dummy's hand is often called "the board."

Somewhere between the picturesque and the practical lies one of my favorite terms—the Yarborough. Named for Charles Anderson Worsley Anderson-Pelham, the second earl of Yarborough (1809–62), it is technically a hand that contains no card higher than a nine. Now the term is used more generally to describe a crappy hand. Most players dread being dealt one. It is considered an unlucky hand, utterly lifeless and boring. But there is a lesson in the Yarborough, one the good earl knew well.

At the whist table, he would bet his opponents £1,000 to £1 that they wouldn't get such a hand. For a true Yarborough is quite rare. The actual odds are 1,827–1. Outrageously bad hands, like outrageously good ones, don't come up very often. In fact, as I alluded to earlier, the chances of drawing any one predetermined hand—thirteen specific cards—is 635,013,559,600–1. So if you'll permit me a minute of armchair philosophizing (and the math majors stifle their yawns), it seems to me that each bridge hand is a minor miracle. In retrospect, the odds of your getting that particular collection of cards are staggering, a once in a lifetime occurrence. So you better make the most of it.

Another choice phrase, which I found flipping through my copy of the *Official Encyclopedia of Bridge,* is the "backwash squeeze." Unlike Yarborough, I have never heard it used at the club, but according to my book it is "a unique type of trump squeeze in which both menaces are in the same hand and the player sitting behind the hand with the menaces holds both guards plus a losing trump, and is caught in the 'backwash' of a squeeze by means of a ruff taken in the hand holding the menaces." Of course I have no idea what that means. The entry stretches for about a page and a half of gibberish. There are some diagrams, one of which shows a devilish declarer putting one of the opponents in a bind with only three cards left to play; no matter what card the defender plays (and two of his three cards are winners in their suits) the declarer has a way to take all three tricks.

A little digging shows that a backwash squeeze almost popped up in Cincinnati in 1994 during the finals of the Vanderbilt Cup. (The declarer came close to getting a chance to execute one, but it became unnecessary due to a defensive error.) In 2006, one will appear in a pairs match at the spring nationals in Dallas. In his syndicated bridge column, Omar Sharif (or perhaps one of his ghostwriters) writes how the defender sitting West was "caught in the backwash of the high trump." Appreciating the beauty of the situation, he continues, "It is almost as if the after-effect of this play is coincidental, not deliberate."

And so while I will most certainly never execute one, I like the sound of a backwash squeeze—the unlikely combination of fighter pilot bravado (you're caught in the jet wash!) and some gruesome dental torture (is it *safe*?). Suffice it to say that I never want to fall victim to one at the table or away.

One night, word goes through class that on Monday the club will be holding a supervised duplicate bridge game for beginners. This is hot news. As it happens, Tina and I are on fire that night, making some big hands that are going down at the other tables, and so, flush with victory, we agree to sign up.

In the sober light of the next morning, I get a call from Tina. She wants to meet at the club this weekend to practice. Duplicate is what the big kids play, and while we're anxious to get a taste of the action, it's pretty scary stuff. It seems even scarier after we get off to a sad start on Saturday, blowing the first couple of hands. Eventually, we begin to play better, but our high is gone. We're not the bridge brains we thought we were.

Twenty-four people show up Monday night, filling six tables. The game starts at seven, though two of our classmates have been there since five thirty studying laminated cheat sheets they made. Tina dismisses them with a nod. "I never cram," she says, though I can tell she is nervous.

There is no shuffling between hands of duplicate bridge. Everyone will play the same hands, though not at the same time. For our game, the cards have been presorted into "boards," which are metal or plastic rectangular trays with one slot on each side (labeled North, South, East, and West). Thirteen cards fit into each slot. Each board (and thus hand) is numbered. The board also tells you which player is the "dealer" (and gets to begin the auction), and which side, if any, is vulnerable. As the board is played, each player keeps his or her cards—tricks are not gathered up by the winners, as they often are in rubber bridge. This allows the cards to go back into their original slots in the board once the hand is over. It is then ready to be passed to another table.

Every pair in the room is either sitting East-West or North-South. During the match, the North-South pairs remain at the table, while the East-West pairs rotate around the room. The boards also rotate, but in the opposite direction. With each board travels a score slip that has a line for every table in the room. Most players also keep track of their score privately. At the end of the night, the person running the game (called the director) will enter the scores into a computer. Since every pair sitting in the same direction got the same cards on the same board, their results can be compared. Thus, all East-West pairs are competing against each other, as are all North-South pairs. They get a "match point" for every pair in their direction that they beat on a particular board and half a point for each pair that they tie. At the end of the night, the pair with the most match points wins. Better yet, each pair's match-point score is converted to a percentage that represents how well they did compared to the theoretical maximum. Scoring above or below 50 percent translates into an above- or below-average game.

Thus the luck of the deal is eliminated. If you bid and make three no-trump, and everyone else in your direction does the same, the board is a wash. But if you make one overtrick, you have the top score.

In a regular duplicate session, the only time the cards are shuffled is at the beginning, when every table makes up some boards that will then circulate around the room. Tonight, as I said, that work has been done for us. We are playing a "supervised game," which means an instructor is on hand to answer questions about the bidding and to make sure everything moves smoothly. Still, for the first time an evening's worth of scores are being tallied, and—most wonderfully of all—there are master points at stake.

By now we have all joined the American Contract Bridge League, or ACBL. Shortly after sending in $26 for a new one-year membership (after the first year, membership is $35), I received a welcoming kit with an *A to Z Member Guide*, information on group dental plans, and two catalogs worth of bridge products—books, playing cards, computer games, electronic shufflers, and a large selection of apparel ranging from windbreakers to aprons ("I Bridge 4 Food") to T-shirts (Lil' Kibitzer, Give Us This Day Our Daily Bridge) to dickeys (no joke). (In the fall of 2006, the ACBL will close its shop and name Baron Barclay Bridge Supplies the licensed distributor of its products.)

Best of all is my new membership card, which bears my very own ACBL number. I can now accumulate master points. Starting with zero, I am officially a Novice. The next rank, at five master points, is Junior Master. It is a long road to the vaunted Life Master plateau (three hundred points)—and even then, there are grades of Life Master, ranging from Bronze Life Master (five hundred points) to the rarified heights of Grand Life Master (ten thousand points). For some people, making Life Master is indeed a life's work; at the other end of the spectrum, in 2006, the country's youngest Life Master becomes a ten-year, forty-three-days-old home-schooled boy named Adam Kaplan, who plays with a bidding system he devised with his dad. It is a dizzying climb and—in the end—one that is utterly meaningless. Yet people go mad for master points. The ACBL has done a brilliant job of creating a demand for something tasteless, odorless, and totally worthless outside of the organization itself. Master points can't be redeemed for food or fortune, only fame—and then only at events where the goal is to get more master points. Master points are an end in themselves. The race for them is endless and self-perpetuating, and yet they are the coin of the realm. Players spend countless hours and dollars chasing them.

At the end of every year, an award is presented to the player who has won the most master points in the past twelve months. Originally called the McKenney trophy, the race was renamed the Barry Crane 500 after the successful television producer and director (*Mission: Impossible, The Six Million Dollar Man*) and fierce bridge addict who died under mysterious circumstances in 1985. Crane was found naked and bludgeoned to death in his garage. To this day, his murder remains unsolved. At the time, he had eleven thousand more master points than his nearest rival. He had won the contest that now bears his name six times, and six times he had come in as the runner-up.

For such a heated competition, many players hire professional partners, and one year, the eventual winner, an amateur, actually paid the two pros on his heels to sit out a few tournaments. In 2005, a fifty-six-year-old auditor from Mountain Home, Arkansas, is taking a shot at the title, having announced he plans to play eighteen games a week for forty-four weeks with a number of partners. Come December 31, he will have attended thirty-five tournaments, crisscrossing the United States and Canada—mainly by car—from Myrtle Beach to Seattle to Dallas to Tulsa to Omaha to Las Vegas to Biloxi to Calgary to Branson to Jackson to Paducah and so on. At the stroke of midnight on New Year's Eve, he will have won some 3,137 master points this year—more than enough to make him a Gold Life Master.

And so that night at the club we bid with vigor. Tina has to play not one but two five-diamond contracts, unfortunately going down each time. Still we are bold, unbowed, and playing a little off the cuff. The scoring of duplicate rewards the brave but punishes the foolish. If you're the only one who dares to overbid your hand, hoping to make the game bonus, and you make it, it's a big swing. But if you don't make it—and everyone else played it safe—you're at the bottom of the pile. In general, Tina and I tend to overbid, but at times we land on our feet.

We're sitting North-South, which means we don't have to move tables. Every three boards, our opponents swap out. Over the course of the night, I feel we're able to establish a little home-field advantage. They're guests in our house, trespassers on our turf, and we initiate the friendly banter—"Hi, I'm Edward. This is Tina. What class are you in? Are you Monday-night people? Have you played duplicate before?"—while keeping coy in our responses. We're seeing the stars from the other weeknight classes; it's the best and the brightest of the Manhattan Bridge

Club beginners, and we—along with our Tuesday-night brethren—are out to do our teachers proud. We nod at our classmates at tables around the room, keeping sprits up. I even manage to give Molly a smile. An indication of how serious it is: I hardly snack, and I never see the restroom.

It's refreshing to play against new blood, like the two girls in their late twenties, one of whom is pregnant. They're hesitant bidders but strong players, and when the round is over we see them off with a nod of respect. Then with relish we trounce the thirty-something redheaded man in a ribbed shirt whose rude partner (a crazy old bat) tells Tina to hurry up. It's thrilling at the end of every hand to know your brilliance (or your opponents' lack thereof) by looking at the score sheet that travels with each board and tells you how the other pairs handled your cards.

As the night wears on, I see a poker game growing in one of the side rooms. There are two busy and boisterous tables holding all sorts of agitated types: a guy in a T-shirt, gold chains, and shades (who "reeks of reefer," according to someone I overhear outside the room), a man in a tie, whose sleeves are rolled up to reveal enormous forearm tattoos, a tubby grizzled guy with wild wiry hair. They're trying to look cool losing $25 a raise; I can't help thinking we're having more fun. In a few months, I will hear a rumor that the club's Saturday-night game was raided by cops who busted in the door, Prohibition-style. All of this will be discussed in hushed tones over the snack table; Tina will wonder if a rival club tipped off the cops. In a rare self-revelatory moment, she tells me she lived through liquor raids on her father's farm, where he made his own wine. At the sight of a strange car coming up the drive, she was instructed to run the booze to a German neighbor over the hill. She says someone was always ratting them out.

Occasionally during our match Tina gets down on herself, thinking all is lost on a hand when it's not. She is a good player, but she lacks confidence. I try to keep the mood light. In social bridge, the dummy is usually free to wander off to the bathroom or fix himself a drink while the declarer plays his cards. At the club, the dummy is technically the only one allowed to touch his hand, and so he has to sit at the table and play the card the declarer tells him to. I am glad for this, because it doesn't feel like you've been abandoned by your partner.

At the end of the night Tina tells me that when she began taking lessons her goal was to play a duplicate game before a year had passed. That morning she looked at her checkbook, and she is proud to say she has done it—albeit supervised—in about half that time. Little does she know that bigger games await her, that only slightly more than a year after our first lesson I will convince her to leave New York and the relative safety of the club and travel with me to Chicago to compete—as unsupervised underdogs—in the national bridge championships.

But for now, we savor our modest triumph. We both feel the thrill of duplicate, knowing that you're not competing against Wanda and Barbara but the Platonic ideal of all the Wandas and Barbaras in the room. The only way to raise your score is to deviate from the pack, display your brilliance, and pull ahead. It is easy to see how the duplicate game quickly becomes addictive, not to mention hypercompetitive. You're playing the whole room. Few games strive to reduce the element of luck. There is a clarity, a certainty to the duplicate table that I can imagine is enormously comforting. The game ends around ten thirty, but everyone is still pumped, clustered around the snack table talking hands and waiting for the scores.

In the end, we win .06 of a master point—a thrilling step on the way to Junior Master. We come in third out of the six pairs sitting North-South, but we finish first in our flight because they end up stratifying the game, as some of the players are much more experienced. As she is posting the scores, the director announces the club is going to host another supervised duplicate game in a month, which happens to be my wife's birthday. Tina's eyes light up, and I don't have the heart to break the news. I am being torn between the two women in my life.

As we wait for the elevator, I am reminded again that Tina might look little and sweet, but she's one tough New York lady. Every night when we leave the club she takes her keys out of her purse and puts them in her pocket in case her bag is snatched on the way home. She is full of such tricks, carrying a wallet but keeping her cash in old envelopes. She is eighty-three years old, though she doesn't like to advertise that fact because, as she says the first time I ask her, "I don't like to tell people. If I tell you, you won't want to do stuff with me."

Tina doesn't bat an eye at walking across town; one night she'll tell me her leg is sore from having hoofed it a mile and a half from First to Tenth Avenue. ("I like to walk," she shrugs.) Even this late, she usually heads home on foot. On nights when she "splurges" and takes the bus, I accompany her half a block to the stop. Both she and the Girls keep themselves pretty active. Earlier tonight, when one of our forty-something opponents said she wished she could retire so she could focus on her bidding, Tina—tough as nails—told her, "I'm really too busy to fit in bridge."

And yet bridge has a way of stealing your hours. Going home, I am distracted on the train—a little too revved up to read, I keep thinking over the night—and it's only when I get out of the subway in Brooklyn that I realize: I've forgotten to eat dinner.

CHAPTER THREE

Kibitzing in Cowtown

Kansas City, Missouri, December 2005

It is Tuesday, December 27, and I'm being driven to the Westin Hotel in downtown Kansas City for the Kansas City Holiday Regional Bridge Tournament. My wife and I are in town spending Christmas with her family. The tournament is attached to a large shopping mall, which means family members want to tag along, part for the bridge spectacle, part for the post-holiday sales. I wonder about the professionalism of this. I doubt Woodward and Bernstein ever brought along their mothers-in-law, but mine has a car, so off we go.

For a place known as "Cowtown"—sometimes a point of pride, sometimes not—I am surprised to learn Kansas City boasts more fountains than any city in the world except Rome, though none are visible as we speed downtown. We are close to the actual geographical center of America (located some 250 miles west of town, just outside Lebanon, Kansas, for you cartographers at home), and I am reminded that Kansas City is an integral part of that most earnest of political clichés, the heartland. It seems fitting that across the street from the tournament is the corporate headquarters of the Hallmark greeting-card company, which was founded in the city almost a century ago.

The Westin is a multitiered hotel complex connected to condominiums and commercial office space; it feeds into a large ritzy shopping center complete with live theater, outdoor ice skating, and a restaurant that delivers your food by model train. In the lobby, there are businessmen on laptops and two lanky kids playing cards (noticeably not bridge). It is a large hotel like any other, filled with the stale serenity of recycled air, the susurration of unseen fountains, gliding glass elevators, and vast plots of potted plants (many decorated for the season). The calm is broken only by the distant caterwauls of loose children. I take an escalator to the ballroom level, passing below the sweat-suited legs of energetic hotel guests—visible only from the waist down—swishing furiously on exercise machines.

When I arrive, the morning game is still wrapping up, though people have begun to circulate. A sign outside one hospitality room says it is open from eleven fifteen to two. At first I wonder why it's empty—it's now almost noon—but then I notice the hours run from P.M. to A.M. This crowd stays up late.

The ballroom is full of people, mainly four to a table, with the occasional kibitzer seated behind. I scan the crowd: lots of Christmas sweaters, gray hair, and bald pates. That said, there seems to be a little of everyone and everything—dowagers in dark suits, twenty-somethings in T-shirts, kids in Harry Potter capes, wiseguys in leather caps and gold chains, and a few senior citizens on scooters. Overall, jeans or khakis appears to be the rule. Comfy is the word—there are lots of button-downs and sweatshirts—though I do spy sport coats, a few furs, and even a clutch of women in stilettos braving the cold to smoke on the veranda. It's noon, and everyone seems to carry a cup of something. In the room, the silence is intense. It is an expectant, almost heated hush. They're hunting those elusive master points.

It is less quiet but equally focused away from the tables. This is my first bridge tournament, and I'm a little overwhelmed. It's like the club scene on crack. The mood is gently manic; everyone seems keyed up, a little slaphappy. It's enough to make a guy jumpy. The complimentary coffee table is a free-for-all. Players form pockets of agitated discussion, clutching painstakingly detailed convention cards and talking clubs, hearts, spades, and diamonds. It's hard to distinguish chatter from a come-on: how does one respond to the question, "Do you play four-way transfers?" In this instance, it is by firing back: "How do you answer a weak two?" New partners? Friends? Lovers? It isn't clear. What matters is that unlike most everyone they meet on the street, at work, or in a bar, these people understand. Around me couples and competitors alike thrill to jabber in the inimitable patter of the bridge dork.

Marti and Chuck Malcolm don't look like crazy people, though at first I assume they are. Who else would want to organize a major bridge tournament over the holidays? (I have plenty of shamefully late shopping these two could do if they really have so much extra time on their hands.) We sit down at an outlying table in the main ballroom. Marti wears a pink turtleneck under a white button-down sweater; she has long blond hair and a nametag with a gold badge on it. Chuck is a big guy with a military bearing; he sports a red shirt, glasses, a mustache, and a cell phone clipped to his belt. It turns out he is a psychologist with the V.A. Medical Center in Topeka, Kansas, where they live. Marti works for the state's Department of Social and Rehabilitation Services.

Some six hundred people have come to Kansas City, which is a good turnout in the Midwest but not as big as things get in Las Vegas or New York. The exact numbers are a little vague, because tournaments aren't measured in people. They're measured by the total number of tables occupied—meaning repeat players get counted more than once—and this year Marti is hoping for 1,150 tables over the course of six days (up 25 from last year). In terms of actual pieces of furniture, there are some two hundred tables covered by white tablecloths with eighthundred-odd bidding boxes standing at the ready beside each red-and-gold chair. How many packs of cards I don't want to know. The logistics seem unbearable.

Players hail from around the Midwest, places such as St. Louis, Chicago, Sioux City, Omaha, Lincoln, and Madison, as well as from far off locales such as Schenectady, Fort Worth, and Calgary. There is a fellow from Yugoslavia (doing a postdoc fellowship in Norman, Oklahoma), a few traveling professionals, plus that man from Mountain Home, Arkansas, who will ring in the New Year with the distinction of having earned more master points in 2005 than anyone else in the country.

The tournament is composed of many events, each of which has no clear favorite to win. It depends on the day—who's in, who's out, and what game they're playing. There are many types of events—some for pairs, some for teams—with intriguing names such as knockout, Swiss teams, and side game series. Marti says, "It's a different game every day, so anybody can win. That's why they come—there's always a chance."

For their chance, players pay $13 a session. The tournament actually makes money, but those profits are pumped back into the three or four sectionals that lose money each year. Anything left over is used to make the holiday tournament a little nicer. These bridge buffs bring a lot of business to Kansas City. Beyond all the shopping and eating, Chuck guesses that during a typically dead week at the hotel the tournament draws in about seven hundred "room nights," which seems a low estimate. Instead of paying for the space, the Malcolms buy a large amount of food from the hotel (say $16,000 worth) and the ballrooms are comped. The food then becomes the late-night snacks. Last night the hospitality suite offered ice cream. Tonight there will be roast beef sandwiches. The room overlooks an ice-skating rink and the mayor's one-hundred-foot-tall Christmas tree; the suite is open between sessions for folks who want to watch bowl games. Champagne is served at the New Year's Eve party pairs, after which there is a party. Marti thinks touches like that make people come back year after year. Chuck says, "It keeps people from just playing and going home, which is what you do at a lot of tournaments." With a somewhat wistful grin, Marti says, "It used to be that bridge players would go out all night and sleep all morning. But we're all getting older."

This is the Malcolms' thirteenth year to head the Kansas City tournament, which they helped start. Amazingly, they organize and play in the tournament at the same time. It's a popular one, partly because Marti and Chuck focus on hospitality, and partly because of the mall attached next door ("People never have to go outside!"). Things usually run smoothly. Still, Marti makes Chuck carry a walkie-talkie.

The Malcolms fly in the face of another old bridge saw, which is that the married couple that plays together rarely stays together. But they met at the bridge table some twenty-three years ago in Cherry Hill, New Jersey, and it seemed like a good thing then and it still does now. At the time they were playing against each other in something called the Midnight Zip (a loosey-goosey late-night game that starts after the evening session). "We were joking around during the game," says Marti. "It was more for fun than anything else."

Playing together remains fun, though Marti admits there's something to the conventional wisdom. "It's tougher to play as husband and wife because the temperament is . . . you know." As she drifts off, Chuck chimes in: "The temperament carries over into the home." He pauses. "It just depends on how competitive you are and how intense you get at the table." Marti adds, "Which is his problem. I'm very calm and easygoing. And he gets really . . ." Chuck smiles sheepishly. "Yeah, I get very intense in a competitive situation. But we've survived."

It is important to note that not every couple does. We're in Kansas City, after all, the scene of perhaps the most famous partnership meltdown in bridge.

John and Myrtle Bennett had been married eleven years. He was the wealthy thirty-six-year-old district manager of the Hudnut perfume company; she had first fallen in love with him in a photograph, then bumped into him on a train during the first World War, when he was in uniform. They lived in a fashionable South Side apartment at 902 Ward Parkway. On Sunday, September 29,

1929, a month before "Black Tuesday," the Bennetts were play-ing what would be remembered as a "very sociable game" of bridge with their neighbors, Mr. and Mrs. Charles M. Hofman. Earlier in the day, the foursome had played golf; as the evening set in, plans to go to the movies were scrapped in favor of a few rubbers of bridge. The stakes were one tenth of a cent a point.

It was around midnight. The Bennetts had gotten off to an early lead but had since slipped behind. Mr. Bennett opened the bidding with a spade; Mrs. Hofman overcalled two diamonds; Mrs. Bennett jumped to four spades, which all passed. After the fact, no one would remember exactly how the cards fell—or even agree on the precise bidding (had Mr. Hofman dou-bled?)—but Mr. Bennett went down two tricks. Mrs. Hofman was later quoted as saying Mrs. Bennett had laid down "a rather good hand" for the dummy, which seems to suggest her hus-band bungled it (by either opening lightly or playing poorly).

Whatever the case, Mrs. Bennett called Mr. Bennett a "bum bridge player," and the couple began to bicker. As tempers flared, Mr. Bennett reached across the cards, grabbed his wife, and slapped her a few times, toppling the table. Mrs. Bennett became hysterical; she shouted, "Only a dirty cur would strike a woman in the face in the presence of friends," a remark which Mr. Bennett had the regrettable gall to try to laugh off. As his wife fled the room, he began packing for a business trip, for which he loudly announced he now would be leaving a day early. He would spend the night in a hotel.

When Mr. Hofman suggested reconciliation was in order, Bennett told him, "Let her alone. She has those brainstorms often," the truth of which was undercut by Mrs. Bennett's reap-pearance with a revolver. When Mr. Bennett spied the gun, he ran and locked himself in the bathroom, barely beating the two bullets that crashed through the door. He slipped out a side pas-sage and was trying to open the front door when Mrs. Bennett felled him with two more shots. She was taken into custody in her golfing attire and charged with first-degree murder.

The trial, almost seventeen months later, was the social event of the season. Minks and suits displaced the court's typically more shabby hangers-on. Mrs. Bennett arrived looking stylish and pale, and in pictures appeared much younger than her thirty-five years, with marcelled hair and thin-set lips. She was defended by former Kansas City mayor James A. Reed, a three-time United States senator and presidential hopeful. The trial was a two-week circus, complete with a dramatic reenactment of the shooting by the defense team, teary testimony from the widow's mother (through which Myrtle—and her lawyer—sobbed uncontrollably), and sensational declarations from the defendant ("I'd rather have been dead myself!"). At the sight of her husband's bloody polo shirt, Mrs. Bennett burst into tears. The day the jury took the case, Senator Reed slugged a newspaper photographer in court.

The defense argued that the shots that killed Mr. Bennett—including the one in his back—were the result of a terrible accident. Mrs. Bennett had been fetching the gun for her husband, who carried it with him on trips, when it went off: twice when she stumbled over a chair and twice (fatally) when he tried to grab it from her, twisting her arm. Mrs. Bennett's first—and contradictory—version of events, the one she gave the police, was not allowed into evidence by the judge. And so it became a case of conflicting versions: close-range mishap or hot-blooded murder? As for the Hofmans, only Charles ever made it to the stand, where his testimony varied from his initial statement; in the end he was no help, claiming he was too shocked by what happened to recall events clearly.

Character witnesses for the defense described a faithful wife and volatile, ill-tempered husband who had previously slapped Mrs. Bennett in public. (The prosecution pointed out the irrelevance of this line of testimony, as the defense claimed the shooting was accidental.) The jury learned of Mrs. Bennett's hardscrabble beginnings in Arkansas, how she cared for her widowed mother, and the depths of her devotion to her husband.

A neighbor early on the scene recalled picking up the smoking gun for fear Mrs. Bennett would do herself injury. Senator Reed's final fifty-five-minute plea to a packed courtroom was a tearjerker: "If you penalize her, you will destroy her."

The jury deliberated for eight and a half hours (during which three members were taught the rudiments of the game), before coming back with a surprising verdict of "not guilty." After a protracted civil suit, Mrs. Bennett collected $30,000 in life insurance.

Thus the price America put on poor play. While the hands were lost to history, bridge wags had a field day printing versions of the supposedly fatal deal—and then demonstrating how through more cunning play Bennett could have saved his life. For a time Mrs. Bennett contemplated writing her autobiography, but negotiations with the ghostwriter fell apart. What seems to be the last report of Mrs. Bennett comes from Algonquin columnist (and Kansas City son) Alexander Woollcott, who reported that Mrs. Bennett found herself hard-pressed to find partners posttrial. One day, a fellow ignorant of her past put down the dummy and apologized for his bid, saying, "Partner, I'm afraid you'll want to shoot me for this." According to Woollcott, Mrs. Bennett "had the good taste to faint."

Back at the tournament, Marti reminds me that not every bridge union must be sundered as spectacularly as the Bennetts'. Sometimes players find they're better partners at the table than they are at the altar. She says, "A lot of the players who are married get divorced—but then they still end up playing with their ex. The partnership outlasts the marriage!" (Then, as an afterthought: "Of course, they probably got divorced in the first place because of bridge.") At this point, a bubbly woman with short gray hair seated at the next table leans over and announces, "I'm proud to be married to my third bridge player. Bridge has held my interest where some of the men haven't." Her current husband, sitting next to her, adds, "I miss your ex-husband. He was a good player." She sighs before focusing again on her table.

"We could tell lots of stories about who's been married to who. You could do a family tree."

I ask Marti and Chuck if they've had any rocky moments, any big blowups. Marti blurts out, "Oh, yeah! But we don't want to tell you about those."

Before I can ask the Malcolms if they have ever heard of the Bennetts, another woman interrupts us. A tournament director's work is never done. This woman has come over to suggest that Marti look into booking a block of rooms at the Hyatt next year. She says they're offering a good rate—plus, people can smoke in their rooms. The Westin, it seems, will go smoke-free on New Year's Day. Marti looks at me and sighs, "Bridge players do smoke, although it's a lot less than it used to be."

By now, people have begun trickling in for the afternoon game. I am curious to stay and watch, so I ask Marti if they ever get spectators. She says a lot of people will wander over from the shopping mall and peek in the door; occasionally someone will draw an extra chair up to the table. Marti says kibitzers are never a bother; they're hardly noticed, given the concentration on the cards. She repeats a story she heard happened at a tournament "somewhere on the East Coast." In the middle of a match, a naked man streaked through the room, only to be disappointed by the result—no one noticed.

There are a few players who draw a crowd, and Bill Gates is one of them. The Microsoft chairman is mad for the game; he frequently partners with another bridge-playing billionaire, Warren Buffett. Because of the tournament's proximity to Omaha (Buffett's hometown), Gates has played the Kansas City regional. That time spectators lined up six-deep. Not everyone was completely starstruck, however; Marti, for one, found the world's richest man disconcertingly short. "I always thought he was big, but he's a small man—I'd say about five-foot-ten max. He has bodyguards, too."

It is now one o'clock, and the afternoon session is set to begin. In adjacent ballrooms, under the light of muted chandeliers, players sit down at tables, the mood cheery and chatty ("It was so good to see you guys in Denver!"). Five minutes later, there is dead silence. The air is heavy, like there's a storm about to break. Marti and Chuck are competing in a compact knockout, which is a shortened team event. In the first match, they've drawn a man from Indianapolis in a black cowboy hat and his white-haired partner. The game begins with friendly goodwill ("Good luck to you today"), though I wonder how much of it is for show (Marti to Chuck: "Behave yourself today—you're being watched!"). Without any fanfare, they pick up the cards and they're off, tossing bids on the table with none of the indecisive stutters that plague us newbies. Chuck passes a bid of one no-trump, much to Marti's disappointment, who goes on to make overtricks. (After the game, there will be quick postmortem mutterings around the table: "Did you take a spade trick?" "You had a normal reverse—why'd you open in no-trump?") The man in the cowboy hat holds his cards beneath the table; it is a common style around the room, perhaps to prevent others from making inferences based on where he pulls the cards from his hand. After Chuck plays a card, he stares into the middle distance. Marti lays hers down with some flair, nonchalantly flipping cards onto the white tablecloth. She frowns a little, and tries to keep an eye on the room at large. Cowboy Hat's partner sighs a lot.

It is a room full of quirky energy: nail chewing, chin stroking, finger tapping, and hand reshuffling are rampant. While there are none of the sunglasses that seem ubiquitous in today's televised poker, I see a lot of ball caps and cowboy hats pulled down low, as well as one outrageous big beige Panama Jack hat.

A Christmas tree stands in one corner, and there are moments of high and low holiday cheer. Overheard at one table: "We helped you out on that one." "Well, it's Christmas, after all." Overheard at another: "We got rid of all the company yesterday and got here as fast as we could." The silence is not absolute, and above the quiet table talk there are small sounds of extroverted release. One woman greets the dummy with a breathless, "Oh, bless you." Across the room, a distinguished-looking older gentleman bursts out, "Acccccccccce . . ." and does a slow-motion karate chop as he plays what surely must be a winner.

Card Kung Fu aside, there are frequent examples of the game's oft-touted good sportsmanship. At my table, Chuck and Marti frequently alert their opponents to the fact that they are making unusual bids. In bridge, the auction is supposed to be perfectly transparent; there are no "secret messages." Any information expressed is supposed to be available to all, so when Chuck and Marti make a bid that employs some sort of special agreement they've made, they must alert their opponents, who can have it explained before the hand is played. After each alert, Chuck and Marti make sure their opponents are on the right page ("This bid says he has an ace or king or both."). At one point, Chuck walks his opponents through every step in the auction. True to form, the players all ignore me.

The other major difference from the way we play at the club is how these competitors finish the hand. Because the players are so adept at counting cards, at some point in every game the outcome becomes a given. Rather than play out all the tricks, they claim or concede what's left. At the club, we do this only occasionally, usually when we're down to the last three or so tricks (and we happen to hold the last of the trump). These people are amazing: not only do they rarely finish the hand, but they often stop with seven or more cards left. Apparently, it's elementary to them; once they've figured out a few unknowns (what cards are offside, how the trumps break, etc.), the outcome is assured—and they're ready for the next hand. (The assumption, of course, is that no one would make a boneheaded mistake.) With the endgame solved, it's time for another puzzle, and they pounce on the boards like junkies ready for the next score. At one point Chuck calls for the last nine tricks, which seems to annoy his white-haired opponent. Later, when he realizes she is guaranteed to make her contract of four no-trump, Chuck concedes very early in the hand. She replies a little archly,

"Yes, but I'd like to play it out—for the fun of it." Strangely, the only ones stopping the hands early are the men, who obviously enjoy going over the cards and divvying up the remaining tricks. Are they showing off? Marti, who is not getting very good cards, reports she is bored with these hands. That afternoon, the Malcolms do not place in the top four. They will do better that night, finishing first in a different team event. They also will play with other partners. At the end of the week, when the master points are totaled up, Chuck comes in seventy-first and Marti one hundred and twenty-ninth out of a field of more than six hundred and fifty people.

CHAPTER FOUR

A Short History of Bridge: From Hoyle to Halloween

Modern contract bridge, the version played today, was developed by Harold Stirling Vanderbilt, renowned railroad heir and yachtsman, while crossing the Panama Canal on the S.S. *Finland* on Halloween 1925. But despite the twentieth-century origins of the modern game, bridge boasts a long and impressive pedigree.

Bridge derives from the British game of whist, a version of which dates to at least 1529, when Hugh Latimer of Cambridge preached an Advent sermon on Christian conduct by way of a card analogy (hearts were trump, naturally). The word "whist" is sometimes said to be derived from an old Celtic word for "silence," though the game was more likely named for the players' habit of whisking cards off the table after each trick—proof that its roots were more spirited than studious. Whist, which involved partnerships winning tricks by following suit—but did not include a dummy—was often played for money. The last card, which was dealt face up, named the trump suit. In 1742, whist was further popularized by Edmond Hoyle and his famed eighty-six-page pamphlet, "A Short Treatise on the Game of Whist, Containing the Laws of the Game, and Also Some Rules Whereby a Beginner May, with Due Attention to Them, Attain to the Playing It Well." Hoyle had established himself as a professional teacher of whist, and his tract, which sold for the then-staggering price of one guinea, was seen as more of a how-to guide (specifically, how to fleece your opponents at whist) than a leisure manual. Thus was born the phrase "according to Hoyle"—generally used to mean "by the book"—though the game's truly great gift to history might have come two decades later, in 1762, when, finding himself hungry but loath to quit the card table, the fourth earl of Sandwich devised his celebrated handheld namesake.

Devotees of whist have included figures both historical (George Washington, Napoleon, Talleyrand) and fictional (Horatio Hornblower, Sherlock Holmes). Whist grew popular in America, and in 1891 an American pair invented the first Kalamazoo tray, or duplicate board, naming it after the city of its birth. (Duplicate games of whist had occurred earlier in the U.K., but cataloging and re-creating the deal by hand had proved cumbersome.) With the advent of duplicate, skill at whist became more measurable, increasing the game's already considerable cachet. No mere pastime, whist was seen as an enlightened endeavor, a rigorous training for the intellect. As early as 1841, Edgar Allan Poe had written in his famous detective story, "The Murders in the Rue Morgue," "The best chessplayer in Christendom may be little more than the best player of chess; but proficiency in whist implies capacity for success in all these more important undertakings where mind struggles with mind."

Poe goes on to give an exalted description of the preternatural apprehension of the whist expert, who demonstrates what would now be called considerable "table presence":

> He examines the countenance of his partner, comparing it carefully with that of each of his opponents. He considers the mode of assorting the cards in each hand; often counting trump by trump, and honor by honor, through the glances bestowed by their holders upon each. He notes every variation of face as the play progresses ... the expression

of certainty, of surprise, of triumph, or chagrin. From the manner of gathering up a trick he judges whether the person taking it can make another in the suit. He recognizes what is played through feint, by the air with which it is thrown upon the table. A casual or inadvertent word; the accidental dropping or turning of a card . . . the counting of the tricks, with the order of their arrangement; embarrassment, hesitation, eagerness or trepidation—all afford, to his apparently intuitive perception, indications of the true state of affairs. The first two or three rounds having been played, he is in full possession of the contents of each hand, and thenceforward puts down his cards with as absolute a precision of purpose as if the rest of the party had turned outward the faces of their own.

The transition from whist to bridge is a murky one, but at some point a variation of whist came along that exposed one hand during play. The idea of a dummy was not new—it had been used in whist to accommodate three-sided games—but bridge made the dummy a permanent feature. The dealer automatically played the hand. He had the right to name the trump suit (or lack thereof), though he could also pass that decision to his partner.

Scholars cannot agree where the name "bridge" came from, though the consensus is that the game entered England from abroad. Some say the new game took its name from the need for British officers in the Crimean War (1853–56) to cross Constantinople's Galata Bridge to reach the coffeehouses where they played cards. Others say it derives from the Russian "biritch," an eastern variant of whist. Still others say in 1894 a British lord brought bridge back from Cairo. On the other hand, there is slight evidence of an earlier English origin—making all those exotic instances exports, not imports—but it is only a vague, passing reference in an 1843 letter.

Regardless of its provenance, bridge began as a distant second fiddle to whist, though in 1895 the first rules of the game were formalized at London's Portland Club. The father of bridge in America was a member of the New York Whist Club named Henry Barbey, who brought the game over in 1893; a year later, some of his fellow clubmen decamped to form their own organization, where they might play more bridge. The game grew in popularity both in America and the U.K., thanks in part to keen enthusiast King Edward VII, who had a habit of berating his partner. The first duplicate bridge game occurred in 1904 at a party in England, with an American husband and wife finishing first.

The next evolutionary step was the appearance of "auction bridge," in which players competed to name the trump suit. By 1908, London clubs had codified rules for that game. Now bridge was no longer entirely dependent on card play; clever bidding began to share the spotlight. In the United States, being a bridge instructor became a socially acceptable position for working women, especially spinsters, though the top experts were typically men. One such player was Joseph Elwell, who left a career selling hardware to become a bridge teacher to the smart set in New York and Newport. Elwell wrote some informative books, but he is most often remembered as the victim of the first unsolved bridge murder. In the summer of 1920, after a late night on the town celebrating a friend's divorce, he was found the next morning dead, sans false teeth and toupee, by his housekeeper. Police unearthed a woman's kimono, plus a list of his bridge students—all female—in his room, though the deed was intimated to be the work of bootleggers upset over an unpaid whiskey tab.

Another early auction bridge luminary was a Philadelphia lawyer named Milton Work, who raised $100,000 for the American Red Cross during World War I by giving lectures on the game. After the peace, he shuttered his law practice and went exclusively into bridge. In 1927, he played in the first match broadcast over the radio (the hands were preprinted in the newspapers for the listeners at home). A year later, Work's services were fetching an astronomical $250 an hour, and he booked a week in May at a Broadway theater where he appeared five times a day. Two other titans of the game were Wilbur C. Whitehead, who founded the influential (but now defunct) Cavendish Bridge Club in New York, and Sidney Lenz, a Chicago timber magnate who retired in his thirties to better apply himself to his hobbies—magic, sports, and cards.

Auction bridge remained the game of choice until 1925, when Harold Stirling Vanderbilt took his historic cruise. The idea of "contract bridge"—the game we play today, in which a side only gets credit for scoring a game if they bid it—was not invented by Vanderbilt. This idea had appeared in France (in a game called *plafond*) and in India (in "S.A.C.C.," a game known by the initials of those who developed it). Vanderbilt's contribution was more refinement than revolution. He developed a superior scoring system that implemented the contract concept (which he knew from *plafond*), and he added the notion of "vulnerability," a term suggested by a female passenger for his idea that a pair who had already made one game toward the rubber should be subject to greater penalties and rewards.

The S.S. *Finland* was anchored outside the city of Balboa, waiting to cross the Panama Canal. Passengers were prohibited from going ashore, and on Halloween night, Vanderbilt debuted his new version of bridge. The first foursome was Vanderbilt and three co-captive friends, Frederic S. Allen, Francis M. Bacon III, and Dudley Pickman Jr. It was a success, and upon returning home, Vanderbilt shared his rules with his circle in Newport and New York. Vanderbilt cut a dashing figure with considerable social clout. The great-grandson of the commodore who had made the family fortune, Vanderbilt was a brilliant yachtsman who would become a three-time defender of the America's Cup during the 1930s. With his enthusiasm, contract bridge caught on with the fashionable set. The game was ready to explode.

CHAPTER FIVE

Gamblers and Grannies

Dallas, Texas, February 2006

Bob Hamman admits up front, "I do like games." And it's a good thing, because few people seem able to pursue their vocation and avocation with such sporting brio that it becomes nearly impossible to differentiate the two. At sixty-seven, Hamman is hardly just a professional bridge player, though he's often regarded as the best in the world. And he's hardly just a businessman, though the curious company he started two decades ago now generates some $35 million in annual sales. Reduce his life and livelihood to the simplest of terms and it's clear: what Hamman does better than anyone else day in and day out, be it at the bridge table or in the boardroom, is his own best advice—"Know what the odds are, then play them."

I am sitting in the headquarters of SCA Promotions, Inc., in Dallas, Texas—my hometown, coincidentally. The name stands for Sports Contests Associates, which operates by the slogan, "Our risk, your reward." Hamman will tell you he's in the business of "risk management," but really he is a very smart, very savvy, and very successful—not to mention perfectly legal—bookie.

Hamman sells insurance, but not the usual policies for flood or fire. Since 1986, Hamman has made a living covering some of the strangest stakes in the land, laying big-time bets on anything from cow-chip tossing to pumpkin growing. He employs about one hundred people worldwide, with offices in Munich,

Calgary, and London. Most notably, his company is behind most of the prize-money sport-spectator contests—those lucrative half-court shots at halftime and Average-Joe million-dollar field goal tries that keep sports fans revved up while their team is in the locker room. Whenever an organization—say, the Chicago White Sox, Anheuser-Busch, Sony, Pepsi, Harley-Davidson, the Dallas Cowboys, or AT&T—wants to hold a blockbuster promotional contest but doesn't want to have to suffer the sting of paying out if lightning strikes (the shot goes in, the kick is good), Hamman's company is ready to step in and insure the sponsor against losing the bet—for a price. Over the past twenty years, Hamman has covered more than $12 billion in prizes and shelled out more than $134 million in claims. But suffice it to say, he makes much more than he pays.

Bob Hamman is a big guy, standing about six-foot-one in navy pants and a white-and-blue-striped button-down with an eyeglasses case bulging out of his shirtfront pocket. He has casually chaotic white hair, furry eyebrows, and a deep friendly voice that has picked up a trace of a Texas accent sometime since he moved to Dallas from California thirty-seven years ago. We sit in black swivel chairs at an oval wooden conference table, with framed scenes of batsmen (Babe Ruth, Mickey Mantle) and ballparks (Dodger Stadium, the Astrodome) behind us on the walls, as Hamman walks me through the business of SCA.

"Well, most of these things are simply a matter of odds, though you almost never have the stats for the exact event," he says. "Sometimes you can back into it, but usually you have to make some adjustments, some computations, and some unscientific wild-ass guesses." That might sound easy enough, but the devil is in the details. Sure, with a little research you might be able to learn the odds of kicking a thirty-five-yard field goal are about 7–1, of draining a half-court shot about 25–1, and of sinking a 175-yard hole-in-one a discouraging 6,500–1. But what about the probability of a certain lucky rubber ducky being first to cross the finish line of a Million-Dollar Duck Race down New

York's East River? Or the likelihood of an angler reeling in the $100,000-tagged salmon at an annual salmon derby in Juneau, Alaska? Or the chances a chocoholic unwraps a Hershey bar worth a Wonka-esque $500,000? Or even the odds a random fan at a major league baseball All-Star Game can throw five baseballs in thirty seconds from the pitcher's mound through a twenty-five-inch hole cut into an eight-foot Taco Bell sign standing at home plate—with a million-dollar prize on the line? That I know, because it was written up in the newspaper. It's 100–1, and SCA set the premium to cover the million-dollar payout at about $35,000. In 2004, a forty-one-year-old owner of a car dealership in Houston beat the odds—and won.

To keep such statistical aberrations at a minimum, SCA employees are not above running experiments. Hamman walks me through an example, which I reproduce here verbatim so readers can experience the wave of drowsy nostalgia I experienced at hearing the words "angular momentum," feeling like I was once again dozing off at the back of my high school physics class:

> Take a hockey shot through a small target hole. First, to put it in perspective, we say, okay, if you had a four-foot-long board—or even just a regular net—what are your chances as an untrained person of putting it in the net from center ice? It's not going to be airborne—airborne you can practically discount—it's going to roll through there. So let's assume the person might be thirty to forty percent to hit an open net. You test that. You have people shoot it. By the way, shooting at the tiny target you're actually going to use is no good because they're going to make so few shots you're never going to get a decent sample. You'd be out there for life. But you can figure out fairly easily what the chances are of hitting a fairly large target. Then if you make the assumption that the distribution of hits along a known target size is relatively random, and you adjust for the target size you're looking at, and take into account how accurate the shot has to be

to go through the target (will it bounce back out or will it get some angular momentum and spin in?)—you can attack it from that standpoint. And, well, it turns out that approach has worked out pretty good for us over the years.

And then there are the sure things, such as what Hamman calls the "ever-popular Elvis-is-alive contest," usually held in Las Vegas or Memphis, in which true believers can win big by providing the sponsor, a radio station, say, with proof of the King's continued existence. The chances of this, Hamman admits, "you assign at virtually zero." That said, Hamman knows you have to win some and lose some, otherwise his phone would never ring. The ideal is the near miss—the sponsor gets the excitement of a close call, but Hamman doesn't have to pay. Thus SCA is the kind of place that employs a director of fishing as well as a director of security, all in the hopes of divining the perfect odds. Still, when you're in the business of cutting it close, you're bound to get hit.

Some losers seem like flukes. When the San Diego Chargers couldn't convert a fourth-quarter first-and-goal series against the Kansas City Chiefs in 1999, it cost SCA some $450,000 to cover the cost to a local electronics store that had promised to refund any purchase over $399 if the Chiefs held their next opponent scoreless. Other cases you bungle because you didn't do all your homework. Hamman remembers, "We did one where if someone grew a thousand-pound pumpkin by Halloween we'd be out fifty grand." When a member of the World Pumpkin Growing Federation showed up with a 1,061-pound gourd, Hamman was dismayed to learn SCA had agreed to cover the contest *after* the growing season had begun—with a record pumpkin well on track. All Hamman will say is, "It was a hell of a pumpkin. We ate pumpkin pie for months."

The business of SCA is not as dramatic as it might appear. Hamman is too smart for that. After taking on a big promotion, SCA often reinsures the risk with larger commercial companies like Lloyd's of London. Hamman also sells less sensational—but no less lucrative—policies such as overredemption protection for companies issuing consumer coupons.

Still, I can't help but wonder what arcane numerologies these people are privy to—what statistical secrets are housed at SCA, what implausible numbers are carefully, craftily crunched? When I walked into the office I noticed what appeared to be a locked Lucite box filled with sacks of money sitting just past the elevator banks. Standing next to it was something that looked like a brightly colored ATM that read, "Mail Yourself a Million." Before I could get my hands on either, I was ushered into reception, which was decorated with a bright panel of sports scenes, framed articles about Hamman, a cardboard cutout of Drew Carey and a Pepsi can, and a handful of big black stage trunks like roadies lug around at rock concerts. As I waited for Hamman, I overheard snatches of a phone conversation coming from a distant office in which a female voice was explaining that by weighing and counting a certain set of boxes she could figure out some strange odds. She went silent at what I assumed was a question from the unseen party, before replying, as she shut the door, "Well, we've developed a mathematical formula for that . . ."

But believe it or not I'm not here to talk insuring offbeat odds, I'm here to talk bridge—though Hamman is willing to admit the two might be related. Long before he even saw the opportunity in a half-court shot, Hamman had been honing his ability to play the percentages at the bridge table, and the same skills that help him line the coffers of SCA have made him a living legend in the game. An eleven-time world champion, Hamman has won more than forty North American bridge titles. He was the first person ever to be named ACBL Player of the Year twice and was inducted into the league's Hall of Fame the first year he was eligible, upon turning sixty. He was the top-ranked Grand Master in the world for almost two decades, stretching from 1985 to the fall of 2004, when he was dethroned by the Italian Lorenzo Lauria. Few believe that will be Hamman's last time at the top.

His friend and admirer Warren Buffett has said, "I could have started playing bridge when I was a three-year-old, and worked at it every day of my life, and I wouldn't be fit to sort his cards."

Hamman was born in 1938 in Pasadena, California. An early bout of rheumatic fever—that had him bedridden on doctor's orders—led to an interest in cards. At age five, he was begging his parents to play gin. By eight, he was taking money off his dad's poker buddies. In high school he got deep into chess, which ruined his grades. Still, his board scores were strong enough to get him a full scholarship to Occidental College in Los Angeles. There he played chess and pool—to the exclusion of almost all else—and lost his scholarship. Hamman dropped out, and in the summer of 1957 he discovered bridge. He enrolled at UCLA and San Fernando Valley State, but he never finished his degree (in mathematics, of course). Instead, he put in long days at UCLA's Kerckhoff Hall, the student lounge, playing bridge from eight in the morning to eleven at night—even when he wasn't technically a student. From there he graduated to the Los Angeles Bridge Club, where he earned his chops while living off odd jobs and the money he made at rubber bridge. He entered his first national tournament in 1959 at the age of twenty-one. Three years later he won a national event. In five years, he was competing for the United States in the world championship.

How Hamman came to Dallas is a curious tale. Indeed, it seems a little strange to bother with bridge in Texas, where ads for the state lottery's new poker scratch-off game interrupt the nightly news. It's called Texas Hold'em, after all, and as legend has it the game was first played some four hundred miles south of us just outside Corpus Christi in a little place called Robstown sometime around 1900. But without a doubt, Dallas is a bridge town, much in part thanks to the patriotic efforts of a multimillionaire 350-pound lapsed-Baptist bridge enthusiast named Ira G. Corn Jr., who ran the Dallas conglomerate Michigan General. In the summer of 1967, Corn was tired of America losing again and again in international competition to the famed

Italian "Blue Team," which had proven invincible for the previous ten years, and so he decided to put together the first full-time professional bridge team just to beat them.

The notion was not entirely without precedent, as Charles Goren, "Mr. Bridge" himself, had believed in paying good players to partner with him as a means of publicizing his books and ideas. But Corn took the idea and ran with it, handpicking six top American players and offering to relocate them and their families to Dallas, where they would be paid a salary plus travel expenses and would dedicate themselves to perfecting the art of bridge. On February 1, 1968, Corn's team reported to work. They were dubbed the "Dallas Aces," later shortened to just the "Aces."

Hamman moved to Dallas in January 1969. Corn had asked him to join the Aces earlier, but Hamman balked, unsure about the merits of this full-time team. A few months later, he witnessed two of the Aces firsthand at the table, and when the invitation to relocate to Dallas came again, he did not decline.

Corn himself didn't compete on the team and stayed mainly out of the way. Instead, he put his players in the hands of a coach, a retired Air Force lieutenant colonel named Joe Musumeci— nicknamed "Moose"—who instituted calisthenics and bed checks. The team practiced sixty hours a week at Corn's mansion—which eventually acquired another wing—and trained using a $2 million SDS 940 computer that analyzed and generated the hands. Play was chronicled by stenographers. Each session ended with an intense performance review that could last hours. It wasn't unusual to discuss every card in a hand and debate every hand in a match; teammates issued color-coded demerits to each other, which were tallied on a blackboard. An Ace could be fined for negligence at the table; he could also be punished for bad behavior away from it. After an evening of competition, there was a two-drink maximum that was vigorously enforced: the first strike cost $50, while the second meant a suspension of thirty days. Curfew was 2 A.M. The team was outfitted in an array of matching blazers and tuxedos. A psychiatrist was brought in to patch up partnership problems. The diligence paid off when, a year after Hamman joined, the Aces won the world championship—and then successfully defended their title the following year. Over time, the Aces' roster would change, but their name remains synonymous with big-time bridge. Ira Corn died in 1982, and a year later the Aces played their final game—but not before winning the world championship in Stockholm, beating the Italians one last time.

Talking to Hamman is an intense exercise. He can flit from boisterous good old boy to bewildering brainiac at the drop of a hat. At one moment he's cracking a joke, at another he's locking eyes and leaning forward with his hand on his chin. He lapses into dry, analytical pauses, yet he seems the kind of guy who'd be at home at a lecture as well as a sports bar. As much as he uses the language of math—peppering his examples with percentages—he uses the language of sport, referring to golf, tennis, and "the odd base hit." He's even unafraid of a little business-speak, such as when he drops the phrase "optimize your percent equity."

We touch on a number of topics, including whether he enjoys playing for money ("Oh, yeah!"). Over the years, he's frequently been spotted at the big game at the Regency Whist Club in New York, where the stakes run $1.00 a point. (Hamman says if someone would organize such a game in Dallas, he'd be there all the time.) He plays poker but doesn't enjoy it as much as bridge, and he blames bridge's steep learning curve for why the recent card craze has passed it by. He thinks that business about not playing bridge with your spouse is hogwash. He plays often with Petra, his wife of nineteen years, who is a former world champion and one of Dallas's top teachers. He plays online only occasionally (usually on Bridge Base), and then mainly only to practice with his partner Paul Soloway, who lives in Washington State and has the most master points ever accumulated. They usually line up an opponent, because "playing against somebody who's totally inept is bad practice."

There is one question I'm dying to ask. Hamman is famous for never sorting his hand—he simply picks up his thirteen cards in whatever order they're in, and he's off to the races. It makes him notoriously difficult to kibitz, since the suits and ranks are scrambled, and it's boggling to me that it doesn't lead to mistakes. So I ask him why. It turns out Hamman's not showing off, or trying to intimidate his opponents—he does it "just because." He simply doesn't need to sort the cards, and by not arranging them in order, he's never in danger of giving anything away. (I, on the other hand, am pretty sure that anyone watching me would be able to divine exactly how many cards I had in each suit just by witnessing my clumsy initial struggle to get all my ducks in a row.)

In general, Hamman seems preoccupied with the concrete limitations of such a conjectural game. Perhaps it is a response to the times. Ask him how bridge has changed over the years, and he simply says, "The game has gotten more complicated." When you ask him how he has been able to stay on top for so long—this is a man who has won national and international titles in five decades—he talks about health and energy. In fact, he uses the word "energy" a lot, but more as a physician or even a physicist than a New Age guru. As a player, you must "conserve your energy"; one problem might be a "matter of energy," while in another, "the energy spent is a sunk cost." He talks about the "psychic swings" players endure during tournaments, which—at, say, twenty boards a match in a twenty-one-match round-robin world championship—can turn into grueling mental marathons. What becomes clear is that he has devoted a considerable amount of brainpower to improving every facet of his game.

Sometimes his thought processes seem to approach the preternatural. I show Hamman a hand I had been puzzling over for some time. It was from last fall's world championship, the 2005 Bermuda Bowl that took place in Portugal. He and Soloway were competing against two members of the Italian team that eventually took home the trophy. Hamman was playing a contract of three no-trump. When the Italians led the eight of clubs, he took one look at the dummy and knew the jig was up—he won the lead and immediately cashed all his diamond winners to go down by two tricks. At the other table, with all the roles reversed, the Italian declarer noticed nothing strange and proceeded to play the hand normally and went down much, much worse. I had studied the hand and the bidding at length, but I still couldn't see what Hamman saw. How did he know he was doomed?

Glancing at the diagram I set before him, Hamman shrugs and says he just knew the ace of hearts was "wrong," meaning sitting on his left instead of his right. I don't follow him exactly, but it seems that somehow based on the bidding, the appearance of the eight of clubs, the position of the moon, the price of prosciutto, the sweat on the Italians, and God knows what else, he figured the wrong man was holding the ace of hearts. It was a gutsy call, one that even after his patient explanation still remains a mystery to me. But Hamman perfectly pictured the other two hands and made the best of a bad situation—for a major swing in points. His final justification is a humble disclaimer: "Effectively, you've got an inference, which in this case was very powerful. Of course sometimes the inferences are wrong and you just look very foolish."

Indeed, Hamman remains genuinely modest, almost to the point of being a bad interview. I ask him—the best player in the world, a man whose brilliance has been dissected time and time again in books, newspapers, and chat rooms across the globe—to look back over all the hands he's played, in all the various places for all the various stakes, and describe the favorites that come to mind. After a pause, Hamman just laughs and says, "The only hands that stand out are shipwrecks. Let's not talk about those."

Since he refuses to dwell on the past, I ask about the future. Is the game of bridge in jeopardy? Hamman admits it is, a little. "The aging of the bridge-playing population is certainly a factor," he says. "I have no objection to the old ladies playing. There's certainly an argument that thinking, reasoning, computing, and so on is much like physical exercise. Use it or lose it. If people shut off their brains at age twenty-two, twenty years later they're not very well prepared to suddenly start using them. So recreations that keep you thinking—even though the topic itself may not be particularly utilitarian in other phases—are good for you. The ability to reason always has some utility. Now, do you expect somebody at age thirty to start worrying about Alzheimer's? No. It may be easier at the end of a day's work to plop yourself in front of the TV and have a beer or two. But bridge is a lot of fun. And most of the people who play it like it—at least briefly, then they get frustrated and go back to gardening."

The problem, as Hamman sees it, is that there has been no new bridge generation. Sure, there are young standouts, but there hasn't been a "hoard of great young players" to supplant the old guard. It's not like in basketball, where eighteen-year-olds are chomping at the bit to skip college and turn pro.

One of the issues seems to be the way bridge is marketed in this country. Hamman takes odds with the ACBL's cumulative-point approach to keeping players interested. "They certainly don't do themselves a favor with this endless proliferation of master points," he says. "The goal should be: 'Learn how to play the game. It's a great competitive activity. Maybe you'll occasionally get a base hit off some good players. Chances are you'll get ground up and spit out—but it doesn't have to be that way.' That's my two cents."

Hamman can't underscore the competitive aspect of the game enough. "It's a mistake to market bridge as a game for little old ladies," he says, getting a little riled up. "You have to bear in mind that you have a psychic stake in the competition, so there's the occasional elbow to the chops or thumb in the eye—metaphorically, of course—and it goes with the territory. If people don't like it, they're not the people you're interested in anyway. Bridge is competition! You're there to beat people. And once in a while they're not going to be all that happy about it. But they'll get over it. And if they don't—let 'em garden!"

On that last note, Hamman pounds the table. He's clearly a competitor. It's the most passionate I've seen him all day. I mention that some of those little old ladies have been known to give me trouble at the table—does he have any advice to a young player starting out? "Don't worry about them," he growls. "You'll be beating them pretty quickly. My advice is pretty much this. Understand as much as you can reasonably absorb what the essence of the game is without totally draining your energy and time. And the essence of the game is . . ." Here Hamman trails off, like a cryptic card-shark Yoda. After a second, he resumes, "Card play is somewhat independent of the type of opponents. Though when you're defending, you have to be aware that certain partners are up to certain types of situations, and others are not. You have to adjust to the game you're in."

As an example, he recalls a hand from the most recent world championship. Again, I will record the gospel of Hamman verbatim (with only minor annotation), so that the truly initiated can marvel at his mind and perhaps send me an e-mail down the line explaining exactly what the dickens he was talking about. It is the story of an auction, a peek into the strenuous psychic shadowboxing the pros perform at the table.

I had one-six-three-three. [Author's note: Meaning he held a hand with one spade, six hearts, three diamonds, and three clubs.] So I bid a heart. West had a spade overcall. Partner bid two spades, which we play as a limit raise or better. And right-hand opponent hit three hearts, which is a game try in spades. Now ideally, my game plan on the hand would be to play four hearts. I might be willing to take the push to five hearts, but I'm not at all sure about it. If I think my opponents are making four spades, I would bid to five hearts. But I'm not in the position to appraise that. So what I did instead of bidding four hearts is I passed three hearts. So now the opponents will declare their intentions. And if they think they're settling for three spades and I get myself pushed into four hearts they might let me play it. And at least I will know that they don't think they can make four when they settle for three, so my equity in going to five hearts—where I rate to go down—becomes less. It's very unlikely if I do go to the five level that they'll take the push to five spades.

So the guy on my left would have to be playing a very deep game to settle for three spades on the anticipation I'm going to later push him. Because chances are that's just where he'll play it, overwhelmingly. They really, as a matter of course, have to reveal their estimate in the hand—unless they're playing a very deep game, and my experience is that if they have no reason to know what you're doing, they're just not going to play that deep a game. You know, it might happen in some other life, but it's not very likely.

So I approached it in that fashion. They bid three spades. I bid four hearts. They came again with four spades. [Which Hamman passed, because he thought he had driven them to a level at which they would fail.] As it happens, we're on for five hearts. [Meaning Hamman could have made five hearts.] So I get a terrible result. [For not going to five hearts.] Had I initially jumped to four hearts, they would have bid to four spades, and I then might have gone five hearts—which would have improved my result dramatically. So by ferreting out the solution to the problem I actually damaged myself.

Everyone still here?

Satisfied by the blank look in my eyes, Hamman abruptly ends the conversation with, "Why don't I take you across the hall and introduce you to some people?"

It turns out Hamman employs a suspicious number of high-level bridge buffs. He shuffles me off to player after player, all enthusiastic to stop what they are doing and swap bridge stories. As we walk the halls, Hamman is hailed right and left by employees young and old with shouts of "Hey, Bob!" He seems a popular boss.

Our first stop is the office of Bart Bramley, the 1997 ACBL Player of the Year and holder of many national titles. Bramley, fifty-eight, wears a plaid button-down. He has an open, friendly face, with shocks of graying curls sprouting from the sides of his balding head. His office is decorated with Yankees' pennants, maps, and a bowl of Jelly Bellies.

Bramley finished second in the Transnational Open Team event at last fall's world championships, but he mainly wants to talk about the great names he's been lucky enough to play with over the years.

The first time he played with Hamman was in 1990 at a national tournament in Fort Worth. Bramley remembers, "We were tossed together at the last minute for a two-day national Swiss Team event at the end of the tournament. We'd been playing with other people all week. But I played with him that weekend and we won the event!"

That was hardly the first time Bramley had bumped into his future boss. As long as Bramley has been playing the game, Hamman has been a force on the scene. Bramley has played against him a number of times, one of which he'll never forget. "One of my best early matches was in 1973," Bramley says. "I played Bob in the Spingold knockout when the Aces were still around, and we beat them in the round of sixteen. It was the only match they lost to an American team all year. They won the Vanderbilt Cup and the Team Trials to lose to Italy in the world championship, but *my* team beat them in the Spingold."

Without much prompting, Bramley spins yarn after yarn about the matches, hands, and people he's played over the past four decades in cities such as Chicago, Geneva, Yokohama, and New York. He remembers competing in the 1998 Par Contest in Lille, France, an infrequently held, hyperintellectual test of bridge theory in which the world's top players are given eight hours to solve twelve fiendishly difficult hands. That year the problems were created by the Swiss mastermind Pietro Bernasconi.

As Bramley remembers it, the contest itself was a pressure cooker: "It's just you against a computer, which shows the hands and the opening lead. Then you play. The computer keeps score and records your time—the faster the better. Every time you make a mistake, it beeps at you. If you make more than three mistakes, your score goes down to zero—and forget it. You're in a room with thirty-five people, each with his own computer. It's terrifying when it happens to you. I got beeped on the first hand."

Despite the lackluster start, Bramley finished in second place, making one fewer error but taking more time than the winner, who graciously suggested speed should not have been a factor. For his efforts, Bramley won what he thought was just a "bunch of French francs," which later turned out to be Swiss francs—or "real money," in his words—worth about $17,500. He says, "It was more than I ever imagined was coming to me!"

Bramley has also had his share of world-class partners. He jokes, "All I play with is Hall of Famers," and indeed the names that come up would make a bridge writer's head spin: longtime partner Lou Bluhm, the original recipient of the ACBL's Distinguished Player Award with whom Bramley won the Vanderbilt Cup the year Bluhm was diagnosed with pancreatic cancer; Hugh Ross, a gifted, gutsy player who won three world titles with three different partners; and the legendary Sidney Lazard, a phenom renowned for his table presence who, until recently, was Bramley's regular partner at national events. Bramley says, "Sidney is a guy with a million stories—and you can tell I have a few of my own—so we hit it off like gangbusters. Every time we get together, instead of talking about our system, we start telling stories."

In 1969, Bramley graduated from MIT, then, as now, a hotbed of the game. Top-notch players such as Lou Reich, Mark Feldman, Chip Martel, and Ken Lebensold were part of Bramley's generation. He had gone to college armed with the ambition to be a famous scientist, but was leaving with the common undergrad's lack of direction. Upon graduation, he faced a tough decision: what's a bridge bum to do? Like many of his bridge-playing friends, he fell into programming. In the 1980s, options trading became popular among the bridge set, and Bramley moved to Chicago, where he traded for nearly two decades. Three years ago he took up the bridge player's latest profession of choice—working for Hamman.

As for what exactly he does at SCA, Bramley says, "I'm one of the guys who figures things out." One of his favorite problems involved a promotion Long John Silver's wanted to run in the winter of 2004, when all eyes were on the twin robot rovers NASA had just landed on Mars. The seafood chain promised to give away one of its new Giant Shrimp to everyone in the country if the rovers found evidence of an ocean on Mars—past or present—by the end of February. When considering the policy, Bramley remembers thinking, "The likelihood of their finding oceans—which we defined as a body of water occupying the same percentage of the Martian surface as the Arctic Ocean, the smallest ocean on Earth, which occupies about five percent—wasn't great. Furthermore, we thought it was extremely unlikely that they could make that determination in about a month. They just wouldn't get far enough."

The clincher came when Bramley had a friend from MIT put him in touch with a man at NASA familiar with the scientists running the mission. "He told us they were not prone to rash statements—that they weren't the type to shoot off their mouths. There might be some professor from Podunk who would look at the evidence and say, 'Oceans!' but not these guys. So we took the case. And it was a best-case scenario the way it turned out. They did find evidence of some water, but the big announcement didn't come until March. So it was kind of a home run for us. Close but no cigar—that's what we're looking for all the time."

As for Long John Silver's, even they seemed happy with the promotional brouhaha. Upon news of the discovery, the company paid up in free shrimp anyway, citing their desire to become the first seafood restaurant on Mars and claiming the discovery represented "one small step for man, and one giant leap for Giant Shrimp."

After another half-dozen stories, my tape recorder shuts off. As I'm switching cassettes, Bramley laughs and says, "You could tell I could give you a few more stories, before we're through"—at which point I hightail it out of there. I'm running late for a date.

But before I go, there is one more stop I have to make. Justin Lall, nineteen, wears the typical teenage uniform of the unconventionally corporate: trim beard, short dark hair, polo shirt, jeans, and flip-flops. Earlier, Hamman raised an eyebrow and described him as "one of the five really good players in the office—a real talent." If you ask Lall about Hamman, he'll laugh and call him "spacey," which says less about Hamman's habits than what passes for spacey in this intense lot. Joking aside, Lall doesn't carry himself with any of the swagger one might think the teenager with the most master points in the country last year—almost twice the number of the runner-up—might. He is unfailingly polite and swallows his sentences like any good teen, despite already having graced the cover of the *Bridge Bulletin*. That was a few months ago, in November 2005, and Lall was holding the trophy he won as a member of the six-man American team that swept the 2005 World Youth Team Championships in Sydney, Australia.

Lall has been messing around at the bridge table since he was ten, when he first filled in on a supervised game for beginners. Skill like his doesn't come out of left field. Lall's father is a national champion, and his mother is an excellent player. He grew up all over—Houston, England, California, Dallas, and San Antonio. His dad is his most regular partner, not to mention office mate, as he also works at SCA. Justin also plays with members of his own generation, like his American junior partner Ari Greenberg and a Canadian named David Granger.

Instead of frequenting the bridge club, he plays online, though usually not with his regular partner, who hasn't had time since starting a job at Google. Lall has played with Hamman a number of times, including at a national event in 2004. He says, "He didn't say a word, really. He didn't yell, he didn't do anything. Most people yell at some point."

Lall is technically a consultant at SCA, not an employee, though the arrangement has lasted longer than expected. His projects include designing promotions for online poker sites and a virtual stock market game. When pressed for details, Lall says, "There's a nondisclosure agreement so there's some things I can't say." I laugh, not because it obviously bothers his good manners to leave my question unanswered, but because I'm thinking about the imposing security keypad outside the door that leads to Lall's office. He works in a secure suite that we'll have to hit a big red button to exit. What secrets does this kid know?

But believe it or not, SCA is really just his day job, a way to make some money on the side. Because, as Lall tells me, "Theoretically, I'm a bridge pro. This is just temporary, sort of a sidetrack. My goal is to be a bridge professional."

Indeed, Lall has no desire to go to college. Alamo Heights High in San Antonio was enough for him. His dream is to be one of the professional elite, the kind of player who could easily pull in $100,000 to $150,000 a year after expenses, says Hamman. To that end, Lall plays professionally with clients—that is, ambitious amateurs looking to improve their game (and win gobs of master points) by paying to play with their betters—as frequently as he can in order to raise his already pretty high profile.

And what are the going rates for a nineteen-year-old pro? An online game costs $30 an hour. For a regional event, Lall charges $250 a session. And at the nationals, he says, "It's more. You take what you can get. But honestly, I'd take $250 a session there, too. Nationals are the only times when bridge pros are in high demand." In a business that seems based on reputation and perception, he probably shouldn't reveal his rates so readily—or advertise his eagerness for work. But Lall is serious about making a go of it. When asked if he would like to travel the tournament circuit full time, spending week after grueling week on the road playing with anyone willing (or wealthy enough) to pay, he responds with bright-eyed enthusiasm. "Most pros have a side job. I don't want to. It's fun going to tournaments. It doesn't really get old. I like traveling. I like the tournament atmosphere."

So far business is good. He has clients "all over," not just in Dallas. He has found players online, too, which is "ideal," he says, "because you just sit in your underwear and get paid to play bridge." Still, the life of a pro isn't all fun and games. Playing with lesser players, your skills suffer—as does the quality of the bridge. Lall reminds me, "If you're playing with a client, it can be sort of a grind. But there are worse things to do to make money."

And what about his social life—do his non-bridge-playing friends understand what he does? Does he have any non-bridge-playing friends? "Um, yeah," he laughs, "but you're right—most of my friends are bridge players." I ask why the rest of his peers seem to prefer poker. "Poker is much easier. The learning curve in bridge is too steep. Most young people don't want to spend a year reading books just to become, like, intermediate. You know, when one of my friends says, 'How do you play bridge?' Well, I just can't tell him. I get that question many times. It's like, I don't know where to begin."

Across town in a historic high-rise apartment building, four fashionable Dallas women of a certain age sit around a card table in an elegantly appointed living room, with spring flowers on the side tables and art on the walls, overlooking a flat cityscape of tree-nestled homes, dead winter grass, and a wooded creek winding slowly south on a brilliant sixty-one-degree early-February day. We'll call the women North, South, East, and Mimi, who is ninety-three years old and the grandmother of one of my high school friends. These are the ladies who are waiting to lunch, as I've arrived a tad late from SCA. Theirs is an every-other-week bridge club, which starts at half past ten and lasts into the afternoon. I am here to meet Mimi's "little foursome," who, she assures me, "play a sociable game."

By the time I show up, they are well into the third rubber. The score has been pretty even so far. Around one o'clock, they break for lunch, which is usually something "simple." Today it's chicken and rice with pimento and capers, hot homemade biscuits, and a chilled cranberry salad with pineapple and apricots, all served on china and washed down with water from crystal goblets. The women agree stopping for lunch is much more civilized. Mimi says, "At some bridge clubs people say, 'We'll bring our sandwich and eat it at the table.' Well, who wants to bring a sandwich? We turn this into a kind of luncheon group, too. That way we can discuss everything we want." I decide not to tell her I usually eat my weight in doughnut holes back at the club.

Mimi is a bubbly white-haired livewire who makes a mean Lebanese kibbe, takes a nap every day, and speaks as fast as an auctioneer in a sweet Southern voice that goes into a high, half-sentence staccato when she gets excited. She was born in a small town in Kentucky in 1912 to parents from Lebanon. She learned the game "way back," in her teens, when a relative visiting from California was stunned to hear her family wasn't playing bridge, which was only a few years old and all the rage. Mimi taught her college friends the game before marrying a Lebanese man who came through Ellis Island and took her to Oklahoma. A few years after he passed away, she moved to Dallas to be near her son's family and began duplicate lessons.

Today she wears a wide-collared striped silk shirt, powder blue pants, and a delicate gold necklace laced with stones. She is worried she overcooked the rice—a new recipe—but it is a hit. Feeding the foursome has become an interesting challenge. One eats no dairy, another no red meat, and another no tomatoes. Only one woman can eat everything, which the woman says, "You can tell just by taking a look!"

The women have been doing this every two weeks for about three years, though all but one of them have been in foursomes before. South, who glitters gold about the neck and ears, says, "We don't see each other all the time. We mix with different groups of people. So this is a way to get together." They usually play until three thirty or so, but East, stylishly decked out in black-and-white, admits, "It sort of depends on who's winning. It's like a poker game. The winners can't go home." North, in her purple cashmere, laughs. At this point I begin to get nervous. On the phone, Mimi mentioned that they play for small stakes, but in Dallas size is relative—see the cars, the houses, the hair—so I had been sure to visit an ATM on the way over. I start to wonder if I am going to leave with my shirt.

Led by Mimi, the women come right at me with questions—about the book, about why I'm in Dallas, about what I do in New York. Once their curiosity is satisfied, we sit around the food and chat about bridge. I pick up bits of philosophy: "You have to be really aggressive." "You can take all the lessons you want, but you won't be worth anything without card sense." "All you need is luck—my friends know I just never get good hands." South tries to remember a joke she recently heard based on a series of double entendres involving a household where the owners are always enjoying a game called "bridge" that "involves rubbers and whatnot"—and thus the maid quits. Mimi finds the joke a bit risqué. South slyly points out, "If you think about it, almost every term in bridge can have a double meaning." I say that some people believe Ely Culbertson, the game's great bygone promoter, intentionally sexed up much of the bridge lingo to make it sound more alluring—thus giving us the squeeze and the elopement, among others.

Most of the women learned the game from their parents. North grew up in a small town and recalls her mother hosting bridge parties for all the ladies in town—except the Baptists—which meant upward of twelve tables. When North got married, she lived in a small town and continued the tradition. Her primary social activity was a couples' bridge club that doubled as a dinner club. The hostess would provide the meat and dessert, while guests supplied the sides. She and her husband enjoyed that for years. Later, Mimi tells me that North's husband is now in poor health, and the game is a good way to get her out of the house.

East is a doctor, who then opened an art gallery. She played a fair amount of bridge when she was younger, but she had to give it up in medical school, when there wasn't the time. She picked the game up again in her retirement. She wonders if the kids still play in college. I am forced to answer for the younger generation, and I confess we're more into poker. East says she loves poker—and watches all the shows on TV—but she thinks it's a much easier game. All the women agree that bridge takes time. One of them mentions a young high-achieving Ivy League son-in-law who became frustrated at his inability to master the game quickly. He gave up eventually, and today "he's not real crazy about bridge." Mimi alternates between asking me to teach her grandson to play and asking me to find him a wife.

Dessert is applesauce-and-date cupcakes served with heart-shaped petit fours, in honor of Valentine's Day. After lunch is cleared, coffee is served, gum is passed, and we sit down to play.

"We play party bridge," says Mimi, meaning the bidding agreements are simple (and sometimes a little shaky), and partners swap out every few rubbers. At the end of the day, everyone has played with everyone else. I suddenly realize this is my first game of social bridge, and it hits me that along with the daunting prospect of having to play well and keep up my end of the conversation, I will be without the familiar tool—that now seems like a crutch—of the club game: the bidding box. Those little plastic cards with their color-coordinated tabs all in a row make keeping track of the bids a piece of cake, and because they're arranged in order there's no need to worry about unintentionally bidding out of line (plus you can see any skip bids). In social bridge, you do it the old-fashioned way—aloud. I'm not sure my powers of concentration are up to the task. It's much easier for me to read the sequence of bids around the table than try to remember them. I've always been more of a visual person; I keep copious lists and I'm terrible with names. Now I'll be the guy who has to keep asking what the contract is.

As we're settling in, Mimi asks, "So, can you play?" She has asked a version of this question every time we've spoken since the very first phone call, when I introduced myself as a friend of her grandson and was met with a charming barrage: "Do I know you? What do you look like? Are you tall, are you dark, are you handsome—what?" The reason she is so interested in my bridge skill is that if she deems me a strong enough player, she has promised to take me to the country club tomorrow for the weekly duplicate game. She used to play every week, but her partner recently died, and it's been six months since she has been back. She says, "It's hard to play with someone you don't know real well," but I can tell she's willing to give me a shot because she misses it. So today, it seems, is a tryout of sorts. Play well, and we're off to the club. Don't, and break a grandmother's heart.

Mimi seats me in her spot at the table and pulls up a chair, saying, "I want to peep over your shoulder." She promises the group, "I won't say anything unless he asks me," at which the women laugh. The cards are nicer and of heavier stock than the ones we use at the club; adorned with tasteful pastel designs, they live in an elaborate box. Two women keep score, "because sometimes one doesn't add right," on scoring pads that boast, "Anytime Is Bridge Time with Mimi."

We begin to play, and in no time Mimi goes from silent observer to subverbal coach, squirming and squeaking not only if I am about to misplay, but if my fingers even happen to brush the wrong card. "Let him play it his own way," grumbles East.

In general, the table etiquette is more relaxed than at the club. The biggest difference—other than the missing bidding boxes—is that the declarer reaches across and plays his or her cards from the dummy, as opposed to asking partner to play them. With Mimi breathing down my neck, I'm really trying to focus, and occasionally I forget and call out for a card. The women begin giving me a hard time. Despite an admonishment from Mimi—"Now y'all be careful and treat this young man well"—it's not long before they're referring to me in the third person as "the little prince."

In spite of the cracks, I'm having a wonderful time. These are lovely ladies, surely the most genial cardsharps in town, and I'm not just saying that because one of them leans over and tells me, with good grandmotherly cheer, "You have the prettiest hair." Today they're chatty, but not overly so, which makes Mimi think they're showing off. "Look at that concentration," she says. "They're on their best behavior!"

Card play aside, the women want to be sure I tell people they're more fun than "just a bunch of old ladies," and they have the patter to prove it. I'm not the only one who gets taunted. When East dislikes the card that is played, she proclaims it "a vulgar display." While being set in three no-trump, South threatens the kind of violence that's only acceptable between friends: "If you put down the king I'm going to hit you." When any of them make a foolish play, the others are quick to quip: "Oh, did you just have a senior moment?" When an unexpected card takes the trick, a surprised South says, "I don't like not remembering things"—to which East fires back: "Like the days of the week?" At one point, North declares, "Y'all just make me sick."

We finish the rubber and it's time to switch partners. I draw South, who says, "You'll like me. I play by the seat of my pants." And so we while away the day in the most pleasant way possible. We play hand after hand, and between the chatting, the laughing, and the stories they tell, I completely lose track of the score.

At afternoon's end, the four elegant women all pull out their big elegant pocketbooks, and my stomach—which had been lulled so gently into a pink petit-four bliss—begins to churn. The twin scorecards are consulted and a debate ensues over the final payout. It's unclear over the cacophony of accents exactly who owes what to whom, but it's certainly a matter of great concern. At one point I hear sixty, at another I hear eighty, and, while a bit high for a social game, these are stakes I can at least afford. Then South, who came out a winner but is now running late to pick up her grandson from school, declares, "Just give me my sixty cents so I can get out of here!" Suddenly a smattering of small change crisscrosses the table. The women pocket their quarters, nickels, and dimes, get their coats, bid their pals adieu, and slip out the door.

I'm flabbergasted. Mimi, who in the confusion apparently covered my forty-cent loss, tells me, "Last time it was a scandalous rout and someone walked off with a dollar." She is cheerful despite having lost twenty cents. As we are settling back into our chairs, she spies a quarter under the table. She swoops down to get it and comes up beaming: "Now I'm up five cents!"

In the new silence, I am hesitant to bring up the trip to the country club, but it seems—after one final bidding quiz ("How many points do you have to have to open two clubs?")—that I pass the test. She thinks we should try our hand at duplicate. She tells me she loves her foursome, and mentions she plays with a few wonderful women on weekends, but clearly she's itching to get back in the big game at the club, where she promises, "They are really tough."

It is after four when I say good-bye, which leaves Mimi just enough time for her late-afternoon nap. She has dinner plans tonight at seven thirty, which earlier provoked East to kid, "Seven thirty? Oh, you are really chic." Mimi never seems lacking for pep. At one point she tells me throwing a lunch for twelve isn't really an effort "if you are used to entertaining." She usually goes to bed around midnight. Late last night her grandson called and said, "Mimi, you're the only one in the family I can talk to after eleven." He swears to me that she's a secret day trader, and rues the day he didn't follow through on one of her stock tips. Faced with the accusation, Mimi demurs, "Oh, I help him one day and he thinks I know something." We laugh, and she adds, "But he chickened out and sold it. I told him, 'Don't sell it!'"

When I ask for her secret, how she manages it all at ninety-three—the friends, the foursomes, the grandchildren, the trading, the cooking, the cleaning, the out-of-town guests—she smiles and says: "Bridge, it keeps you young."

And so after a late night of last-minute practice on the computer, the next day it's off to the country club in my best club-wear (shirt and slacks, no jacket required). On my way, I pick up Mimi, who sports a jaunty red-and-white scarf and is eager to run over our bidding strategy as I navigate the long and leafy Dallas streets. It seems a case of too little too late, but she offers animated advice ("Take your time") and reassurance ("We'll have fun!") as well as the occasionally ominous tip ("Don't let them get into your head—they can read your hand before you say anything.").

She ended yesterday with a game "We'll try it," but today Mimi seems all business, making sure I know how to play Black-wood and weak two-bids. I'm reminded she has a rep to protect and a partner's memory to uphold and I'm just some chump in uncomfortable shoes.

We show up at the club just as the game is about to start. To make matters more complicated, we learn we are to be a roving North-South pair, meaning we'll have to sub in and out in a com-plicated movement, a diagram of which the director hands me on a well-worn card. At least we get to sit the first round out, afford-ing Mimi a chance to work the crowd while I pound a Coke.

The room is lovely, dark, and clubby, with wood paneling, bookshelves, and a fireplace. I have been here before, as my par-ents are members. On one side stands a bar with soft drinks, iced tea, water, coffee, and napkins that announce the club was established in 1896 (which is old for Dallas, a city founded in 1841). Unlike at the Manhattan Bridge Club, this bar is manned by a uniformed waiter, which lends an air of civility to the con-stant caffeine crush. (This is to say nothing of the restroom, which boasts fine linens, gilded soap dispensers, and mouth-wash.) Curtains are drawn against the tall, bright windows overlooking the golf course; outside, duffers putter about in the sunshine. The room hums with a comfy Texas twang. There are eleven tables draped in felt; counting us, there are forty-six players. I'm the youngest in the room by some fifteen years.

Play begins at one sharp; we're supposed to finish sometime around a quarter to five. Most of the pairs seem to have met at the club beforehand for lunch, making this a game for those with only the freest of calendars.

On the very first hand, Mimi and I bid our way up to a three no-trump contract. It is only after the auction is over that I realize I am the one who has to play it. My heart pounds and my fingers shake—as they will for most of the afternoon, independent of the all-you-can-drink cola—but somehow I manage to eek out the necessary nine tricks. My success comes more by chance than cunning; rather than take the time to figure the angles, I play my cards at what I think is a respectable pace and hope for the best.

There is little time for relief, however, because immediately we are on to the next board. Across the room, tables seem to be working quickly and quietly, but still the no-nonsense director stalks the room, calling out "Hush!" and "Hurry up!" Despite the fact that I'm not very strong at keeping score, I am in charge of recording the hands, meaning I phrase each result as a question and wait for the opponents to correct me. If no one says anything, after a respectful sip of my drink, I mark the scorecard with my stubby gold-embossed pencil.

It is only one of many awkward moments. While the faces and the cards change, there are certain clumsy beats that replay at every table. When we sit down our opponents take one look and peg me for a ringer, thinking Mimi must have gone and hired herself a pro. (The other option, that I'm a golddigger, doesn't occur to me until we're leaning against the bar and Mimi whispers, "They're all going to think I'm robbing the cradle!") Our opponents' initial confusion at seeing me is second only to my other favorite moment, when during the round I make the invariable boneheaded play and our opponents pause, trying to fathom my reasoning, wondering if I'm doing something inspired, even visionary. They strain to see what only I can see, but soon it becomes clear: I'm just a dope in over my head.

When I first picked up Mimi, she seemed agitated, like she wanted to discuss something she was too polite to discuss. After a few blocks, she caved. In a very diplomatic, offhand way, she eventually got around to suggesting that I keep my book project under wraps. She doesn't want to unnerve the club members. I am happy to comply, but once we're at the table Mimi ends up telling them anyway. She begins by introducing me as "a good friend of the family" or, more mysteriously, as "my guest," but usually before we can finish the round her bubbly enthusiasm wins over and she has me spill the beans. It's a conspiratorial progression: "Edward, why don't you tell them where you live . . . Edward, why don't you tell them what you do . . . Well, Edward, why don't you just tell them? They won't say a peep!" Mimi might love a secret, but she loves sharing one all the more.

Mimi is a popular gal. The members and staff all know her; they stop by our table to inquire after her recent absence. It seems everyone has a warm word for Mimi. At the table, she exhibits far more signs of life than I do, slouched as I am, with my Coke and dazed look. It's hard to believe she dates to the Taft administration. She is the belle of the ball—so many are glad to see her—and she has a high time, relishing each victory and worrying over each defeat. She is an enthusiastic bidder and an excellent player. She wears glasses at the table, along with what looks like a huge opal pinkie ring, with which she fiddles from time to time. When she's thinking or counting, she turns her head to the side and taps out a syncopated beat—then proceeds to play her cards briskly and brilliantly. Her hands are almost always in motion. She seems pleased to put out the word that she's seeking a partner once again. I imagine she will be in high demand.

Our opponents are a friendly, intimidating lot. There are white-haired women with big diamonds and bigger bouffants, bright makeup and brighter blazers; I spot more shoulder pads than in a locker room. The younger women dress smartly in fitted leather jackets and stylish skirt suits; they sport shorter but no less artfully arranged coifs. If I had to guess, I'd say 85 percent of their clothes came from Neiman Marcus (a Dallas institution since 1907). The men wear sport coats but no ties. There is a person on a walker with a tube up her nose. Everyone is full of warm, Southern charm, and they play ruthlessly.

After muddling through a few rounds without giving Mimi reason to dump her iced tea on me, we move to a table by the windows to battle two wobbly old ladies, one of whom seems barely able to see over the table. They're sweet, if a little disinterested in us. Despite the dazzling late winter sun, the curtains behind us are drawn tight—to fight the glare, they protest, when Mimi asks me to open them a bit. The ladies win the first auction, and before her partner plays the hand, the woman on my right calls out all the cards on the dummy, pointing to them one by one for her apparently hard-of-seeing friend. She does this just once before her partner proceeds to kick our ass. It is a rout. Looking back, the hands—at the time so distinct, so crucial—tend to blur, but some humbling experiences stick in your mind. I had heard a lot about these hardly harmless L.O.L.s (little old ladies), as they're sometimes called, but never did I expect to encounter them my first time out. After three swift, bloody boards, the smaller of the two sends us packing with a barely audible, but somehow brazen, "Thank you." Is she talking trash? I still don't know.

In general, however, we seem to be holding our own. The intensity of play is matched by the cheerfulness of the chatter. I am told over and over how wonderful it is "to have a young man at the table." Everyone is all smiles and interest. I feel I could announce I was a freelance assassin, and it would be greeted with "Isn't that nice?" I imagine good old-fashioned Southern aplomb makes for brilliant bluffing, but I'm too worried about making a mistake to spot any bogus bids.

I end up having to play the hand a lot. Whenever there's doubt about the contract, Mimi's solution seems to be to put the final bid in my hand, making me the declarer. I think she's testing me. But that doesn't make me nervous. What makes me nervous is the presence of the director, that specter arbiter who runs the game and enforces fair play and haunts the dreams of us newbies. At the Manhattan Bridge Club, we peer out into the big room and watch as players shoot up their hands—sometimes with a smile, sometimes with a sneer—and sing out, "Director!" Any unsanctioned play, breach of protocol, or even honest mistake can be cause to call the dreaded director, who glides over to dispense justice cold and clear. Any time we hear the call, we look up, as it almost always promises a fair amount of drama. In general, I imagine directors get a bad rap, like baseball umpires and low-level inquisitors. (In some circles it is considered rude to call one over unless it's absolutely the last resort.) But here, at the country club, I'm afraid of this woman who—in an effort to speed up the game—reaches over our hands and grabs the finished boards while we're still in the middle of playing.

So on board number nineteen, playing against two women I'll call "Intimidating Posture" and "the Swede," when the Swede starts off by leading out of turn, dropping a heart on the table when it wasn't her play, Intimidating Posture has no choice but to pronounce the word that makes my blood run cold: "Director!" She appears in an instant, ready to adjudicate, but only after rebuking the Swede ("Again?!"). Even though I'm not at fault, I'm sweating. As a penalty, the director outlines a host of complicated options I can take; it's like listening to a waiter recite the evening's specials—I forget all but the last one. So with all eyes on me, I opt for the penalty freshest from her mouth, that of letting the bad lead stand and making my hand—instead of Mimi's—be the dummy. There are a few reasons this doesn't seem like a half-bad idea: 1) Mimi has the better cards (since she opened the bidding), and this way they will be concealed from our opponents; 2) Mimi will now have to play the hand, thus getting me off the hook; and 3) I'm not about to ask the director to repeat herself. So I put my hand down as dummy, which in the end I think helps us, as we get an above average score on that board.

We seem to be playing well, I guess. It's hard to tell in the heat of battle, though afterward there will be plenty of statistics. We'll get one printout comparing our board-by-board results to those of the other North-South pairs and another showing our place in the field overall. Right now, I'm just amazed at myself for having made it this far. After three hours of concentrated, no-talking, heart-pounding card playing, I am utterly exhausted. I think I have an inkling of what Hamman meant when he spoke of psychic swings. And so, on the second to the last board, as I'm shakily on my way to making an easy, lay-down-the-cards four-heart contract, calamity strikes.

My right hand opponent leads a club. Bloodied but unbowed, I am determined to finish this thing—for Mimi. The cards swim before me. I have a vague idea to trump the club in the dummy, so I throw away a diamond from my hand. The table pauses. A little gasp escapes Mimi's lips. Suddenly, there in the dummy I see a long line of low clubs. I can't trump it—I have to follow suit! Like a boxer in the last round, I've gone blind in one eye. The opponents take an easy trick, and the game falls apart. The next thing I know I'm down three and our opponents—who now will receive a nice fat bonus, as surely I'm the only soul in the room who didn't make the hand—are actually thanking me profusely. I've bungled it. And we were vulnerable.

Mimi, as always, remains gracious. While we wait for the scores to be tallied, she tells me again and again that this is the toughest game in Dallas. (Indeed, one of the players sitting North-South is a national champ.) She even attempts to shoulder some of the blame, saying sometimes she would jump my bid just to end the auction and let me play the hand. As it turns out, that second-to-last hand was enough of a blunder to drop us down one place in the rankings—to second to last. It's not good enough to win us any master points, but I'm still thrilled with our result. Ever since I first spoke to Mimi, she has said that if she took me to the club it wouldn't matter to her if we "finished at the bottom of the heap." Then she told me again.

And again. And I began to realize it might matter a little. So Mimi is pleased, too. She studies our results carefully, happy to see we scored the top on not one, but two boards. (She will call me first thing the following day, too, for further discussion.) After I apologize again for that dismal ending, she says not to worry. She's just thrilled so many people stopped and said hello. The winners of the day are two bridge teachers who seem to have coached most of the teams in the room.

I leave Mimi in a chair by the entrance and head to the parking lot to get the car. In the next room, they're preparing for what looks like a Valentine's Day ball, but my heart is filled with less than love as I glance at those mercenary, possibly trash-talking L.O.L.s who whipped us so badly, now patiently waiting for the valet. I can't help but notice they're chatty and I'm worn out. I feel punch drunk, like I've swum a thousand laps or been awake for a week. I'm dying for fresh air. Mimi, for the record, hasn't flagged in her vigor.

As we drive home, I glance up at the light to make a left turn, and—just for an instant—I see a card. I mean I actually envision—hallucinate might be a better term—a giant ace of diamonds floating among the branches of an old pecan tree. Why diamonds, I don't know—it's those vanishing clubs that will haunt me. I've heard of this before: bridge players who begin counting obsessively to thirteen, the number of cards in a suit, or who measure out their lives in increments of fifty-two. But seeing a card up in the trees?

Meanwhile Mimi, oblivious to my delirium and its distracted effect on my driving, is chatting amiably. She tells me, "Well, that sure was a lot of fun. It was good to see everyone." Then she pauses, perhaps thinking of partners past, and adds, "But you know, the faces are changing." As I drop her off at her apartment, she offers one final piece of advice. "Listen, when you speak to anyone and they ask, 'How'd you two come out?' you just tell them we came in third."

CHAPTER SIX

A Short History of Bridge: From Ballyhoo to Mr. Bridge

The spread of contract bridge was evangelical. Half a year after Vanderbilt's voyage, a notice appeared in the *Los Angeles Times* announcing a Chicago woman was suing her husband for divorce on the inexcusable grounds that he trumped her ace. Within two years there were organized tournaments, the most famous of which, the Vanderbilt Knockout Team Championship, lives on today as part of the spring North American Bridge Championships. Not only did Harold S. Vanderbilt donate the magnificent cup that still bears his name, but he established an endowment to provide the winners with silver replicas in perpetuity.

The game seized the imagination of the country, a good part of which would soon find itself long on free time and short on cash. Bridge was at once cheap and glamorous, the game of tycoons available to any foursome with a deck of cards. In 1931, the two top-selling books were both on bridge. It became the companionable—and inexpensive—way to pass a Depression-era evening. Much of that fervor can be attributed to one man, the P. T. Barnum of bridge, Ely Culbertson.

Culbertson was born in the Carpathian Mountains of Romania in 1891 (by coincidence, the year Barnum died) to an oil-prospecting father from Pennsylvania and a Cossack princess mother. Bertrand Russell would call Culbertson "the most remarkable, or at any rate psychologically interesting, man it has ever been my good fortune to know." Ely's father made a fortune in oil, allowing for his son's remarkable real-world education. In the first thirty years of his life—as he bounced between Russia, America, Mexico, Havana, Spain, and Paris—Culbertson would be an anarchist, labor agitator, hobo, revolutionary, Yale man, Cornell man (though he didn't last long at either university), womanizer, gambler, sailor, Bowery bum, brothel brawler, house gambler, and, eventually, professional bridge player. He came to bridge by way of vint, a Russian variant of the game, which he had picked up at age eighteen from a condemned comrade while imprisoned in the Russian town of Sochi on the Black Sea, where he was trying to seek vengeance for his revolutionary girlfriend, who was strangled to death in a political assassination. Culbertson spoke many languages and had a mind for mathematics, which he studied to better his card play.

With his family's wealth lost in the 1917 Russian revolution, he returned to New York in 1921 broke but determined to get by as a bridge teacher, an occupation he had read about abroad. He scratched out a living playing at the cheaper clubs in Greenwich Village before moving up to the private Knickerbocker Whist Club, which hosted a sizable money game. At the club, he met a young widow named Josephine Murphy Dillon, who was the secretary of Wilbur Whitehead, the renowned card player. In 1923, Ely and Jo were married. Despite the smart match, Ely was an outsider to the clubby world of the gentleman card player. He was also something of a strong personality. Two years later, when Whitehead established his own club, the Cavendish, he informed his former secretary that she was welcome to join, as long as her husband did not. (Years later, when Ely did join, some members jumped ship.)

In the grand American tradition, Culbertson was determined to radically self-invent himself as the country's greatest bridge celebrity. He was a born huckster and hustler, and he was full of "scientific" ideas—some sound, others not—that he wanted to bring to the game, particularly in the realm of bidding. He converted his wife, herself an accomplished player, to his own homegrown system, which he had long been developing and now wanted to simplify so that the average social player could learn it. Unfortunately, he was unable to find financial backing for his ambitious schemes, but in 1929 he self-incorporated and took an office on West Fifty-fourth Street. The month the market crashed, he founded a magazine, *The Bridge World*, which survived the collapse thanks in part to its devotion to controversy and gossip. Culbertson criticized the outmoded ways of such sacred cows as Whitehead and Work (whose own bridge magazine had just folded), and provided sensational coverage of the Kansas City Bennett bridge murder. He dubbed his bidding style the Approach-Forcing System, a name he picked for its vague connotations of sex.

Culbertson formed a team consisting of himself, Jo, and two talented younger men, Theodore Lightner and Waldemar von Zedtwitz (perhaps the only player who boasted as colorful a biography as Culbertson, von Zedtwitz had already fought a war, abdicated a German baronage, and reclaimed a Kentucky family fortune). In 1930, the foursome played a grudge match against a British team, and the event—which Ely hyped to the hilt—became the great Anglo-American bridge match, considered to be the first international bridge competition. To pay for his team's passage, Culbertson presold copies of a book he hadn't written. It was to be the synthesis of his vaunted system, and he advertised it heavily in his magazine, offering it at a discounted $1.50 a copy. He worked down to the wire, dictating the book seventeen hours a day to three secretaries and finishing it in a cab en route to the pier. Halfway through the match, Culbertson received a telegram stating that three printings of *The Blue Book* had already sold out—the first in a mere twenty-four hours. He had made a fortune. To top it all off, the Americans won the match.

Culbertson used his newfound fame and fortune to create a

so-called "bridge laboratory," the Culbertson National Studios, which certified a corps of (mostly female) teachers to spread the gospel of the Approach-Forcing System—which soon would be used by some 84 percent of the 20 million bridge players in America. *The Bridge World* now reached forty thousand readers. Ely was everywhere. The backlash was on its way. A cabal of influential players, many predating the days of contract bridge, was formed to combat the Culbertson epidemic. They established the Bridge Headquarters, from which they promulgated their brainchild, the Official System, which was a standardization of the methods of the various members, who included such luminaries as Wilbur Whitehead, Milton Work, and Sidney Lenz. Adding insult to injury, they invited Culbertson into their fold.

The feud was fierce and public. In July 1931, a challenge was issued in the pages of *The Bridge World.* It was to be the "Battle of the Century"—Ely and Jo against the Bridge Headquarters' best, Lenz, and a player of his choice in 150 rubbers of bridge. Culbertson's ambitious careerism (not to mention his domination of the bridge world), rankled Lenz's sensibilities of the genteel clubman. He accepted, picking for his partner a brilliant Brooklyn-born young man named Oswald Jacoby.

On the evening of December 7, 1931—a date Culbertson suggested to the press might be more important than the Armistice—the event got under way after something of a late start (Ely got lost and Jo misplaced her glasses) in a pink-and-green salon on the tenth floor of New York's Hotel Chatham. Only the officials, a discreet butler (who emptied the ashtrays), and certain favored bystanders were allowed beyond the well-guarded doors. On the street below, police held back the curious crowds, among which a rumor circulated that Chicagoland gangsters on loan from Al Capone had been brought in to keep the peace. The National Broadcasting Company carried the opening speeches and hands over the radio.

During the next six weeks, as many as thirty stenographers

at a time would work in the suite. Six Western Union telegraph operators stood on call twenty-four hours a day. A new pack of cards was used for each deal. The *New York Times* covered the match hand by hand, often supplying trick-by-trick analysis and keeping a running tally of the number of aces and kings held by each side. Results were cabled daily to papers across the Atlantic.

From the get-go it was pure bridge ballyhoo. Lenz did card tricks, Ely pontificated, and everyone posed for the newsreel and press photographers. The players bickered at the table—with the exception of Jo—and every sharp word showed up in the press. After the Culbertsons took a considerable lead, Ely cited his opponents' ungentlemanly "petty squabbling," claiming they might prove themselves "the world's worst losers." Lenz complained about Ely's slow play, at one point "falling asleep" at the table. When the referee, a young bridge-playing Army lieutenant named Alfred M. Gruenther, woke him, Lenz initiated a heated exchange with Culbertson, eventually storming out of the room (after asking to be notified by telegram the next time Ely played). Adding insult to injury, when Lenz's chips were down, the president of the Bridge Headquarters, F. Dudley Courtenay, withdrew his support, saying Lenz was not representing the group as a whole.

On December 18, Jo excused herself for a few days to do her holiday shopping, at which point Ely played with another of his usual partners, Theodore Lightner. When the boys wanted to compete on Christmas Eve, Jo nixed the idea. Ely would also partner with Waldemar von Zedtwitz, Michael Gottlieb, and Howard Schenken for one night apiece—the latter two being something of a publicity stunt, as Ely had never played with the young up-and-comers.

Culbertson fans sent their team good-luck wreaths, figurines, wishbones, rabbits' feet, and a four-leaf clover. Ely gave his opponents copies of *The Blue Book* for Christmas. Halfway through the match, the game was moved to the Waldorf-Astoria Hotel, where a wing on the fifth floor was dedicated to the proceedings. (Even the press had its own private card room.) After a nasty verbal altercation, Ely nearly came to blows with a friend of Lenz's, Sir Derrick Wernher, who dramatically challenged Ely to a match. Despite the fact that Wernher outweighed him by a hundred pounds and stood six inches taller, Ely called the man a "big yellow beefsteak." The rumble was forestalled by the appearance of Mrs. Culbertson. Other kibitzers were typically more casual, including Chico Marx, who cracked jokes for the spectators, many of whom wore evening dress.

After 103 rubbers, Jacoby would resign as Lenz's partner, citing the older man's constant criticism. The two had incompatible styles of play. Commander Winfield Liggett Jr., was brought in to finish the contest, which, despite a final push from the Lenz team, was not very close. The match ended after midnight on the morning of Saturday, January 9. After 879 deals and 150 rubbers, Ely and Jo finished ahead by 8,980 points. At the conclusion of the match, Ely and Lenz did not shake hands.

Ely took to the airwaves at 12:45 A.M. to claim his victory, telling listeners the contest only confirmed what he already knew. According to him, the Approach-Forcing System was worth on average an extra two hundred points a rubber. Next up for the Culbertsons: a family vacation to Havana.

The newspapers reported the cards were very even. The Culbertson side held 3,520 aces and kings to their opponents' 3,512. In the public eye, the Culbertson system had emerged triumphant. Wrigley gum sponsored a series of Culbertson radio programs, and Chesterfield cigarettes paid $10,000 to include in each pack a tiny bridge guide bearing the Culbertson seal of approval. Ely and Jo made six short films for which they received $270,000. A speaking appearance by Ely might fetch an audience of three thousand. Twice more a Culbertson team ventured to England to defeat the British, taking home a trophy donated by steel baron Charles M. Schwab. During the darkest Depression years, the Culbertsons' income topped $350,000.

And yet for all his success, Ely remained at times an outsider.

When the master point system was introduced in 1936, ten players were named Life Masters. Ely was not among them. His last important match would be in 1937 in Budapest, though he continued to influence the game. He grew concerned with global politics during the 1940s, and died in Vermont in 1955. Nine years later, when the ACBL Hall of Fame was established, Ely was the first to be inducted.

Today, the Culbertson-Lenz match is considered more a triumph of a well-coordinated partnership (or partnerships) than a superior bidding system. In fact, history has sided with the losers. To evaluate a hand, Culbertson's system employed a complicated "honor trick" method, which has long since disappeared; meanwhile, the Official System used the simple 4-3-2-1 point count advocated by Milton Work—which is similar to what we bid with today.

It would take a while for the country to get out from under Culbertson's long shadow. In the meantime, America's love for the game flourished. In Hollywood, bridge had become the pastime of stars and studio heads—to the point that Buster Keaton labeled the game Hollywood's second favorite "indoor sport." Movie moguls such as Louis B. Mayer, Irving Thalberg, Hiram Abrams, Joseph Schenck, and Samuel Goldwyn all played for big money. As early as 1930, the Marx Brothers caper *Animal Crackers* showed Harpo and Chico running amok at a society bridge table (Chico's lunatic bidding is questioned by an opponent: "One." "One what?" "That's all right, you'll find out."). The same year the game provided comic fodder for the Mack Sennett short *He Trumped Her Ace.* Other short comedies would follow, including the 1932 *Bridge Wives*, directed by Roscoe "Fatty" Arbuckle, concerning a husband driven to desperate acts by his wife's obsession with bridge. A year later Sennett would hit the nail more squarely on the head with *Don't Play Bridge with Your Wife.* The Culbertson-Lenz match was lampooned in the feature-length comedy *Grand Slam* (1933), wherein a waiter invents a bidding system with no rules that he believes will restore marital bliss to the bridge table. The game played a prominent role in the 1939 Jimmy Stewart screwball comedy, *It's a Wonderful World,* in which Stewart uses some psychic bidding to escape from the bridge-playing police detail delivering him to prison. (That an audience would understand Stewart's ploy—and buy the idea of idle cops sitting down for a rubber—hints at the game's thorough saturation of the culture.) Perhaps one of the most memorable silver-screen bridge parties is also the briefest; in the 1950 Hollywood noir *Sunset Boulevard,* Buster Keaton made a ghostly appearance with fellow silent stars Anna Q. Nilsson and H. B. Warner to form Gloria Swanson's collection of bridge-playing "waxworks."

The craze peaked in the 1940s, when the game was played in 44 percent of American homes. Every heyday needs its giant, and the country soon began to worship at the feet of a Philadelphia lawyer named Charles H. Goren. Goren became determined to prove himself at bridge at twenty-two while attending McGill University. A Montreal hostess laughed at the young law student's ineptitude at the auction bridge table, and he decided not to play again until he had mastered the game. (Goren had grown up poor in Philadelphia, and perhaps the woman's laughter cut various ways.) After some diligent study (particularly the books of Milton Work), Goren finally entered—and won— a duplicate game in Philadelphia.

Before long, law was a thing of the past. Goren was working with his mentor, Work, even ghostwriting the master's bridge columns. In 1936, Goren published his first book. A year later, he won the most master points of any player in the country— for the first of eight times. (He would hold the title five years straight from 1947–51.) In 1942, he published his influential book, *Better Bridge for Better Players.* In 1944, he became the syndicated bridge columnist for the *Chicago Tribune* (replacing Culbertson). And in 1949, his landmark *Point Count Bidding in Contract Bridge* swept the nation, becoming a bestseller (at $1.00 a copy). Its emphasis on the point-count system (including assigning points for distribution) drove the nail in the coffin of Culbertson's "honor tricks." For countless living-room players, Goren simplified and standardized bidding. Suddenly everyone "played Goren," and perhaps not since Hoyle have so many statements been made "according to."

In 1950, Goren's team won the inaugural World Team Championships, dubbed the Bermuda Bowl after the tournament's tropical location. (The event and its nickname endure, though the host country changes.) The father of "Standard American" bidding, Goren became known as "Mr. Bridge." He was a prolific writer, turning out nearly forty titles (including such classics as *Contract Bridge Complete* and *The Standard Book of Bidding*). In his lifetime, he sold more than 10 million books, the introductions to which were penned by the likes of playwright George S. Kaufman and writer Somerset Maugham, with whom he played. He was also just as likely to sit down for a rubber with comedian George Burns or a few of the Brooklyn Dodgers. His preferred tournament partner was Helen Sobel, one of the greatest female players ever, who happened to have picked up the game as a chorus girl in *Animal Crackers*. Goren never married, living mainly in Manhattan and Miami Beach. He was a guest at the White House at the request of Bess Truman. He played with the Duchess of Windsor and Dwight D. Eisenhower. In 1958, his face was pasted over the king of hearts and put on the cover of *Time* magazine. The story was called "King of Aces" and claimed bridge as the country's top card game, with 35 million players. Goren wrote weekly for *Sports Illustrated* and monthly for *McCall's*. His TV show, "Championship Bridge with Charles Goren," ran on ABC from 1959 to 1964. Every Sunday afternoon, after the dulcet tones of the theme "Music to Play Bridge By," Goren would sit down with Groucho and Chico Marx, bandleader Les Brown, and other celebrity guests, a colorful cross-section that might include diplomats, tennis players, corporate executives, and football coaches. In the late 1960s, Goren gave up the game when his memory began to suffer. Some say he had Alzheimer's. He cut back his schedule, though his empire continued thanks to his tireless underlings. In the 1970s and 1980s, he lived in the care of his nephew in California. Charles Goren died of a heart attack in 1991 at age ninety.

In the intervening decades, the game has gone on, growing more complex and sophisticated, as theorists correct the mistakes of the past. In his autobiography, Hamman writes, "My level of play with the Aces when they were at their peak wouldn't be good enough to win as often as I win today. The progression of knowledge is such that the best players of the 1930s and 1940s would be blown out by good amateurs today."

And yet, since Mr. Bridge bowed out, no one has filled his shoes.

CHAPTER SEVEN

A Manhattan Interlude

They say bridge is about partnership, and it's true. Beyond mere strengths and weaknesses, you must grasp your partner's style, his philosophy, his outlook on life: how optimistic is he? Does he prefer to play it safe or go for the long shot? Is he excitable, overconfident, vindictive? How does he react to setbacks—does he become a mouse or a lion? Bridge is in part an extended exercise in empathy. And while I am learning a lot on the road—tips and tricks I am eager to share with Tina—I find myself spending my afternoons and nights back at the club trying to get to know her better. This is no easy task; Tina is a very private person. In time, I begin to tease out her life story.

She was born in a North Italian neighborhood in Greenwich Village in 1923. Her parents had emigrated from Italy through Canada, gaining entry into the United States when a stranger in line in front of them lent them a $50 gold piece to prove to the border officials that they were not indigent. When Tina was six, her family moved to a farm in Somerset County, New Jersey. Her parents ran a boardinghouse and a working farm. As a girl, she was shy; she used to love the sound of the cicadas because it meant summer was ending, and she would no longer have to wait on the boarders. She went to Wilson College, a women's college in Pennsylvania. Afterward she returned to New York City and attended a secretarial school in Times Square. With two friends, she took an apartment in the Village in 1946, which she describes as a wonderful time. ("The war was over—we were hopeful.") Trained to be a French secretary, she worked for the French mission to the UN, after which she held a number of unrelated jobs (including one as a junior buyer for a department store) before getting a position as an English secretary at the drug company Bristol-Myers. For twenty-five years, she worked for the president of the company in a big office on Park Avenue.

She was married and divorced in what she once called a "legalized affair." Neither of them wanted kids, though she thinks she would have been a good mother. An only child, she says she "lost the decade of the 1960s" taking care of her parents when they both became ill. She left the Village and moved into the apartment she still lives in today because it was only seven minutes from work—at a light jog—and she could literally run home on her lunch break to check on her mother. In 1982, Tina was diagnosed with ovarian cancer. The doctors said it would kill her, and they "took out everything that wasn't nailed down." After doing her own research in the drug company's library, she put a stop to what she felt was overly aggressive treatment, saying she knew when enough was enough. They told her she wouldn't live—now it's twenty-four years later.

Tina remains circumspect about her health. Only after a while does she tell me she has tremors in her right hand, which get worse when she's agitated or nervous. Her physical therapist says the best thing is for her to have a drink, which she says "only means I end up an alcoholic with two shaky hands." Many days it is hard for her to grip large objects.

Tina is a hard-nosed freethinker, a left-leaning liberal. She is concerned about politics in a way that used to be called "socially responsible." She remains cynical but hopeful. She says, "I can see the light at the end of the tunnel," but she worries about the environment and her own energy consumption because, she tells me, "It's all for you guys." Given her political and cultural involvement, I find it ironic that she says to me again and again, "You're the one who's in the world. I'm not."

Over the months, Tina grows more focused on our play, perhaps because her game with the Girls has started to fall apart. After my return from Dallas, she delivers some unfortunate news. I have been unable to attend Tommy's class for weeks, and when I ask after the Girls, Tina tells me Eru died just before Christmas. Nobody knows what happened—Eru just stopped showing up. Kathy had her number, which she called for weeks before speaking to a relative. The women are frank about their friend's death. There is no mincing of words, no hushed tones or sad smiles, just a matter-of-factness that seems to come from having had a stream of friends pass away. I am ashamed how little I actually know about Eru. She was a bridge club friend; I spent a surprising number of hours with her to not know how to spell her name. That much I learn through her obituary, which I look up in the *Times*. I read her family has dedicated a cherry blossom tree in her honor.

CHAPTER EIGHT

The Kids Are Alright in Gatlinburg

Gatlinburg, Tennessee, April 2006

Over and over I hear it: if you want to see a bridge phenomenon, go to Gatlinburg. Gatlinburg is the Tennessee home of the Smoky Mountain Mid-Atlantic Bridge Conference Regional Bridge Tournament, a seven-day affair held every April. In terms of regional tournaments, Gatlinburg is a monster—more than twice the size of the next largest, usually Las Vegas. In 2005, it set the regional attendance record with 9,096 tables. There is a dizzying schedule of events, many with charming down-home names such as "Rocky Top Side Game," "Sugarlands Midnight Knockouts," and "Redbud Stratified Pairs." Games start at 9 A.M. and run all night. No one is entirely sure why so many people flock to Gatlinburg, but, boy, do they flock.

Unfortunately for me, I start calling for a room only three weeks out. The first two places I try are booked solid. The third can give me a room Monday night and Saturday night—the first and last nights of the tournament—with nothing in between. I dial again and again with no luck, but at least I'm enjoying the Tennessee drawls. On the fifteenth call I end up with a room at the local Howard Johnson, which doesn't exactly thrill my wife, who decides to tag along when she discovers that Dollywood, the Dolly Parton theme park based in Dolly's hometown, is some six miles down the road.

What I know about Gatlinburg going in:

Gatlinburg (population around 3,700) is a two-by-five-mile Smoky Mountain resort town that got its name in the 1850s when the owner of the general store, Radford Gatlin, agreed to accept the mail. The town was mentioned in the country song "A Boy Named Sue," made famous by Johnny Cash. Gatlinburg stands at the foot of the Great Smoky Mountains National Park, which straddles the border between Tennessee and North Carolina and receives 9 million visitors a year. The park boasts eight hundred square miles of bountiful wilderness, with some twelve hundred campsites, seven hundred miles of streams, and eleven picnic grounds, and is home to more than ten thousand recorded species of flora and fauna, with perhaps as many as nine times that remaining undocumented. There are warblers and wildflowers, mussels and madtoms, foxes and fungi, bobcats and box turtles, and a record variety of lungless salamanders. Twenty-five percent of the park's forests are old growth. It has more species of native trees than all of northern Europe.

Of course, the region's most famous resident is the black bear. The most recent census estimated there were about sixteen hundred of them in the park, which gives us a bear density of about two per square mile. This seems notable from a visitor's point of view. (Were Gatlinburg suddenly to become part of the park, it would stand to have twenty bears roaming the streets.) The National Park Service Web site lists a number of fun facts: bears see in color, smell well, and can sprint thirty miles an hour. In 1999, there were 166 "bear-related incidents" in the park. A "Safety in Bear Country" leaflet offers further helpful hints like, "If you see a bear, remain watchful." Unfortunately, many of the animals have become panhandlers, and there seems to be no clear consensus on what to do if bothered by a bear—one plan involved finding a "stout stick." If that fails, and, God forbid, you are physically attacked, the Park Service suggests you "fight back aggressively with any available object." The leaflet ends by providing a phone number to report a bear incident.

Bold bears aside, we approach Gatlinburg anticipating a

real Appalachian spring. On a beautiful afternoon, we drive in from the east, crossing the mountains on a sun-dappled road with great green views of the Smokies and critters scampering through the brush. The radio plays a fifties country station while we marvel at shop signs advertising "videos and picnic supplies," "sewing and taxidermy." Then, as we approach town, something happens. Suddenly there's a proliferation of RV parks, "Tiffany" glass shops, and crappy craft stores—with a heavy emphasis on lawn art. Just as we're entertaining suspicions we aren't in a bucolic backwoods anymore, downtown hits us like a hot funnel cake in the face, with its greasy food shacks, go-cart tracks, and Hard Rock Café. Stores line the street, every one calling itself a "shoppe" or featuring kooky alliteration or both (hats off to you, Karmelkorn Shoppe). Apparently, the town does a brisk business in weddings—there are tuxedo rentals, bridal shops, a marriage license center, and a string of hokey wedding chapels ("Walk-ins Welcome"). Later, I'll pick up a brochure for a "Hillbilly minister," who will marry couples just about anywhere. Passing a parking lot a few days later, I'll catch a glimpse of a bride standing next to her car, sloughing off her dress and wriggling into jeans.

We cruise the main strip, passing stoplights helpfully numbered one through ten, which end up being surprisingly useful landmarks, as the side streets blur together into a seamless wall of kitsch. Traffic is slow going. Impeding our progress are throngs of flabby tourists in shorts and sandals, cameras slung around necks, who lead their children through the chaos with the oblivious air of ducks on parade. They cross and recross the road with no regard for lights or crosswalks. At one point, I watch a man stop traffic by pushing a stroller into the oncoming lane—with his child strapped inside. As for the sidewalks, they're clogged by flocks of red hatters trying to cut through veritable phalanxes of morbidly obese people on power chairs. Outside the Hard Rock, there is a line of thirty or so kids in matching white T-shirts squealing in anticipation—more so for the hot fudge sundaes, no doubt, than a chance to behold Tom Petty's harmonica.

For less star-studded dining, Gatlinburg offers what must be described as an obscene number of pancake restaurants—even to a man whose favorite meal is breakfast. Upon further investigation, the places serve the same, overpriced fare; perhaps there is a central kitchen bunker running underneath the town, turning out cardboard flapjacks by the ton, which are then carted up through a network of tunnels.

In terms of lodging, the town boasts more than ten thousand rooms, practically none of which are arranged in anything as simple as a single interconnected structure with a parking lot. No, Gatlinburg is the home of the small-time blockbuster; growing up here, one would think by definition a hotel has to have a waterslide, windmill, or miniature golf course. By these standards, our HoJo is downright plain, though it does have a pancake house and overlooks a Ferris wheel.

After checking into the hotel, we decide to head to a national park visitor center located just outside of town. Suddenly, not more than a quarter of a mile from the last wedding chapel, we're back in pristine wilderness—the majesty of the park sneaking up on us with head-spinning schizophrenia. At the center we collect handfuls of brochures on Gatlinburg, most of which simply list the national park alongside other area attractions such as black-light mini golf and "Earthquake: The Ride."

Forearmed, we decide to tackle Gatlinburg on foot, which is not for the faint of heart. Walking the strip, one gets propositioned every few feet by a freshly scrubbed youth; they're like drug hustlers in Mexico, but here they're peddling horseback rides or tickets to a hillbilly music show. To a one, the stores are tacky and touristy, innumerable and interchangeable little monuments to the can-do consumerism of Clark Griswold. Where else can one pick up a puzzle of the Last Supper and a Confederate-flag placemat? There are myriad magnet marts, kandy kitchens, shirt shops, and a World of Swords. In fact, for such a family-oriented place, weapons are surprisingly easy to come by. There are knife stores selling blades of all kinds: Asian, elfin, and commando. Amazingly, the toughest thing to find in Gatlinburg is hiking equipment; it's easier to get your hands on a shot glass than a water bottle. (Never mind that the Appalachian Trail winds through the nearby national park.) Of course, ATMs are the most ubiquitous of all. After a while, my disappointed wife sums up the shopping as "stuff obsessive freaks collect," meaning bears, blades, guns, mugs, Christmas candles, Beanie Babies, Thomas Kinkade paintings, and so on. I don't ask where bridge and I fit in.

That said, Heather is enticed by the scooter rentals. I can't picture riding a scooter in the Smokies; I only imagine they make tasty little meals on wheels for bloodthirsty bears. But Gatlinburg is something of a shrine to lunatic locomotion, home as it is to TV's original Batmobile and *The Dukes of Hazzard*'s General Lee.

Those are hardly the town's only big-name attractions. The place seems to be firmly under the thumb of a Ripley's Believe It or Not! mafia, as evidenced by the Ripley's Believe It or Not! Museum, Ripley's Aquarium of the Smokies, Ripley's Moving Theater, Ripley's Haunted Adventure, Ripley's Super Fun Zone, and something called Ripley's Davy Crockett Mini-Golf ("36 Holes of Whimsical Family Fun!"). There is also a Guinness World of Records Museum, which—according to the fine print—is also run by the Ripley empire.

But of all the mind-bending sights on the strip, I find it hardest to believe the "Help Wanted" sign posted in a store window that insists only people "with English as their first language" need apply. I couldn't exactly picture a lot of disappointed (but fluent!) Frenchmen being turned away. Perhaps this wasn't indicative of a vile xenophobia, but I had already noticed a strange absence of minorities in Gatlinburg—tourists or otherwise. According to the 2000 national census, the last available, Gatlinburg is overwhelmingly white, with only five—five!—African Americans, though there were about twelve times as many Asians and Hispanics.

But Gatlinburg is a baffling town. Besides the variety of ghost tours and haunted houses, other curious attractions include Cooter's, a museum named after the crusty mechanic on *The Dukes of Hazzard* that houses costumes, scripts, props, and, yes, the aforementioned 1969 orange Dodge Charger. There is also a place advertised as "The World's Largest As Seen on TV Item Store." And for those with more serious devotions, there is Christus Gardens, "America's #1 Inspirational Attraction," with its "precious gems of the Bible" exhibit, religious dioramas, and face of Jesus carved in a six-ton Carrara marble block, which, according to the brochure, is "the single most-photographed object in Gatlinburg."

And I'm just getting started. At one end of the strip rises a 407-foot neon-lit Space Needle that offers visitors panoramic views above and laser tag below. Down the street, adults can fork over $12 to ride the Sky Lift, a ten-minute alpine chair lift that ascends to . . . a four-thousand-square-foot gift shop. But perhaps the most staggering absurdity of all is the appearance—in the middle of that woodsy and wonderful Smoky Mountain air—of an oxygen bar.

By now it's getting dark. We eat a bland, overpriced dinner at a Mexican place whose name must have been Spanish slang for "evacuation," and head back to the HoJo, pausing only to consider the perverse pulsings of a nightclub called the Party Hut. Such places aside, Gatlinburg nightlife seems pretty PG. On a midnight stroll for ice cream (a long shot, we knew), the only other soul on the street is a very drunk maintenance man whose wife left him two years ago after two decades of marriage. Tennessee born and bred, he rambles on with such a thick Appalachian accent that I half expect him to spirit us up to his still for a secret swig of moonshine. Instead, he invites us to karaoke.

Considered from the upper balconies of the HoJo, Gatlinburg at night is a neon gash in the Smokies. The sounds of the strip lull us to sleep.

The next day I'm back on the street, walking to the bridge

tournament, which is being held in the convention center that anchors one end of town. I have an interview scheduled, so I'm trying to think about bridge, but I can't help but notice that along the short way I could get my Old Tyme portrait taken as many as six times over. To be fair, I have a bit of a bad taste in my mouth, having been victim to an early-morning pilgrimage to Dollywood, in nearby Pigeon Forge.

In summing up the charms of Pigeon Forge, I will mention only two of the many showbiz attractions that compete with the behemoth that is Dollywood. First, there is the newly opened Miracle Theater, showcasing nightly (except Sundays) a faith-based musical blockbuster billed as "the ultimate battle between good and evil" involving live camels, swashbuckling angels, and the crucifixion. A Jumbotron outside proclaims: "He's ready!" (and shows a glowing guy in white robes) . . . "He's waiting!" (cut to a close-up of red devil eyes) . . . "The battle begins!" (as an armor-clad archangel brandishes a sword). Sharing the same giant parking lot is the Alabama Grill, featuring the food, memorabilia, and music of the eighties supergroup Alabama.

And then there's Dollywood, those 125 acres of down-home Tennessee theme park dedicated to the bosomy genius, with its incongruous "Festival of Nations" event, Dolly Dollars, and Doggywood Kennel. It's a story for another book. I had been excited to visit, especially after learning the park had a dress code (shirts buttoned up two thirds of the way, no partially bared buttocks) that expressly forbade "character-type costumes." Was this a problem? How interesting. In reality, Dollywood was a disappointment. The "Kinfolks Show" had the day off, and the roller coasters were pretty puny. Even the world's largest wind chime seemed small. After a few hours, we left, having spent $45.70 apiece to see a blacksmith and a few bald eagles. Even Heather was a bit disenchanted, and this is a woman who has an incredibly strong Pavlovian response to "Coat of Many Colors"—only a few bars and she bursts into tears.

In short, I found Pigeon Forge, with its hundreds of lawn

chairs set along the main drag so people can sit a few feet from the three-lane divided highway and watch traffic, to be Gatlinburg's fraternal twin—a unique but equally harrowing hellhole. On our drive back, we got caught in some strange lunchtime gridlock, and it took forty minutes to travel the six miles to Gatlinburg.

And so I'm in something of a Smoky Mountain daze as I approach the convention center. Suddenly I notice signs in the stores that say WELCOME, BRIDGE PLAYERS, and there they are, swimming against the schools of tourists—bridge players. I can spot my own a mile away, with their furrowed brows and clipped, curious conversations ("I had a stiff heart, and when I saw dummy, I knew I was cooked!"). They are everywhere, buying fudge and basking in the sun on the convention center veranda, from where they make catcalls to friends on the street, shouting over a crowd of confused middle school choristers: "Hey, Leonard, you win some, you lose some!"

Leonard does not reply, and I head into the convention center, pushing past two men who—as soon as they're through the door—start puffing angrily on cigarettes and jabbering in Italian. There is quite a crowd in the lobby: men in cowboy hats and tennis shoes, a woman in a leopard-print skirt suit and a black beret, people in ladybug T-shirts. There is a tall, very tan woman with two forty-something guys in ponytails standing next to a dapper old gent in a seersucker suit and baby blue tie. A teen in a T-shirt lights up on the veranda though he barely looks old enough to smoke. Bridge-themed sweaters are everywhere, and I am impressed to see a woman wearing a full-length dress decked out in cards. Still, she is one-upped by a white-haired woman in a motley pantsuit printed head to toe in playing cards—and topped with a matching painter's cap.

I descend an escalator to the main floor, passing a fellow in hiking shorts and a big backpack; perhaps he wandered in off the trail. Seeing him, it dawns on me that one way to tell tourists from bridge players is that, for the main, bridge players wear pants.

On the lower level, I pass a row of vendors selling patches, purses, and jewelry, much of it bridge themed, as well as wool blankets, doggie hats, and T-shirts that read "World's Greatest Bridge Player" and "If Card Playing Is a Sport, I'm an Athlete." On a bulletin board is tacked a rogues' gallery of the tournament's newest Life Masters, the snapshots revealing delighted but drained faces caught in the afterglow of reaching a milestone. Next to the information table, I see a message board covered with handwritten yellow Post-its. The notes are pretty standard, people looking for rides to the airport and such, plus a few souls searching for encounters more social ("Any BBO or Zone players want to meet for drinks?") or strange ("Archie, I need a parrot joke fix—Barbara").

I poke my head into the great hall, where I assume the action to be, and I'm overwhelmed at the sight: some 67,000 square feet of bridge marked off into areas by big red banners ("Intermediate/Novice," "Senior Entries"). A third of the way down, the room is divided by a long gray partition covered with brackets and scores. The ceilings are thirty feet tall; the space is cavernous and eerily silent. There must be thousands of people seated in green and silver folding chairs, four to a table, in rows and rows and rows, but the tournament's directors are able to walk the aisles and—with a low shout—make their instructions heard. I notice most of the bidding boxes are Tennessee orange; I wonder if that's a coincidence. In the corners stand giant red clocks—like timers at a basketball game—ready to count down the minutes left in the round. A kid in a long pointy Rip Van Winkle beard and black skull-and-crossbones T-shirt walks about, delivering cards. I am utterly fascinated by this colorful well-behaved mob—a model of cooperation and concentration—but I can't stay. I have an appointment to keep.

Marlene Wass has been running the tournament in Gatlinburg so long she can't remember when she started. Her cochair, Judy Nolan, says that Marlene brought her on board some thirteen or fourteen years ago, so it must be longer than that. Even for Judy, "the years run together." Ask the women why they do it, and they're quicker with an answer: "Because we're fooools!"—pronounced with an extra few lingering o's, Tennessee-style, before they burst into laughter.

Marlene has red hair and wears a purple shirt, gray slacks, glasses, and black sandals. She seems to be in her sixties, though I'm not about to ask for specifics. Judy has white hair, a white sweater, black pants, and stylish gold brooches on her shoes. Around their necks they wear gold medals that read "2004 ACBL Volunteer of the Year." They both were nominated by Bruce Reeve, the friendly man in glasses who sits on their left. Reeve is a past president of the ACBL and the current director of district seven, which includes Georgia, North and South Carolina, and eastern Tennessee. In a deep Carolina drawl, he says, "These two were the first recipients of that award. It might even have been created with them in mind."

From their demeanor, you would never guess that these two women run the most successful regional tournament in the country. They display good Southern graces, refusing not only to brag, but revealing a certain charming reluctance to divulge too much about themselves or their tournament. The closest I get to a boast comes from Marlene, when, in asking a question, I round up the difference between last year's attendance in Gatlinburg and the figures from the recent spring national tournament, which just ended in Dallas. Before I can finish the question, she's all over my numbers, saying, "Now I'm not sure Dallas had quite that much . . ."

The Gatlinburg tournament was not always so big. Marlene remembers that the year it really "blew up"—or at least for the first time, as the tournament seems annually to break its own attendance record—was 1990, when the convention center opened and the games were moved under one roof. Previously, the tournament had been divided between two locations. This year attendance is up 5 percent, with players coming from Sweden, Poland, Australia, Canada, England, Mexico, Bermuda, and forty-nine of the fifty states (let's get with it, Wyoming!).

When I ask the women their secret, Judy says, "Basically, we have a great location in the Smoky Mountains. The convention center is convenient. There are some nice hotels, but it's fairly reasonable for people to stay." Marlene adds, "They can bring their spouses and families. And if they don't play bridge, they can go off and golf, tour the mountains, go to a show, or go to Dollywood."

It is funny to think that the holiday tournament in Kansas City—also a regional—seemed impressive at the time. Gatlinburg is more than eight times as big. The logistics are staggering. In addition to the great hall below, the tournament uses six upstairs rooms, giving it a total playing area of 71,078 square feet, or about one and a half football fields. The players use somewhere around nine thousand decks of cards and some twelve thousand bidding boxes. Each morning, the tournament publishes anywhere from 500 to 1,500 copies of the *Daily Bulletin,* which ranges from fourteen- to eighteen-stapled oversized pages. The bulletins contain short articles, announcements, scores, and schedules. They are written by a director who gets the day's results sometime after midnight and heads back to his hotel, where he e-mails his work to a printer in Pigeon Forge. First thing in the morning, Marlene's husband, Bill, goes and picks them up.

At my prompting, Marlene walks me through one mystery that has been bugging me since I got here: how the cards are set up at the start of each match. More than fifty tournament directors—the men and women in charge of the various sessions—report to Gatlinburg from all over the United States and Canada. Each is responsible for bringing a certain number of cases of boards with cards already in them. At the start of each session, a handful of boards are put on each table, and the participants sit down and sort the cards into suits. The directors then pass out the predetermined hand records, and the players themselves duplicate the hands. When everyone is finished, the stacks of boards are passed down a certain number of tables, ensuring that the players will never meet the boards they just made. Everyone then plays thirteen or so rounds at two boards a round (for which they have fifteen minutes). Marlene concludes, "And that's just for a pair event."

While we're going over this, a volunteer comes in to report that the upstairs ladies' room needs attention; a toilet is clogged, and players are complaining that the floors and sinks are sloppy. Judy puts out a distress call. When she's finished, she says, "You should see this place Sunday night. I mean it's cleaned daily, but at the end of the week they have to clear the tables and come in here with a forklift. There are mountains of trash. Bridge players are messy. They're just like little kids."

I ask for a wild story from years past, and Judy says, "Tell him about the wedding," which cracks up the room. When everyone is settled, Marlene starts in: "They met online playing bridge. He was from Texas, she was from Florida. They agreed to meet at a tournament. Within two months they decided to get married—here. I didn't even know them, but they got in touch and said they wanted us to make the arrangements.

"I happened to know a bridge player who was a Baptist minister. I called him, but he didn't know if he wanted to do it. He wanted to talk to the couple; he wanted to be sure they were ready to get married. And so he came down and met them. In the end, the only problem he had was that they wanted him to wear a Gatlinburg T-shirt. They were going to be wearing Gatlinburg T-shirts, and they wanted the minister to match.

"Well, the reception was going to be in the convention center. We arranged for a room upstairs. The couple asked that we put an invitation in the bulletin, inviting everyone to the wedding. We also contacted the local TV station, and they agreed to come."

At this point, Judy jumps in. "On the day of the wedding, the woman went out to the grocery store and got a cake. Now he was white and she was black. But when she picked up the cake, the little bride and groom statues on top were both black. So when she got back she came right in here and asked to borrow some Wite-Out and fixed the cake."

Now it's Bill's turn. "The minister compromised by wearing a Gatlinburg T-shirt with a black coat. All the bridge players who formed the audience wore the T-shirts. There was no organ or anything, so everyone sang a cappella. What exactly it was, I don't remember—probably 'Here Comes the Bride.' "

Judy finishes up. "They came back the next year, but we haven't seen them since. If they're still married, we just don't know."

This is just a spectacular example of the kind of small-time affairs the women have to deal with on a daily basis. We are talking in the prize room, which serves as a command center of sorts, and over the course of the afternoon our conversation will be interrupted constantly by people looking for the lost and found, directors with problems, and stray volunteers. The women take everything—from lost car keys to personality clashes—in stride. They're remarkably calm and collected. Judy says, "People can get worked up over the simplest things. We can't do anything about most of it, but we listen."

The entry fee is $10 per person a session. Of that, the tournament gets $3—to run the event, provide hospitality for the players, and so on. The rest goes to the ACBL and the MABC, or Mid-Atlantic Bridge Conference (which is comprised of districts six and seven). Still, Judy admits, "This tournament makes a lot of money." The tournament gives out a lot of freebies, including a "table favor" every night. Marlene says, "We pass out taffy all the time, plus pencils, convention card holders, dollar-off chits at the concession stand, and chocolate. There's free food a lot of nights. Tonight it's ice cream bars. Last night there was fresh fruit. Tomorrow there will be a chicken finger buffet and tiny hot dogs." At registration, every player received a stainless steel travel mug with the tournament's name on it. The mugs came from California; the shipping alone cost $1,600.

But the players came for more than the mugs, and I ask the women why all these people are here. Judy says, "Because they have a different temperament than most people—they like to win. Sure, they get points at a tournament like this, but they like the thrill of beating you." Marlene nods. "They're competitive."

But surely folks are more friendly than that in Gatlinburg, which, according to the Visitors and Convention Bureau Web site, is "The Heart of the Smokies." Is there a regional flavor to the game in Tennessee? Judy, who is from Maryville, a small town south of Knoxville, where she plays with the mayor's mother, thinks for a while before responding. Eventually she says, "Well, people will maybe be a little nicer." After another pause, she adds, "You'd be surprised how many people move into this area, and I don't think they understand eastern Tennessee for a while. People don't forget—or forgive. They won't do anything, but they remember. You might pay for something ten years down the road. And I'm talking about bridge people—the regular east Tennessee players." At the look of surprise on my face, she says, "But really, it's more laid back than in other places."

Marlene and Judy learned to play bridge in college. Neither of their husbands plays; the women agree it's best not to play with one's spouse. ("Or at least not duplicate," warns Judy.) The women are too busy running the tournament to play in it, though they tried that once, some three or four years ago. Marlene says they were "zombies." They don't even have time to kibitz, which is a shame, as they would like to see some of the top professionals who show up. Judy tells me she hears, "Some of them play very slow. Their computers are slow. Now these young kids, they can do it like that!" (She snaps.) "They're the ones that are coming on."

The problem, of course, is that there aren't that many young people coming on. Judy tells her son bridge would improve his poker, but he doesn't listen.

When they're not actively running the Gatlinburg tournament, the women are planning for the next one. It is a job they work on twelve months a year. In fact, before the week is over they will meet to set the schedule of events for 2007—they want to start printing flyers as soon as possible. Tournament chairs across the country ask Marlene for advice on how to grow their events like Gatlinburg, and she tells them all the same thing: advertise. She says, "Sure, we get a lot of word of mouth, but we still send flyers to every tournament imaginable." By June, she wants to begin papering the country.

For all their work, the women are quick to pass on credit. Some fifty volunteers work the tournament, and Judy says it could never run without them. "Basically, they're people who like to do things for other people with nothing in return. They drive up here and pay to stay to volunteer. They might get a free entry and a dinner—we host an Italian dinner at the hotel to thank them—but that's it." Marlene says over the years certain volunteers have practically become cochairs in their own right. There's a medical doctor who hands out the prizes, a woman who has run the registration for many, many years, and two friends who oversee the partnership desk. There are also the grunts who come in early Monday morning to help set up—people who drive their own trucks full of supplies from Knoxville and build the section signs and hang the banners.

And then there are the caddies. Technically, they're not volunteers, as they get paid, but Judy and Marlene brag about them just the same. Caddies are the people—more often than not youngsters—who pick up score slips, move the boards from table to table, and perform a mix of menial tasks at the bidding of the caddy master. Judy says, "We house them. We give them chits to buy things from the concession center. We give them junk to eat and drink. We have five sessions a day. Some of the caddies are working three sessions, so they're making good money, but they're tired—hopefully too tired to go out and run around all night. The caddies have certain rules and regulations they have to follow, and if they don't follow them—they're gone."

There are caddies and there are players, and here in Gatlinburg you're either one or the other. The pecking order is firm, the caste system set. If you're a player, you're entitled to complain about the folding chairs, the food, the air-conditioning, or the slowness of the caddy. In short, you're entitled to complain about everything. Sometimes you're just plain entitled. If you're a caddy, you're allowed to gripe about one thing and one thing only—bridge players—and even then only under your breath. But that's okay, because you know who really runs the show.

The man in charge of the caddies is Jay Bates, thirty-five, a Bronze Life Master from Durham, North Carolina, whose nametag reads "Chief of Caddy Operations." I meet Jay outside the caddy shack, basically a storage closet off the main room marked "Caddies Only." Next to the door is a handwritten list of the caddies who have won the most master points in the tournament so far. Jay is not there when I first arrive, so I duck my head in. There is a cooler of soda, a picked-over Italian sub, bags of taffy, and a surly youth who eyes me suspiciously.

When Jay shows up, I tell him I'm interested in working as a caddy. He looks at my shoes and asks, "Can you run in those?" When I promise I can, he says he'll take me on board for the evening session, which should be pretty tame. In the meantime, he'll give me a crash course in caddying while we "walk the room."

Jay has a friendly face with a five o'clock shadow and short dark hair that is balding in back. He wears a white T-shirt, green shorts, and white sneakers with white socks. He has been playing bridge seriously for five years, but it is not his only hobby. He says he used to be very into the *Star Trek* card game and that he and his girlfriend, Darleen, still travel around playing Dungeons & Dragons with old high school friends. His e-mail address involves the phrase "Jedi Knight." That said, bridge is his passion. It is how he met Darleen, who takes a week off her job as a schoolteacher to help wrangle the Gatlinburg caddies. She's also Jay's bridge partner, and together they run a weekly game in Durham. In a few weeks, Jay says he is going to ask her to marry him.

This is Jay's third year to work the tournament and his second as caddy master, and as we wind through the massive hall, he explains many things. He points out the orientation of the tables, how some rows are situated as "squares" and others as "diamonds," so as to facilitate the flow of caddies. He indicates how sections are marked by tall stanchions bearing a letter or two of the alphabet (there being more than twenty-six sections, the A, B, C's eventually give way to AA, BB, CC's and so on). He says a good caddy can cover four to five sections, depending on the type of game being played.

But what exactly does a caddy do?

During a session, caddies are responsible for picking up the boards after they've been played and moving them from one table to another. But it's not so simple as passing the boards straight down the line—there are often complex movements, involving various teams in various sections sitting in various directions at various tables. And then there are the score slips that need to be picked up and taken to the scoring tables, where they are entered into a computer. As Jay tries to explain the nuances of working a "board-a-match" event as compared to a pairs game—something he says any good caddy knows—my head begins to spin. All I take away is that the directors need the results as fast as possible, so they don't use those traveling score slips we use at the club that get passed around with each board and allow you to compare your score with everyone else's once the hand is over. That kind of postmortem table talk would slow down a match considerably—just take thirty seconds for each board and multiply by the number of boards in an event and factor in all the tables and you can begin to imagine the gridlock that could grip the huge room. It's a race, Jay tells you; the directors have so much to do—so many scores to tally—that not a second can be wasted. And hence the need for good running shoes.

For their efforts, caddies get paid $25 a session if they want to work piecemeal, or $100 a day (consisting of three sessions) if they agree to work the whole week. There are about twenty-five caddies, fewer than last year, but it's an elite bunch. None of the caddies are local. Most of them are bridge brats, with parents who run or play in the big bridge events across the country. The caddies are housed three or four to a room in a hotel paid for by the tournament. During the workday, they're under the watchful eye of Jay and Darleen; as to what happens after hours, Jay shrugs, "They're eighteen, so basically it's not my concern." That is, all but the one fourteen-year-old, whom Jay has to make sure gets back to his parents by 11 P.M., as Gatlinburg has a curfew for minors. The rest mainly seem to be in their late teens or early twenties, though a few of the women are older than Jay. These women, he promises, "may not be the fastest on their feet, but they're solid."

As we move through the tournament, Jay is a whirlwind, solving problems, directing latecomers, finding last-minute partners, even sitting down to play a hand until Darleen shows up to take his spot. "I do what I have to do to keep the game going," he says. Indeed, the problem with "walking the room" with Jay is that he rarely walks. Speed is ever a concern to him, and he'll say things like, "Let's motor!" as he bobs and weaves through the tangle of tables, chairs, bags, stanchions, and scooters like a fish in a pond. I am nowhere near as nimble and often bump shoulders and trip on chair legs. Meanwhile, Jay ducks in and out picking up entry forms. He's one of those guys with an honest-to-God spring in his step who practically launches himself airborne after each footfall. At his normal pace, he is hard to keep up with. When he's really in a hurry, he breaks into a high-hopping elbow-pumping jog, dropping low into a crouch to turn the corners.

Thus an interview with Jay tends to happen in intervals, more like we're passing notes than having an actual conversation. While we're talking, he keeps running away. If we notice a player in need of the director, our job is to rush to the table, raise our hand, and bellow, "Director!" At the word "Caddy!" Jay is gone—zipping off to do another of his peculiar wind sprints: pick up a handful of used boards, dash down four or five tables, swap them for a fresh batch, then reverse the lap and deposit the new boards—all before coming back to me and picking up his sentence where he left off. So, in bits and pieces, I learn that in his day job, Jay is a nicotine research specialist at Duke University Medical Center, a position he has held for about nine years. He could have advanced beyond that, he tells me, but he doesn't want to. The job leaves him time for bridge. His goal is to become a tournament director.

We are interrupted by a caddy, who comes over to report that twenty entry slips have gone missing. Jay dispatches someone to investigate. He says you never know what problems will come up. During the afternoon game, the fire alarm went off, and the entire building had to be cleared mid-match. It was only a false alarm, and before long Jay was standing outside shouting, "All clear! All clear!" Last night a woman took two boards home in her purse by mistake; she was so embarrassed she sent her husband to return them. Earlier in the day, a woman was hit by a falling ceiling tile. Jay was first on the scene. The woman was fine.

With all the games finally underway, Jay informs me my duty of the evening will be to serve as his "guard" as he makes the rounds handing out tonight's table favor—white plastic rain ponchos with the tournament logo printed in orange. It sounds vaguely dangerous, but basically we are to wind our way through the room carrying a box of ponchos, delivering four to a table while trying not to upset cards, drinks, and players.

I look at the room. There are around 600 tables in play, meaning at least 2,400 people—maybe more. A few days ago Jay says they had some 3,000 people playing at the same time, which he thinks has to be some kind of single-session record. I stare out at the vast space and consider the smallness of me and Jay and our cart piled with boxes holding—according to the packing slip—2,500 ponchos. Where do we begin? I can't even do this!

Jay plunges right in, often carrying a box on his head like the Carmen Miranda of wet-wear. He gives shout-outs to what he calls his "bridge family" as we make the rounds, telling me stories of matches played with and against these folk. He points out the big professionals and a few legends in the game, men like Mike Cappelletti Sr., who have conventions named after them. I tag along, plopping down ponchos ahead of and behind him whenever I get a chance. My helter-skelter delivery bothers Jay. After a few sections, he politely proposes a more efficient system in which we divide up to tackle every two rows, passing out ponchos on both sides. Spoken like a true caddy.

The boxes aren't light, and soon I'm sweating. Jay says he's on his second shirt of the day. As I deliver my ponchos, I am reminded of what one caddy said to me earlier when I told him I was writing a book: "Please remind players that we hate interrupting them even more than they hate being interrupted." Indeed, the reactions I get range from stone-cold silence to disappointment ("Is it edible?") to "Thank you, hon!" to "Where were you yesterday when it poured?" Some players are grabby, others are polite, but most make the "Where were you yesterday?" joke, which gets old after about the fiftieth time. Jay says there had been a debate whether to hand out the ponchos the first night, but he says, "We couldn't trust the players to hang on to them." Tomorrow, I will feel vindicated when we're under a tornado watch.

While practical, the ponchos aren't as big a hit as previous nights' freebies like the bags of chocolate or dollar-off drink chits, which Jay passed out by himself. "You'd think they were gold," he says. At this point, an older woman comes over to present to us what she believes to be a better system of distributing the ponchos. After she's gone, a caddy within earshot sighs, "Oh, players, they think they know everything."

At ten, while in the novice section, we run out of ponchos. It seems more than twenty-five hundred people showed up tonight. It's not a big deal, but Jay says, "Trust me—we'll hear about it." And we do. But just as we're about to be overrun by disgruntled grannies, the snack bar starts handing out free ice cream and the mob moves on. At this, Jay says, "Bridge players are pigs. Just look at the floor when we're done." A tournament director wanders over and adds, "Oh, are the cards going to be stuck together tomorrow!"

Jay runs an exceedingly tight ship. As for the caddies, they take things seriously but carry themselves with greater nonchalance. In general, they remind me of a high school theater group, fighting and flirting with each other; I wouldn't be surprised if a back-rub chain broke out. And so Jay's role seems part camp counselor, part diplomat; when a teenage girl stops him to complain about how annoying she finds a particular boy, Jay simply says, "Well, he has his own style." When the girl is gone, I ask if it's hard breaking in new caddies. He says, "As long as they use their heads, they'll be fine. If they can use their feet, even better."

Soon one of the old hands, "Jen," nineteen, latches on to me, the newcomer. (Some names have been changed to protect the caddies.) She begs to read my reporter's notebook before trying to grab it. She will pester me about writing a note in it until I relent. In bubbly script she writes: "Jen is an awesome player. She made her contract of three no-trump with one overtrick," followed by two smiley-face exclamation points.

Not all of the caddies are so young. One enthusiastic first-timer in her forties has never played the game but is having fun as a caddy. When I ask how she's getting on in Gatlinburg, she tells me, "Pairs games I can handle, but in knockouts, it's like everything's exploded at once. You just try to make it out alive."

About ten of the caddies are "national caddies," meaning they are qualified to work the national tournaments. National caddies are the cool kids. They wear gray T-shirts that say, "Who's UR caddy?" and tend to stick together, making inside jokes as they weave through their sections. They throw fake punches when they pass each other and sometimes wrestle around on the floor. They know all the top young players, and have opinions on who's going places. They're impressed in spite of themselves by the salaries some of these kids can command as professionals. In understated awe, they repeat the numbers: one young pro charges $400 a day with a one-week minimum, while another is said to take in $600 a day, plus expenses.

Ahren, a tall blond twenty-something from Minnetonka, Minnesota, is one of the head caddies. Despite his laid-back manner, Ahren is described by Jay as "the Energizer bunny," which of course says a lot. He is clearly the gang's ringleader. His dad is a tournament director, and his two brothers are also caddies. He tells me, "I only do regionals and nationals." In essence, Ahren is a professional caddy. Jay estimates he is home only six to eight weeks a year—the rest of the time he's on the road.

The phenomenon of a pro caddy is relatively new. Caddies used to be culled almost entirely from local talent, but now there's a group that travels the tournament circuit full time. As a friendly kid with fishhooks in his hat tells me, "In three days here I can earn as much as a week at Starbucks." Of course money isn't the only draw, but while some caddies have aspirations to one day sit at the big tables, not all of them are players. In fact, a caddy named Greg tells me, "Some hate the game."

Greg, thirty-three, has been caddying on and off for twenty years. He has dark hair and a deliberate, thoughtful manner. He points out that Gatlinburg attracts a lot of top caddies because it pays better than the national tournaments and puts people up in hotels. (At other tournaments, caddies sometimes squeeze twelve-plus to a room—to save money—which inevitably leads to problems with the management.) In Gatlinburg, there are also more games—to both work and play—than at most tournaments. The only complaint here, says Greg, is that the caddies' feet get sore—because the floor is concrete.

Greg is not a full-time pro caddy, but he tells me, "I think it says something about the economy that people are making a living doing this. There are so few jobs. That's the lure. That and it gives some of the younger guys access to high school girls they otherwise wouldn't meet."

Greg is finally coming around on bridge. After growing up around the game—both his father and godfather are names in the bridge world—Greg started playing in earnest a year ago, after running into some young players at the national tournament he was working who made the game look fun and interesting. He tells me you only get a youth scene like this at big tournaments like nationals and regionals. He says a sectional event—one step down in size from a regional—will be filled with nothing but senior citizens.

As far along as I am into my research, I'm surprised to learn bridge has its own bunch of migratory fans, kids who blow around the country going wherever the action is. They are the ACBL equivalent of Deadheads, only with less patchouli and no parking-lot scene (and perhaps more partial Ph.D.s). These caddies speak their own language, go by their own nicknames, and even have their own secret Web site—the address of which I am bound by oath never to reveal.

The main part of the site is a forum to "bitch about bridge players." There are postings on work ("What other tournaments worth working at are coming up? I still have not found a job.") and play ("Buy a bottle of absinthe for Atlanta."). In general, the forum covers more or less what you'd expect from a bunch of red-blooded eighteen-and-over peripatetic American (and Canadian) kids: *Star Wars*, the soup in Denver, twenty-four-hour diners in Dallas, the age of legal consent in various states, caddy pay, cheap flights, marijuana laws, who's hot, who's not, who's hooking up, who's not, and drinking, drinking, drinking. There are topic threads titled "Motion to Strike," "Why did Denver suck??" and "Sluts." In one post, the feasibility of a laxative prank is raised, only to be scuttled by the observation: "The geriatric nature of bridge tournaments means there is already enough going on in the bathroom."

In the bristling cyber-banter, cool kids pick on less cool kids, and everyone craps on the "local nimrods" who sometimes caddy hometown tournaments. There are allusions to drinking and drugs and getting kicked out of hotels—scrapes with the law that the Jays and Darleens of the world are likely to know nothing about. Some questions are earnest: "What the fuck does it mean when your boyfriend says, 'I don't mind if you want to make out with other people.' Please translate this one for me. He says that he wants to get marryed [*sic*] next fall." Others are not: "Will this administration ever bring the Hamburglar to justice?"

There are even a few philosophical musings on the nature of caddies and players. One reads, "Bridge is a good outlet for competitive people who need to feel better and smarter than other people. Many of them probably got picked on a lot for being unathletic or unattractive as kids. This helped me understand why so many of them are jerks to caddies." Another states, "Caddying is kind of like rushing a fraternity. You are put in a stressful situation with a group of other people and then treated badly by another group of people. You are asked to do silly tasks for long periods of time and then you party in between. Going thru this with a group of others brings you all closer together faster than normal."

They are certainly a tight-knit bunch. Early in the day, when I approach a gang lounging around a table, a short girl of indeterminate age with black-tipped blond hair looks up and snarls to the guy whose lap she's on, "Who's he?" Suddenly I feel like a narc.

A caddy's world-weary scorn is born of battle, the defensive disdain of the second-class citizen. Caddy abuse is rampant. In one session, Greg sits in to play with an intermediate woman whose partner hasn't appeared by the game's start. Up front she tells him that if he's not any good she'd rather just withdraw and be done with it. As it turns out her partner shows up halfway through the first hand, and rather than let Greg finish it out, the woman sends him away, leaving her partner to pick up the strange cards and—with no idea of what has been played, or how the bidding went—muddle through blindly.

Upon hearing this story, "Rebecca," who says she could count the points in a bridge hand as a toddler and has been caddying since she was eight, says, "Players are just big overweight babies." Now twenty-three and one of the head caddies, she repeats what a lot of people have said to me: the less experienced the player, the nicer they are to caddies. To get back at some of the more obnoxious experts, caddies have been know to give them nicknames, like the guy they call "Drinking Problem" to honor his after-hours antics.

Caddies are not the exclusive targets of a bridge player's temper. As the session winds up, I see a woman in her sixties pull her husband away from the table and loudly bawl him out—for bawling her out ("I don't *ever* want to hear you telling me I misdefended the hand!"). To be fair, she shows more decorum than most, who get into it right at the table.

Perhaps it's past this lady's bedtime. We're all a little cranky, except Jay, who continues checking off what needs to be done on little slips of paper written in caddy code: the tables that have to be moved, the boards still in use that need to be correctly stacked and stored for tomorrow, the room that needs to be broken down, the equipment that must be shifted to the loading dock.

The time draws near for the midnight knockout, which actually starts at eleven thirty. The late-night game is a caddy's best chance to play, and all day I had been hearing the caddies talk smack: who was going to win, who was going to drink, who was going to take advantage of the drunks, and so on. At any hour, the knockout format is by far the most popular. The lineup essentially looks like a March Madness bracket, with teams advancing round by round through head-to-head elimination until one team is left victorious. Knockouts offer the most master points, which explains their wide popularity. In Gatlinburg, some take place over as many as four sessions, with the winners in the top division walking away with some sixty-odd master points—more than a fifth of what's needed to become a Life Master.

While a handful of points are on the line, the midnight knockout is hardly so serious. People tend to drink and cut loose, and that goes double for the caddies. Enterprising Jen has put me on her team. She's rounded up quite a group. In addition to us, she's added Tim, an exceptional young player who is one of the tournament directors, and a twenty-three-year-old guy from Florida in a red T-shirt, flip-flops, and shorts, who she doesn't know very well but turns out to be Rob Meckstroth, a son of Jeff Meckstroth, one of the best players in the world. I will be playing with Rob. When Jen sees the look on my face, she tells me, "It's okay. We usually get knocked out early."

Knockouts are a team game, which means Rob and I will sit North-South at one table, while Jen and Tim sit East-West at another. Our opponents will fill in the gaps. Since we play the same hands at both tables, the scores can be compared—with the overall winner advancing to the next round. Tonight there are thirty teams. I don't think we have a prayer.

Rob is a former caddy and sometime bridge pro, though not this week—he's just "playing for fun." He drove here from Florida, where in the fall he will go to graduate school to study decision information sciences. He's not the stereotypical bridge nerd. He describes himself as a jock ("I play all sports") and seems outgoing and affable, not to mention slightly ADD, as he talks quickly and leaves half his sentences unfinished. Rob learned bridge when he was ten, but he only started playing seriously about five years ago. His father discouraged him from becoming a professional because in Rob's words, "He wants me to have a life." He says, "I felt no pressure to play. My dad didn't want me to get involved in bridge because he dropped out of college for it. He was worried I would get addicted to it, want to become a pro, drop out of school, and become a bum. So growing up he kept me separate from it. I traveled to tournaments, but just caddying."

When I ask for advice on our match, Rob offers, "Hope they're drunk." At this point, I catch a whiff of hops and wonder if Rob might be a bit under the influence himself. He soon admits he was just in a bar, where he downed forty-four ounces of local brew.

At this point our opponents sit down: two gruff no-nonsense Tennessee guys who—it becomes clear almost immediately—can't stand us. I'm guessing they've pegged us for caddies. Forty-something and fat, one of them barks at me while I'm considering what to play: "Do you know it's a fast game?" I do, but I'm nervous, playing with the son of a legend, and I botch the first two hands. Luckily, Rob hardly cares that we seem to be losing, despite one good result on a board when Rob makes a false no-trump overcall to disrupt the opponents' bidding. Later, the men call the director on us when Rob unintentionally fails to follow suit—despite the fact that it's clear what the penalty should be. At the mistake, the guys get all crabby. Rob knows the rules better than they, and the director upholds what Rob said—which only makes them angrier. In the end, Rob throws up his hands and concedes them an extra trick, for no apparent reason.

I'm amused, because if these two knew who Rob was, they'd be kissing his butt. Rob has about a thousand master points, half of which he's racked up over the past year. He's won about eighty so far in Gatlinburg and by tournament's end will finish 101st overall (out of a field of 3,819 people who managed to win points). He has won the second most master points of any junior (i.e., under twenty-five) player in the country so far this year. In conversation two days later, I'll ask him what it's like to be at a tournament when your father is one of the most famous bridge players in the world. Rob says, "It's interesting. You walk around and everyone knows who he is. Random people point at him in restaurants and say, 'Oh, that's the world champion bridge player!' It's the opposite of life at home where no one knows who he is. It's funny to be famous in this one little world, but out in normal life no one really cares." Still, tonight, in this room, these guys would definitely care who Rob was—if only they knew. Instead, they treat us like punk kids.

While we're finishing up, a friend of Rob's brings him a beer. It seems the concession stand is still open. Our team loses the round but not by much, and we end up advancing because of the narrow margin. Next Rob and I face off against a sweet old married couple. The husband keeps joking about sneaking sips from one of the two beers that now sit on Rob's side of the table. The wife takes one look at us and says, "You're caddies, right?" Despite their friendliness, the couple creams us. Rob is really good but probably a little drunk, and I keep trying to settle the contract in his hand, which doesn't always go so well. In the end, Rob says our defeat is partly his fault, but he's being generous. I'm clearly to blame. After the round, he juggles packs of cards.

Now that we're out of the knockout, it's time to socialize. At night, the caddies exhibit a level of ownership over the tournament that would be unimaginable during the day. It's their house, so they have no problem throwing cards and swilling beers. Kids walk around dangling six-packs in plastic bags. One of the professionals, who's young and drunk, offers to tell me all about the drug culture in bridge. Unfortunately, the conversation never takes place. Instead, a crowd gathers around Rob and his tall beer-buying friend, who seem to know everybody. The friend, tipsy, explains to me that he's here playing professionally, though he admits, "I have more money than most of my clients. Financially, I'm all set. I don't have to work. I just want to fuck around." It's hard to tell what's talk and what's not, but he says his outfit is part of being a pro. He wears designer jeans, loafers, a T-shirt, a backward Jack Daniel's hat, and a blazer that he says cost $800. He's twenty-three and he tells me, "No one dresses well in junior bridge. I always tell everyone you can make more money—even as a bad player—if you just dress up."

Soon he is joined by another friend, "Alex," an eighteen-year-old Asian American. The caddies say this guy is taking eleven classes a semester at the University of Virginia in an effort to finish his undergraduate degree as fast as possible—perhaps in only one year. He has taken a week off school to come to the tournament. Often seen wearing a backpack, he runs to do homework between sessions. One of his friends tells me Alex is getting paid to play, but it's hardly enough to cover gas and expenses. Tonight he skipped the midnight knockouts in order to beg Internet access off one of the hotels. He told them he had to turn in assignments, and they let him online. Alex turns out to be a friendly but aggressive ambassador for the game. When he tells me he went to the number-one public high school in the country, he points out, "We're the only public high school with a big bridge club—is this a coincidence?"

As more kids get knocked out, the circle grows. The consensus seems to be that the midnight games have gone downhill ever since the tournament started awarding master points in them. A caddy gripes, "It used to be a great way to blow off steam, shoot for ridiculous contracts, and have a few beers. But now people care." Perhaps to illustrate the point of how much they just *don't* care, a handful of drunk or drinking youngsters tell me of their midnight exploits at various national events: tales of boozy excess that seem more likely to come from a frat house than a bridge tournament. First, there's the one about the young pro who downed a bottle of Grey Goose and threw up all over the playing floor, and how "hilarious" it was the next day to see world-class bridge players standing around in what they had no idea was dried vomit. Next they debate the past outcomes of certain late-night "shot-a-round" pair games, where—despite downing double shots—one of them displayed the remarkable ability to puke everywhere but on his cards. Apparently everyone gambles, and as the nights wear on the wagering devolves into bets on coin tosses—heads or tails at $50 a flip—or high-stakes games of high card, low card.

These are not the only young guns here. I have tried repeatedly to corner what many call the "hot" young couple of bridge, Jenny Ryman (from Sweden) and Gavin Wolpert (from Canada), two engaged, good-looking twenty-somethings who met at a world championship in 2003. Together they won the prestigious Blue Ribbon Pairs in Denver last fall. At twenty, Ryman became the youngest player ever to win the event, which prompted Bob Hamman to say to the *New York Times*, "It shows the face of bridge is changing."

Despite my efforts, the wonder couple proves elusive. They never seem to hang out; somehow I only see them when they're sitting at the table. And so I find myself, as the hours grow late, standing outside by the curb with a mix of caddies and pros as they hang around smoking and talking and not wanting to go to bed. In the morning, they'll be back at work, playing cards with older people who are paying for their company or shuffling boards around the thankless tournament machine. But tonight they're kids. They talk about boyfriends and girlfriends. Jen says she's engaged to be married in two years. In the meantime, her friends joke about setting her up with Alex. The idea of an early marriage is scoffed at by the boys. They ask when I got married. I say when I was twenty-eight. The guys all agree that that distant age sounds about right—certainly no sooner. We disband around two A.M. As Rob and his friends walk down the street back to the hotel, they loudly lament, "We have to play at nine!"

Two days later, I, too, would be playing at nine. Jay has agreed to free Greg from his caddy duties to play with me in the Sunrise Stratified Pairs. With about ten master points, Greg is more advanced than I. The night before we filled out a convention card together, going over our agreements. We sat at an unused table, part of a pack of the momentarily idle, as caddies came and went, grousing about their sections, shooting players looks, and chatting about crazy conventions. We were an intimidating bunch. I felt like one of the gang.

This morning I'm not so sure. I had tried to go to bed early, but there is some sort of high school band convention in town, and hoodlums were setting off car alarms in the HoJo parking lot all night. I'm bleary-eyed and nervous—this isn't a midnight game, this is serious.

Caddies play for free, and they slide me in under the radar. It's Saturday, the second to last day, and the tournament is emptying out. At Gatlinburg, by the end of the week people have gone home; they have either tired themselves out (some by playing five sessions a day) or have picked up the number of master points they came here to win. (Or, in the case of my wife, they have to get back to work.) Even with the slowdown, the tournament is up more than four hundred tables over this point last year. By the last day, some 3,943 players will have come to the tournament—more than the population of Gatlinburg itself. The final attendance (in terms of total tables) will reach 9,564 tables, thus shattering last year's record by nearly 500 tables and making Gatlinburg 2006 the biggest regional tournament ever. It is essentially the size of last year's spring national, held in Pittsburgh, which was a full four days longer.

Greg and I are signed up for the stratified game, which means we'll be competing against people with roughly the same number of master points. I show up ten minutes before nine, and there's no sign of Greg. Eventually I go looking for him and find him already seated at a table. It turns out I was waiting in the wrong area, and now we're off to a late start—we'll have to rush through the first few rounds to catch up.

In general, our opponents are understanding and accommodating. The Canadian pair is by far the friendliest; they say a great many of them made the drive down, and the only thing they have to complain about is construction in Kentucky. The Canucks don't even call the director when I unintentionally fail to follow suit—we simply correct the error, which didn't effect the outcome, and move on.

Next we play two nice Knoxville ladies in loud floral prints.

One of them marks her scores with a pencil bedazzled with cards made of glitter. The women are impressed that Greg and I are playing together for the first time. They agree that finding a partner through the partnership desk can be iffy. The lady on my right says she once saw a woman get paired with a man whose first question was how many master points she had. When she said she had two, he refused to play with her. It turns out he had three.

Despite some blunders on my part, we manage to defend one hand brilliantly, setting one unlucky woman from Tennessee terribly. I worry a little about what Judy said about eastern Tennessee bridge feuds. I try to remember this woman's face in case I ever return to Gatlinburg.

Greg is working on about five hours of sleep, having stayed up late playing in last night's midnight knockouts. He pulls his baseball hat low and chugs coffee. Despite his efforts, out of eleven pairs in our division we finish dead last. After three hours and twenty-four boards, we have no top scores, five bottom ones, and a bunch of average results. Neither of us thought we were doing that poorly; we assumed we were more middle of the pack. I am ashamed, but Greg takes it in stride. One of the caddies teases us over our score. We repair to a side table to lick our wounds.

Greg lives in Ohio, where he went to college. A biology major, he was pursuing a Ph.D. in neuroscience before he "got tired of killing rats" and gave it up. Since then, he has held an assortment of jobs, from doing diabetes research in a lab to managing a band in New Mexico. Now he works as a community organizer and serves as the caretaker of a mansion. Looking out over the room, he says, "People play bridge because it is a world unto itself. At the table they focus so intently that they can escape from the misery of their lives." He also points out that the game offers a safe, structured social interaction for people who, he says, "have serious social issues." Maybe he's taking our loss harder than I thought.

As to why Greg is beginning to play the game after some twenty years of sitting on the sidelines, he says he likes being around smart, young, interesting people, for whom he admits he's a little socially starved living in Wooster, Ohio. By now, lunch is being served at the food court. Greg suggests the home-made soups; he has stayed away from the sandwiches ever since the year some bad egg salad made a lot of players sick. As we sit talking, the lunch line grows. Greg looks it over and says, "Some of these people will never leave this building."

I, on the other hand, need to clear my head after three hours of apparently appalling bridge. It happens to be Earth Day, so I get into my rental car and pull onto something called a "motor nature trail," which seems just about right for Gatlinburg. (Later, I read that the force behind the creation of the national park in the 1930s was not tree-huggers but motorists, who wanted a scenic area to tour in their cars.) The trail starts just up the block from the convention center and winds a couple of miles into the Great Smoky Mountains National Park. The storms have passed. It is a dramatic sky, the dogwoods are blooming, the creeks are swollen, and so at 5 mph—with the radio off and the windows down—I cruise the trail, taking in moss, mud, rocks, butterflies, and an endless forest of tall straight trees. I pass a picturesque waterfall. At one point I pull over and—keeping an eye on the nearest stout stick—listen to the first songbirds I've heard in Gatlinburg. The sun breaks through for just an instant, and it's glorious. Then it's back to the tournament.

Today's soup is chicken gumbo, and indeed it's good. There is a decent spread to choose from: sandwiches and salads, hot dogs and pretzels, and lots of fruit and cookies. I find an empty table and eat my lunch furtively, as Jay had mentioned something earlier about having me work the pairs game.

Soon I bump into Rob again. I haven't seen him since our midnight debacle, and he admits that the 9 A.M. game indeed had been rough. Rob points out that there are a lot of kids in Gatlinburg, and there will be more in Chicago, at the summer national tournament. There, "Every night's a party," he says. "The midnight games here are nothing—wait until nationals."

Today Rob is wearing a polo shirt for a poker Web site, and so I ask if he plays. It turns out he does—to the tune of $30,000 in winnings over the past two years. Poker kept him from having to get a job during college, leaving him plenty of time to party. I ask if he ever got up a bridge game in the dorm. He laughs. "I heard ninety-five percent of college students know how to play Texas Hold'em. I'd say less than one percent know how to play bridge." Ask which he prefers, and it's bridge hands down. "Bridge requires so much more skill. Sure, there's a lot of skill in poker, but it's easy to master that skill. It's easy to become a good poker player. It's hard to become a good bridge player. I have a whole bunch of friends that are all successful at poker. They would not be successful at bridge."

I ask Rob if he's playing the midnight game tonight. He's not sure. He drove from Gainesville, and it's a long way home. He also points out that he doesn't live solely for tournaments. He says, "It's nice when it's all over. I go home and the bridge stuff is totally gone. I have a very normal life that has nothing to do with bridge. I can't stick around tomorrow—I have a final-four intramural football game to get back to."

After the afternoon session, I crash the caddy pizza party, which is taking place at a motel across the street from the convention center. The room is strewn with pizza boxes and two-liter bottles of soda; there is a cake for Darleen, who's celebrating a birthday. Everywhere caddies casually sprawl on chairs. Bill is there to stand in for his wife, Marlene, the tournament cochair, who's attending another meeting. He kicks off the party by clearing his throat and making a short speech thanking the caddies for their efforts. It's been another banner year for them—many players have commented on their speed and efficiency. He asks that everyone send Jay his or her contact information come winter, as this year they had some trouble tracking people down through old addresses and e-mails. He closes by telling the group, "Have a good time—this is your party!"

With Bill gone, the conversation shifts to the best way to break into the convention center after dark so as to get a jump on the final cleanup. People would rather work all night than get up early tomorrow. Tonight will be the final round of midnight knockouts. The game is free, and if you lose, you can keep reentering the losers' bracket as long as there's someone awake to play. Greg tells me it's a crazy scene: people get drunk and balance boards on their heads. The caddies discuss the teams for tonight, and the pizza boxes begin to empty. A girl offers to demonstrate how to explode a soda bottle using a pack of Mentos. This prompts an argument over whether the proper term is "soda" or "pop," the sides forming along strictly geographic lines. The girl's trick is never performed. The talk drifts to what kind of complicated bidding systems people want to play one day when they're really, really good.

One caddy mentions he plans to sleep an entire week. Not everyone gets that luxury. Tomorrow Ahren leaves for the Fort Lauderdale regional, which starts on Monday. He always drives between tournaments, preferably straight without stopping. Ahren isn't sure exactly how many weeks he'll be away from home this year, but he knows he's booked solid caddying for months. Ask him why he does it, and Ahren shrugs. "There's no way I'll get rich doing this," he says. "I know that. But getting in a midnight game every night and playing for free—that I like a lot."

A few of the other caddies are heading to Fort Lauderdale, too. Others will be at nationals in Chicago in July. Some won't see anyone until they're back in Gatlinburg next year. The sun comes out again and eventually the party moves outside to dangle feet in the pool. Not everyone will work tomorrow, the final day. The numbers begin to dwindle as people take leave of the group, shouting, "Good-bye forever!"

Soon it's my turn to go. As I get into the car and begin crawling the clogged, slow strip back to my hotel, I'm not sure I'm going to make it to tonight's midnight knockouts. I'm tired of all the traffic, tourists, knickknacks, and fudgeries. And, yes, I'm a little sick of bridge. So at the HoJo I put on some shorts and go out for a run. Pounding down the road, I catch my first sight of real wildlife since coming to Gatlinburg: a large brown hawk swooping low overheard. Like me, he's heading straight out of town.

CHAPTER NINE

Social Studies

On a handsome block between Central Park and Madison Avenue on Manhattan's Upper East Side stands 15 East Sixty-seventh Street. The six-story Beaux Arts townhouse is unmarked, save for a brass sign standing at the curb requesting trucks not block the entrance and a curious emblem on three sides of the plain gray awning, above which the number fifteen is carved in an elaborate marble cartouche. The emblem is an outline of a spade in green bearing the initials RWC, which, among the world's card cognoscenti, stand for the Regency Whist Club.

For decades the club has operated out of sight of most New Yorkers. It is the only private bridge club left in Manhattan, and it is very private indeed. Its membership rolls past and present read like a Who's Who of the game, including, among many others, Waldemar von Zedtwitz, Theodore Lightner, Charles Goren, Oswald Jacoby, Sam Fry, and Harold S. Vanderbilt, the man who started it all. The Regency is an unabashed Old World holdover, perhaps the last haven of card-shark robber barons and titans of industry, who come to while away long afternoons playing rubber bridge with each other. To this day, it remains the home of the city's—and some say the world's—biggest money bridge game.

In 1936, the Regency became Manhattan's third bridge club. First was the Cavendish, which was founded in 1925 by Wilbur Whitehead as a card club that the city's women could join. Second was Crockford's Club, which was established by Ely Culbertson in 1932. The appearance of the new Regency Club, as it was then known, created something of a stir. It was formed by a foursome led by Mrs. T. Charles Farrelly, who had been the social director at Crockford's. As the story goes, she and Ely had an argument over her salary, and he—emboldened in part by a biography he was reading of King Frances I of France—dared her to quit and declare war, which she promptly did, establishing her own club five blocks away and driving his into ruin in two short years. Culbertson didn't go without a fight. The defection led to suits and countersuits, which ultimately were dropped in 1938, after Crockford's shut its doors. (Culbertson claimed the Regency had been poaching his well-heeled members, which was true—in those two years Crockford's membership declined from more than six hundred to a mere two hundred.) The Regency quickly became one of the city's toniest clubs, operating its own French restaurant and entertaining the cream of society's card players. In 1964, the nine hundred members of the Regency Club merged with the seventy-five (all male) members of New York's historic Whist Club (established 1893) to form the Regency Whist Club.

Today the club is home to modern moguls such as James E. Cayne, national bridge champ and chairman and CEO of Bear Stearns, who used to play with Warren Buffett on a team known as C.A.S.H. (Corporate America's Six Honchos). Cayne's Bear Stearns predecessor, Wall Street legend—and accomplished amateur magician—Alan "Ace" Greenberg (who remains chairman of the firm's executive committee) is said to appear daily at four. As with any club, membership is discreet, though over the years the regulars have been reported to include Jack Dreyfus (founder of the Dreyfus Fund) and the late tablemates Laurence A. Tisch (chief of CBS and cofounder of Loews Corporation) and Milton J. Petrie (retail giant).

Such deep pockets tend to draw the top pros, many of whom can't pass up a game when they're in town. The club is a favor-

ite for good-time gamblers such as Bob Hamman and the international sensation Zia Mahmood, arguably the most popular
player in the world. The Regency also employs a top-flight staff
of house players. Without a doubt, the club offers the premiere
social game in the country, both in terms of the caliber of play
and the size of the stakes. I had been told that in the big game—
which is by invitation only—hands are played for $1.00 a point.
At that level, things get interesting quickly. Bidding and making
a slam in six spades, say, nets a player nearly $1,000. And that's
just on one deal lasting anywhere from five to ten minutes. Sure,
slams don't come around every day, but making a vulnerable
game—perhaps a more modest three no-trump—is worth $600.

I stride up the same six steps on which Vanderbilt trod and
pass through the door, leaving behind the bright Manhattan
afternoon for the club's soft interior glow. A woman waves me
through the formidable wrought-iron gate, where I am met by
Bob Yellis, fifty-five, the club's card manager. As he leads me to
the back of the club, I can almost imagine the ghosts of bridge
greats past haunting these halls, whispering, "Let's cut for partners," or, "You idiot—what a bad lead."

I had met Bob last week at the Manhattan Bridge Club, and
he invited me to the Regency. As we bid farewell, he said, "Don't
wear a tie, but"—pointing to my jeans—"you can't show up in
those." Bob wears a green jacket with the club insignia on the
pocket, a purple shirt, and a green tie. We sit down in the dining room, which is unoccupied at this hour, as most members
are finishing up their lunch in the barroom. That said, the room
stands ready, the tables covered with brilliant white cloths and
every place carefully set with gleaming silverware. Mirrors run
along the walls, and chandeliers dangle from the ceiling.

As Bob settles into one of the red velvet–cushioned chairs,
he says, "The problem with rubber bridge is that it's a dying
sport." He sighs. "And this is basically a rubber bridge club. We
have a few duplicate games, which are very well attended, but
we're mostly a rubber bridge club. We're the only one left. But

whereas we used to make all our money collecting card fees for rubber bridge, now it's almost a fifty-fifty split between those games and duplicate."

Without much prompting, he continues, "When I first learned to play, as a kid out in Great Neck, Long Island, I loved duplicate, the scoring, the competition—I couldn't understand rubber bridge at all. But rubber bridge is more sociable and friendly. You play four hands with one partner and then you switch. You don't get the antagonism. Sure, some of the members here have been playing against each other for forty years, so there is some, you know, built-in hostility. But normally you have to be nice to your opponents because you're going to be playing with them in twenty minutes."

Bob has been the card manager at the club for nineteen years, and before that he worked there as a director part time. He is in charge of all the games and the club's eight or nine pros. He says, "Our main job is that if there are three people and they want to play, one of us plays."

That is not entirely as cushy as it sounds—there is no fleecing the members. Bob explains, "When I play with them, I'm playing for nothing." He is a gambler, having grown up playing poker with his friends, but he likes his bridge with nothing on the line. He says, "I don't want to play for anything. I enjoy the game without playing for money. I grew up on duplicate, but I love the sociability of rubber bridge, the kidding around. At duplicate clubs, if you even say hello to people in the big game they freak out. Here, we joke around. We're easygoing and relaxed. No one is trying to make their living at the table. Everyone is here to have a good time."

This brings us to Bob's other job, which is to keep the peace among members, a task he believes is easier at the Regency than at other bridge clubs. Bad behavior is greatly frowned upon, though at times, talking about his charges, Bob sounds more like a schoolteacher than a bridge pro. The club has cracked down on feuding, forcing members to play nicely with each other or not play at all. The only members barred from sitting at the same table are husbands and wives, but the reasons are more economic than social. "What's the sense of it?" Bob asks. "If one is winning and the other is losing, it's really the same thing. That's the only kind of discrimination we have."

I laugh, thinking of the social strata the club pulls from, but Bob leans in and says, "I'll tell you something. Before I got here, I had heard it was a stuffy old club. And then the first time I played here, this woman told me to drop dead. There's a lot of joking around. If someone leads out of turn, he usually just takes the card back—no big fuss. It's a gentleman's game. You're playing with the same people five days a week for fifty years. You can't be a prick. You have to be nice—it's a means of survival."

The club boasts about 250 members, many of whom play every day, and it's open seven days a week. The busiest days are midweek, while weekends (including Friday) are slow. People begin filtering in around one for lunch, after which they head upstairs for a game.

On a regular day, the club draws some thirty or forty rubber players. The Tuesday and Thursday afternoon duplicate games are very well attended. They are limited to a hundred players, and they often fill up. There is a smaller duplicate game on Sundays of about forty people. As a rule, turnout is seasonal, with members traveling in the summer and heading to warmer climes in the winter.

The club closes when the last member leaves, but Bob says, "By seven it's pretty quiet around here. People may use the dining room until nine or so entertaining their guests, but this crowd is getting older and they don't like to stay late. At night this club is basically dead."

That hasn't always been so. Bob remembers at one time they had a hundred junior members; now they have five. A junior member is a member under forty. Bob tells me about a member who is ninety-four, a Syrian man "as stubborn as they come."

Bob says, "He won't use the bidding boxes, even though he can't hear." The man is a tenacious bidder—with or without support from his partner—and he tends to end up in three no-trump. Bob remembers, "A couple of years ago there was a question of whether he would go to a retirement home. Instead, he comes here every day for lunch and bridge. He's in at one and goes home at five. It's a really good thing."

Bob is clearly fond of the members, who, he says, "play until the day before they die." He jokes, "Sometimes you don't know if they're sleeping or thinking, and when they start bringing in the oxygen tanks and the nurses, you know you're in trouble." But their dedication to the club is remarkable, and Bob tells me, "One woman I used to teach was ill and knew she had to go into the hospital on Sunday, and she did—right after the duplicate game."

In recent years the club has tried to attract new members, inviting young professionals in for cocktails and lessons, but Bob says, "You're dealing with a very movable subject. What happens with the young members is that a lot of them have babies, move away, change jobs, and they just can't come to the club. Plus, most of our action is during the daytime, and most of these younger people work."

Still, Bob insists the scene at the Regency is hardly as moribund as it has been at other New York clubs: "I remember this one woman joined the Cavendish Club—back when it was still in business—when she was maybe forty years old. Twenty years later she was still one of the youngest members!"

Indeed, the Regency tries to keep up with the times, though in the world of private card clubs, the notion is somewhat relative. In rubber bridge, conventions are usually kept simple, as players are often playing in makeshift partnerships. Many clubs like the Regency forbid the use of complicated systems, keeping the emphasis on skillful card play rather than convoluted bidding. In recent years, the house rules at the Regency have changed. In late 2001, what Bob calls "the new guard" staged a "coup" and let in a few basic conventions. The restrictions on the duplicate game are even more lax, though for the most part no one plays any wildly artificial system.

I ask Bob for details on the club's legendary big game—whether it's true, as rumor holds, that it's played for $1.00 a point. "Well, maybe, I don't know," he demurs, the model of discretion. "Some of the members play for different stakes." Then he smiles, as if I'm only seeing the tip of the iceberg, and adds a seeming non sequitur: "You know, you can always make side bets with people. Even if you're playing for a small amount of money, you can always bet someone $5.00 a point on the side."

Bob continues diplomatically, "You know, the very good players come here, but so do the people who play for social reasons. Crawford and Jacoby and Vanderbilt—all the old bridge names played here. Sam Stayman used to play here. In fact, that was his wife who walked in and waved at us a few minutes ago."

In time, we join Mrs. Stayman in the barroom, where she is finishing a lunch of salad. She wears a green sweater over a white collared shirt, with a stylish red-beaded necklace tied around her neck. Next to her sits a friend in a beautiful scarf. A plate of small cookies goes untouched on the table while the women sip their coffee.

A member of the ACBL Hall of Fame, Samuel Stayman won numerous championships and was part of Charles Goren's 1950 winning Bermuda Bowl team. His name lives on today in the ubiquitous no-trump convention I mentioned earlier. "Stayman," as it's called, is one of the first conventions a beginner learns—it is a name known to nearly every bridge player in the United States.

Mrs. Stayman is a fashionable and friendly woman who, to her friends, goes by "Tubby." Later, when I ask what her real name is, no one in the room will remember until the bartender supplies "Josephine."

When Mrs. Stayman met her husband, she didn't play bridge. He arranged for her to take lessons from his friend, the irrepressible Victor Mitchell, who died in 1995 (after which he was inducted into the bridge Hall of Fame). Mitchell was happy to take over the education of Mrs. Stayman. On the first lesson, he took her by subway to Belmont Park. She remembers, "I didn't learn a lot about bidding that day, but I learned something about horses." Mrs. Stayman smiles. "Oh, he was a character. He lived on cigarettes and coffee. We had such experiences with Victor. He was truly beloved."

We are the only ones left in the barroom, save for a woman eating alone at a small table by the front windows. The room is elevated slightly above street level—enough to be beyond the usual sidewalk fray, but not completely removed from the life of the city on a brilliant sunny day. The curtains are parted to let light fall on the dark wood of the bar, which has a brass rail and is backed by polished mirrors. A lone dish of pretzels sits on the bar. At one end, folded newspapers are tucked into baskets. Deep red leather banquettes line the walls. The carpet is green; the chairs have black leather backs. Around the room, urban scenes are painted on panels. Above the marble fireplace a mirror stretches up toward the tall white ceiling.

A woman with her hair in a bun and a plaid suit walks in. She is joined by a friend in a red silk shirt and scarf. The women all bear the last names of or can be linked to bygone bridge champions. I expect they are excellent players in their own right, and my suspicion is confirmed by the arrival of their fourth, slightly younger friend, who tells me, "They are all sharks." This woman met her husband at the club; Bob says, "She got married here," which causes the woman to laugh, "Well, not *here*." The ladies meet regularly for what they call a "women's game." Mrs. Stayman explains, "We do let men play, but they don't last very long!"

When I ask why she plays bridge, Mrs. Stayman tells me, "Of course, I loved the game so much when my husband was alive. I still do. I also happen to be the kind of person who likes to learn new things. So I try to keep up with the game today. I go onto bridgebase.com and watch the pros play. I'm a widow. I'm alone. But I can go online at night and be thoroughly entertained."

Cookies now gone, we escort the women to the second floor, where they'll play their game. The building was built in 1904 by famed architect Ernest Flagg, who was also responsible for New York's Scribner and Singer buildings and Washington's Corcoran Gallery. There is a beautiful marble floor in the entryway and a sweeping open staircase that rises through the center of the townhouse in the grand old Manhattan style. Before we ascend, I spy a list of the club's officers hanging on a wall. There seem to be a surprising many, but Bob chimes in, "You know, the Grievance Committee hasn't met in ten years."

The stairs are wide and carpeted and flanked by a dark wooden banister. On the landing before the second floor a chalkboard lists the pairs for yesterday's duplicate. Mrs. Stayman points out that this is also where the club Christmas tree goes every year. Games are spread through the club on the second, third, and fourth floors, depending on the level of skill and size of the stakes. Duplicate is always played on the third and fourth floors. The women make their way into the library, an elegantly appointed room at the front of the club with black-and-white carpet, wood paneling, and a glassed-in collection of shiny silver trophies that rises to the ceiling. On the far side of the room, a quiet foursome of men in suits are well into a game. I notice both the cards and the scoring pads carry the club's logo. As the women arrange their bidding boxes, Mrs. Stayman apologizes but says she won't play without lipstick on ("It's bad luck for everyone."). I recall that someone once told me her husband was one of the best-dressed men in the game. Problem solved, the women settle in to play.

One of the older gentlemen waves Bob over. When he gets to the table, he bends down, and the two exchange hushed words. I see Bob glance in my direction. Then he straightens and motions for me to follow him out the door. Apparently, one of the older members objects to my not wearing a tie. I think I look quite clubby in a conservative sport coat and slacks. Bob apologizes for telling me to show up without neckwear. He says, "You know, you never can tell."

We continue our tour. The back of the third floor holds a blue-and-white room often used for teaching. Across the landing, on the south and sunny side, is a pink salon with high windows and blue curtains. This is the site of the big game. A backgammon table stands in the corner. The room is empty right now, but I take a moment to ponder the fortunes won and lost within these cheerful walls. I wonder if Tina and I will ever make our way here. For our sakes, I certainly hope not.

In a room on the fourth floor with green-striped walls and a plush green carpet, a group of women are meeting for a private game. Eight women in their sixties in stylish suits and jewels fill two tables. Bob and I peek in, then cross the hall to the accounting office, which holds computers, two women at work, and a wine rack. The club rents the fifth- and sixth-floor apartments as offices. As we're heading downstairs, one of the women from the private game stops Bob with a bidding question. As he explains to her why she should bid three hearts, an insistent dinging begins to issue from the green room. It carries down the stairs and into the carpeted hush of the lower club. On tables in each room I had noticed discreet silver desk bells, and I had wondered at their function. The prompt arrival of a blue-coated waiter solves the mystery.

Bob likes people, and he loves to teach. He has been a bridge instructor since high school, and these days he teaches as many as sixteen classes a week in private homes and clubs mainly in Greenwich, Connecticut. The secret, he says, is to be upbeat. At the Regency, everyone jokes with Bob and Bob jokes with everyone, from members to waiters to bartenders. Most of the staff has been there a while. We walk downstairs with the waiter, who tells me he has worked at the club for twenty-eight years. When we reach the second floor, the dinging begins again. Bob gives him a sympathetic look and says, "I don't think you'll be getting a tip."

As I remain tieless, we skirt the library and make our way to the back room on the second floor. Two tables of dark-suited men in their fifties, sixties, and seventies sit at opposite ends. Bob announces to the room, "He's thinking of buying the place." From the corner, a disgruntled voice calls out: "He can have my share." At no point does anyone look up from his cards.

Back at the bar, Bob says, "We don't work because we get paid a lot. And we don't work for tips." Pouring himself a soda, he says, "It's the working conditions. I've been everywhere, and I know—this is the last club I'm working at."

Despite his love for the Regency, Bob plays duplicate games in other clubs. He competes almost exclusively with an eighty-eight-year-old woman whom he says he "inherited." The daughter of one of America's grand families, she used to play with his mentor, Murray Schnee, who died in 1979.

Bob hands me a short history of the club printed on purple paper. It is excerpted from an upcoming edition of the club book. He is proud of the place he works and its dedication to the game. Taking in the room, he says, "This is the pinnacle club. In fact, Zia Mahmood once told me this is the nicest club in the world. If anyone would know, he would."

As we're standing there, a member sidles up to the bar. He says he came down to meet me; he heard a rumor I was interested in buying the place. He says this with a perfectly straight face, and I can't tell if he's joking. After a few pleasantries, he leaves, though not before offering a handshake and the call of the clubman: "If I can help you in any way, look me up in the book."

That the Regency Whist Club might serve as a nexus of bridge and high finance is no casual coincidence. The game has long appealed to competitive, analytical types who are good with numbers. Bridge also attracts a wide array of the persuasive and powerful, from playboy Hugh Hefner to Supreme Court Justice John Paul Stevens, who is a Life Master. In fact, bridge and the law seem to go hand in hand; until Chief Justice William

Rehnquist died and Justice Sandra Day O'Connor retired some four months apart in 2005 and 2006, one-third of the country's highest court played bridge. Federal Judge Amalya Lyle Kearse of the U.S. Court of Appeals for the Second Circuit is in the ACBL Hall of Fame. Other card-carrying luminaries include F.W. de Klerk, Clint Eastwood, Martina Navratilova, Sting, Senator Kay Bailey Hutchison, Isaac Mizrahi, and the band Radiohead.

For years, Egyptian-born actor Omar Sharif was the bridge world's most recognizable star. He raised the profile of the game in the late 1960s and early 1970s, sponsoring a touring "Bridge Circus" that held highly publicized exhibition matches throughout Europe and North America, plus a high-stakes rubber match in which Sharif took home $18,000. These days, he is less of an ambassador for the game. In 2003, Sharif told a reporter that he had given up bridge because he "didn't want to be a slave to any passion any longer"—and that his widely syndicated column was never written by him, but by entrepreneurial friends using his name.

The majority of bold-faced bridge names seem to belong to businessmen. Frank T. Nickell, the president and CEO of Kelso & Company, the New York private equity firm, sponsors—and plays for—one of the game's most formidable teams. Peter Lynch, the legendary stock picker who ran Fidelity Investments' Magellan Fund for thirteen years, has advised would-be market barons, "Play bridge, poker, or hearts. Chess is not a good game for the stock market, because everything is known." According to the ACBL, Lynch and his wife are members.

Today the young lions of business play poker—some New York hedge funds even boast in-office card tables—but bridge is still the game of a certain older investor set. One thirty-something trader on the American Stock Exchange told me that on the floor, there is a distinct bridge-playing subculture. In his words, "On the Street, you're either part of the mainstream or the math club. The bridge guys aren't your typical

Wall Street hotshots; they're strange disheveled rich men in their mid- to late forties who trade derivatives all day and then go compete all night at bridge parties. When I worked with them, I felt like an outsider. I was a loudmouth who wanted to go to the bar and meet girls; they spent their weekends at tournaments."

Bridge Hall of Fame member Michael Becker has said, "There is a relationship between playing bridge and trading options. They both involve coolness under pressure and the ability to play well when you're ahead or when you're behind." Becker started out as a bridge professional, but in 1979, his partner, Ron Rubin, convinced him to give options trading a go. Becker found success on the floor, and in time trained a bevy of championship bridge players to follow in his steps. In 1990, four years before he retired, he told a journalist he had a stake in 11 percent of the traders on the AMEX.

But by far the most famous bridge-playing pair is the world's two richest men, Bill Gates and Warren Buffett, who met at a picnic in 1991.

Buffett, the septuagenarian "Oracle of Omaha," remains the populist hero of American investing. He drinks Cherry Coke, eats Dairy Queen, and lives in the same house he bought in 1959. He is worth some $46 billion, which puts him at number two on *Forbes'* worldwide billionaire list (though he has since pledged to donate some $31 billion of his fortune to the Bill and Melinda Gates Foundation). He picked up the game in college, and today he remains a serious addict. I can only wonder what it costs the economy (and shareholders of Berkshire Hathaway) every time Buffett sits down to the table for a few hours. He calculates that bridge consumes more than 10 percent of his productive time, or roughly twelve hours a week. He is serious about his cards. In a casual game, he once ate a bad score sheet that his sister threatened to frame. He is known to use a deck that reads "Make Checks Payable to Warren Buffett." In 1989, 1990, 1993, and 1996, Buffett captained the "Corporate America" team in a charity match against a team from Congress. The corporate raiders won every time. In 2006, he sponsored the inaugural Warren Buffett Cup, a transatlantic bridge contest modeled on both the Anglo-American battles of the 1930s and golf's Ryder Cup. The event precedes the Ryder Cup and features America's top dozen bridge players against Europe's.

Gates, the Microsoft mogul and the world's richest man—to the tune of $53 billion—has been known to appear at ACBL tournaments, where he competes and kibitzes like anyone else. He picked up bridge from his father. Twenty-five years younger than Buffett, Gates is a keen but still green competitor. He is working to improve his game.

How the billionaires became bridge buddies is a story known best to two-time world champion Sharon Osberg. Osberg, fifty-five, is Buffett's bridge partner. "He's completely hooked," she tells me on the phone from San Francisco. She met Buffett in the early 1990s at a bridge contest held in the Empire State Building. She was playing with *Fortune* magazine writer Carol Loomis, a friend of Buffett's. Osberg remembers, "Carol and I started playing in tournaments when I was back East. Warren thought this was pretty interesting, and he said the next time I was traveling to stop in Omaha and we'd play bridge. Well, I didn't even know where Omaha was. I'd lived in New Jersey and California, and all the stuff in between was the same to me. But I said, 'Okay.' So, scared to death on my next business trip, I actually did stop in Omaha and played bridge. And we became very good friends."

At the beginning, their chances to play bridge were few and far between—until Osberg pressured Buffett into getting a computer, something his friends had been trying to do for years. "It wasn't easy," she remembers. "Bill Gates already had volunteered to deliver one personally to him!" But it was bridge that broke the billionaire's back. Osberg says, "I travel to New York a lot on business, and whenever we overlapped there on trips we'd get together a bridge game. One day I said, 'You know, Warren, you could play this game from your living room in your pajamas.' I tried that twice, gently at first, and finally the third time he said, 'Okay, okay, let's set it up.'"

And so the two became pioneers of the online game. Osberg says, "We began playing on a proprietary service before it was even the Internet, so this was maybe 1992 or 1993." Osberg worked at Wells Fargo for years, a company that did business with Microsoft. Buffett suggested that the next time she was in Seattle, she might set up Gates's father, Bill Sr., on a computer so that the two men could play bridge. Gates Sr., had recently lost his wife, and Buffett thought he might be at loose ends. From that encounter, Osberg befriended Bill Jr., who began to show an interest in bridge.

And so Buffett loaned out his bridge partner-slash-coach, and Osberg and Gates began competing in ACBL events. Twice they have competed in a world championship pairs event, finishing 319th and 258th overall. Osberg says, "I've been teaching him. He's so smart—if he had more time, he'd be a very fine player." And so what do you give the world's richest man on his fiftieth birthday? If you're his wife, Melinda, it's a free pass to play in a tournament with Osberg.

Osberg and Buffett play three to four times a week online. Gates joins them as often he can, which is about every four to six weeks. ("He has a lot of things vying for his time," says Osberg.) Gates usually partners with Fred Gitelman, one of the founders of Bridge Base, or David Smith, Osberg's ex-husband. In the online world, Buffett competes under the nom de guerre "T-bone" (his usual at Gorat's, his hometown steakhouse), while Gates's Internet handle is "Chalengr" (short for "Challenger," the type of private jet he flies). I ask if Gates plays his games on the Microsoft Network, and Osberg drops a bombshell: "Actually, he doesn't. His friends don't. MSN is a great site, but it's more for beginner bridge players. We play on Bridge Base and OKbridge."

When I was in Kansas City, tournament chair Marti Malcolm admitted to running across Bill Gates in cyberspace. She said, "When I first joined OKbridge, I was trying it out, and he was in there lurking, playing, whatever. I really didn't think much about it." It turns out she beat him, though she assured me with good Midwestern humility, "Yeah, well, he's just starting out."

When they can't line up a foursome, Osberg and Buffett will join a random game, something users of both sites have gotten used to. She says, "Everybody knows who Warren is. In the early days, we drew a crowd, but now it's only when Bill logs on that people pay attention."

Like many professionals, Osberg prefers to play bridge live at the table. She says, "When I play online I do things like do my laundry and feed my cats. It's not quite as serious for me. Warren takes it much more seriously; he's very focused. If you ask him, he would probably prefer playing online because there are less distractions."

The billionaires only rarely face off in person, though Osberg can recall some memorable battles. She says, "Once every few years Bill gets together a few of his friends and takes them on a trip. He's taken them to China, Africa, and so on. One year, he took them through Alaska on this very special train that traveled down through the Northwest to Colorado. As a surprise for Warren, he brought me in, and I brought Fred Gitelman. We joined the train in some godawful place in Montana, and we played twenty-four hours of bridge. We spent a day and a half on the train. Warren was completely surprised; he had no idea."

When I ask Osberg who won, she hesitates a little before confessing, "Warren and I usually win." She contrasts her two students: "Warren is certainly the more experienced player. He's probably more intuitive; he has a more natural style. Bill, as you would expect, has a much more scientific approach; he's more a student of the game."

Osberg sees a correlation between bridge and finance. She says, "A lot of what makes you successful in the business world would make you successful in the bridge world. The calculation, the bluffs, being able to read your opponents, being able to push them around . . . There are a lot of macho traits in bridge. It's just a beautiful game."

I ask about the word "macho," which I've often heard applied to the professional game. She says, "I found being a woman in bridge way more difficult than being a woman in business. Way more. In bridge, the prejudices and biases are much more deeply ingrained. In general, it's harder to find strong female players—for whatever reason. The same is true in chess and most of the hard sciences. But in bridge, even when you find a woman who can play, there are built-in problems. For instance, it is very difficult for a man to sit down and play with a woman if he has a wife. It becomes tricky to find a partner or a team. I've been barred from teams purely because of my sex, because other women don't want their husbands playing on a team with a woman. It's unbelievable. Basically, it's why I stopped competing as much."

Osberg is very satisfied with her role as the billionaire's bridge coach. She laughs, "It is certainly a completely different world for me. Warren has absolutely changed my life." In 2005, Buffett and Gates announced they would put up $1 million to fund bridge programs in public schools. They put Osberg in charge of the effort, which didn't immediately meet with success. That winter, she told me, "I don't have kids, so I guess I didn't really understand how bureaucratic and difficult it is to work through school organizations. I would love to get public schools involved, but so far I've been rebuffed without so much as acknowledgment—even using Bill's and Warren's names. I told people the $1 million was 'initial funding'—these are deep pockets! I wrote an Op-Ed in the *New York Times* as my last great hope. I never realized it was this hard to give away money."

About nine months later, in the fall of 2006, things were looking up. During the last school semester, Osberg had ten programs up and running, and this year she was expecting to roll out some two hundred more. She also had formed a partnership with a large children's community service league. That summer, at the Nebraska regional tournament, Buffett and Gates ate burgers and fries with more than two dozen schoolchildren participating in programs funded by the duo. Most of the kids came from Nebraska or Iowa, though one group had learned the game at a summer enrichment program in Atlanta, where the tables and cards were supplied by the billionaires. After lunch, the budding players had their T-shirts and dollar bills signed by the world's two richest men.

Osberg believes her mission is critical. She says, "If we don't do something, bridge is history." As for what her partners themselves think, Mr. Gates declines to comment, though perhaps I shouldn't have sent my request from a mac.com e-mail address. (Later, Mr. Gates responds in a courteous letter, again declining to participate but saying he hopes I will continue to enjoy the game as much as he does.) Mr. Buffett, on the other hand, is more forthcoming. After responding to my letter with a handwritten note, he agreed to answer a few questions over e-mail. He did so one afternoon in brief bulletpoints, making me wonder if he was anxious to join Osberg online.

When asked to divine the future, the Oracle of Omaha comes across as cautiously (and modestly) bullish on bridge. He writes, "Participation in bridge has been falling for some time. I don't think it is exacerbated by the poker phenomenon. There is some work being done with young people to try to reverse the trend."

He says the game fascinates him because, "I like solving a new problem every seven to eight minutes," and the secret to good bridge is also the key to good business—"Using all possible facts and inferences to make decisions, and working with a partner."

And what does he enjoy more—playing bridge or making money? Mr. Buffett writes back, "I love them both."

CHAPTER TEN

Fear and Loafing in Las Vegas

Las Vegas, Nevada, May 2006
While down in Tennessee, I had heard people refer to Gatlinburg as "the Las Vegas of the Smokies," but nothing, of course,
can compare to the real thing when it's staring you in the face
on a hot ninety-something-degree desert day: the Manhattan
skyline, the Eiffel Tower, King Arthur's castle, Aladdin's palace,
the canals of Venice, an Egyptian pyramid, the Barbary Coast,
and more—a strip of stately pleasure domes dropped into the
middle of the Nevada desert, lined in neon, and swarming with
gamblers, tourists, hookers, and wiseguys all trying to hit it big.
The sight is either energizing or overwhelming, depending on
one's constitution. Personally, staring at the beast that is Las
Vegas, I feel on the verge of epileptic seizures, like a kid watching Japanese cartoons.

It is early May, and I am in town for the thirty-second annual
Cavendish Invitational, arguably the most prestigious—and
undoubtedly the most lucrative—bridge tournament in the
country. The event originally was held at New York's Cavendish Club, an exclusive establishment as old as the game itself.
Opened in 1925, the year Harold Stirling Vanderbilt codified
his famous rules, and shuttered in 1991, because of financial
woes, the Cavendish was a mecca of the rubber game, where
upper-crust members gathered to pad about on thick red pile
carpets and wager on cards played on dark brown felt. The first

Cavendish Invitational Pairs event was held in 1975. It began with what is known in betting circles as a Calcutta auction, in which pairs are "sold" to the highest bidder. Money from the auction is put into a pool, which is divided at the end by those who purchased the top finishers. The first Cavendish Calcutta raised $50,000. Originally a share was given to charity, but that practice has since been dropped. These days the auction usually fetches around $1 million. In addition, there is a smaller players' pool that holds the entry fees paid by all the players; from it, prizes are awarded directly to the winning pairs. Because of its noble pedigree and exclusive entry policy—one must be invited to take part in the tournament—the Cavendish retains something of an Old World aura about it, an idea of luxury and class, glamour and opulence. It's not so much the money you win, but the elegance with which you win it. As one very young professional player rhapsodized to me with laughable snobbery—and utter sincerity—"Ah, the Cavendish—bridge at its finest."

For the past ten years the Cavendish has been held in Las Vegas, which has given it a certain Sin City flair. This is my first trip to Vegas, and as our plane soars over the brown lunarscape of the desert, I can't help but wonder if this really was the most logical place to put all those golf courses and all-you-can-eat buffets. Such thoughts are swept aside by our arrival at the airport, with its larger-than-life baggage claim, where flat screens blast ads for everyone from Celine Dion to Carrot Top. There are Starbucks and slot machines—all blinking and buzzing—but what speaks loudest to me are the dribbles of vomit in the men's room urinals, little crusted reminders that—as the official Las Vegas tourist authority slogan goes—"What happens here, stays here."

The guy driving my taxi is something of a friendly mother hen. He tells me there are some thirty thousand people in town for a hardware convention, which is "just enough for us cabbies to notice." He warns me that in Las Vegas the buildings are so big—and the desert so bare—that distances are deceptive. Things that look close can be very far away. He points to a huge casino that seems to loom just up the block. "That," he says, "is two miles away." As he drops me at my hotel, he imparts his most important advice, "Drink lots of water," and, yelling out the window as he drives off, "Pace yourself!"

I am staying at the Tropicana, the historic casino built in 1957 that not only offered Las Vegas's first swim-up blackjack table but still boasts the longest running show in town, the *Folies Bergere*—a showgirl cabaret that debuted in 1959 and made the Tropicana the "Home of the Most Beautiful Women in the World." In the film *Diamonds Are Forever*, the hotel even gets a nod from that notorious tomcat, James Bond, who—in the person of Sean Connery—drolly remarks, "I hear the hotel Tropicana is quite comfortable." That was 1971. In 2006, it's a dump. Case in point: the lobby of the Bellagio boasts two thousand hand-blown glass flowers; the Trop plays Bryan Adams.

So it seems of all the swank places to stay in Las Vegas, I have found what the uninformed and mean-spirited might call the bridge club of casinos. The clientele is hopelessly older and helplessly sedate. This goes double for the cocktail waitresses; apparently the Tropicana serves as a kind of Elysian Fields for barmaids, where—I regret to report—just because the ladies are a little long in the tooth, the skirts aren't any less short. Surveying a clutch of aged chain-smokers in wheelchairs, I realize this is a far cry from the pool scene at the Hard Rock, which more than one person described to me as a "Puffy video." I shouldn't be surprised, however. I know why the senior citizens come to the Tropicana. It is cheap, and, like me, they're stingy. Pensions and book advances don't allow for much in the way of extravagance.

I am given a room in the bowels of the hotel next to an unmarked room that will suspiciously emit a low hum, day and night, for the next 144 hours. I also can hear the sounds of the pool, where they play the Backstreet Boys all day until 6 P.M., when it closes. The hotel is a thirty-four-acre, 1,878-room labyrinth centered on a 61,000 square-foot casino designed to confuse and confound, all in the hopes that—struggling to find your way back to your room—you'll eventually surrender and sit down at a slot. I spend a lot of time wandering lost, and on my first exploratory outing the Tropicana gets $13 of self-pity out of me.

I find it hard to fall asleep at the Tropicana, with its paper-thin walls and nocturnal bands of losers and lost souls lurching down the halls. That said, I wake at an ungodly hour because of the time difference from New York. I am hardly invigorated. Many before me have detailed the gonzo lunacy that is Las Vegas—see Hunter S. Thompson, et al.—but let's just say that few things inspire fear and loathing like midweek mornings at the Tropicana. Imagine creeping through the casino at 7:30 A.M. and seeing flocks of elderly early birds shooting craps, or watching one lonely old biddy ritualistically flutter her fingers across the window of a slot machine—trying to cast some sad solitary spell—as she loses nickel after nickel on each pull of the lever.

Discouraged, I venture back toward my room only to find two amorous drunks attempting to find privacy in an elevator that only travels between three floors. They mumble "next car, please" but it's no use; there is only one car and precious few floors, so, their valiant efforts with the "close door" button notwithstanding, I—and soon others—get treated to the gruesome sight of them again and again. Eventually the couple topples out into the hall.

But perhaps the most disheartening display greets me upon the return from an early-morning jog along the strip, when I—sweaty and stinking in the already scorching sun—am propositioned by a hooker. I guess you have to admire her gumption.

The strip itself is teeming with humanity, most of whom seem to want to sell you a trip to the Grand Canyon. (Even the guy in the food court at the mall is running a special for $99.) Unless you're in a casino, everyone is trying to get you to go somewhere else. As for the people around you, they seem pretty proud to be exactly where they are. Perhaps it's some human need to assert oneself in the midst of such overwhelming surroundings, but there are a lot of magnificently loud T-shirts, some spouting the usual stupid slogans ("Blarney spoken here!") but a surprising majority splashed with big bold letters that read LAS VEGAS. Personally, I was brought up to believe that this is a fashion no-no, like wearing the shirt of the band whose concert you are attending.

To be fair, I'm in a particularly easy place to play the misanthrope. My hotel sits at the intersection of Tropicana Avenue and Las Vegas Boulevard, a nexus of such intense foot traffic that one cannot cross the road at street level, but is forced to use a somewhat annoying system of pedestrian skywalks. Each corner holds a monolithic casino; traveling counterclockwise from the Tropicana you hit the MGM Grand, New York-New York, and Excalibur, which means all I have to do is turn my head to see a forty-five-foot 100,000-pound bronze lion, a 150-foot faux Statue of Liberty standing before a one-third-scale Manhattan skyline, and a magical castle whose restaurants reportedly run through 44,100 Cornish game hens a month. All together, there are a whopping 12,926 hotel rooms and 415,000 square feet of casino games at this intersection, with each property touting its own pimped-out poker room, full of free drinks, no-limit tables, and plasma TVs.

But I'm here for bridge, and it's time to head to the Cavendish, which, thankfully, is being held about fifteen minutes south of the strip at a swank hotel, spa, and casino complex called the Green Valley Ranch Resort. On my way there, the cabbie tells me it's technically not in Las Vegas but in a town called Henderson, Nevada. The casino, he says, is more of a place for laid-back locals and upmarket travelers. It offers a mix of high and low entertainment, ranging from high-stakes tables to cheap slots to a movie theater to fine dining to a food court— all of which, after the hubbub of the Tropicana, seems an oasis of taste and charm. As for the hotel, it's niftily appointed in a southwestern theme, all warm leathery browns and sandstone beiges, with an abundance of overstuffed couches, deep leather chairs, and grand chandeliers.

The Cavendish is being held in several of the large ballrooms called "Estancias," which the concierge pronounces not with a Latin "s" but a hard "ch"— "Estanchias"—like they're supposed to be Italian or something. Outside the Estancias, small LED screens announce the tournament, but there is no one inside.

I push through a set of doors and step onto a terrace. If the decor inside is Old World hacienda, outside it's trendy OC. A manicured palm-dotted lawn leads to a large infinity-edge pool spanned by a curving white bridge and bordered by private cabanas and a prim, perfectly raked beach. I wonder how I will spot the Cavendish competitors. It would be hard on the strip, where an international bridge player might easily be confused with a high roller—indeed, many are both—but here, at this chic resort, it should be simpler. And it is. There, by an outdoor buffet, are my bridge players: pale and puffy, forking fruit into their mouths and squinting into laptops, smoking cigars and lounging alfresco in shaded cube-shaped beds—cutting a sharp contrast to the lithe lines of hotel guests baking their bronzed, artfully arranged flesh beside the pool.

The opening brunch of the Cavendish Invitational is in full swing as players mingle under white umbrellas surrounded by low pruned hedges, pink ceramic planters, and rectilinear cushioned couches. Young players slouch late into brunch; they pick up plates and plop down into the sunny mod seats shunned by the older hands, who already roost comfortably at tables in full shade. A boisterous bunch of Italians separates itself and takes over a padded cube. In general, it seems that bridge players tend to huddle tighter than the average human grouping, as if constantly sharing secrets. It is a magnificent day, full of birdsong and sun. At poolside, sprinklers in the palm trees rain down a fine mist on silent sunbathers. The mountains rise in the distance. It's amazing to think we will stay indoors for the rest of the day.

The Cavendish kicks off with a three-session tournament called the John Roberts Teams that—while awarding $50,000 to the first-place squad—is essentially a warm-up to the pairs event. It is played this afternoon, tonight, and tomorrow morning, wrapping up before the grand Calcutta auction. On my way in from the pool, I bump into Bob Blanchard, fifty-four, the New York businessman who—along with fellow competitors Bob Hamman and Roy Welland and organizer Bill Rosenbaum—runs the tournament.

Blanchard wears a red-striped button-down open to show some neck, tan dress pants with cuffs, brown shoes, glasses, and a silver-and-gold watch. He has dark hair and a trim mustache, and either it's my overactive imagination or the dry desert heat but he seems to bear a slight resemblance to Moe Greene, the Vegas casino owner who gets whacked in *The Godfather.* I expect him to start complaining about Fredo, but instead he asks for directions, as he can't find his way to the playing room. When we start down the hall, he gets a call on his cell. It's Zia Mahmood, the star international player. It turns out he's lost, too.

The Cavendish Invitation Pairs are held every year over Mother's Day weekend, because—according to the tournament literature—bridge players are "widely rumored not to have mothers, having devoured them at birth." Past winners include some of the best in the game. It costs $2,500 to enter a pair, which goes into the players' pool. This year there are forty-four pairs. The event lasts five sessions over three days, with a session consisting of nine three-board rounds.

Players are given twenty-five minutes to complete a round, which works out to eight minutes and twenty seconds a board. Slow play is not tolerated. After a two-minute grace period, the offending team gets a written warning. For every infraction after that, they are penalized in points. There are also penalties for tardiness, discussing a hand during a round, and comparing results in the playing area. Some rulings may be appealed—at a price of $50 an appeal, which goes unrefunded if the appeal is dismissed. "Appropriate dress" by players and kibitzers is required.

At the Cavendish, conventions are kept simple. If an uncommon convention cannot be explained in ten seconds it is not allowed. In general, overly artificial bidding systems are banned. Not surprisingly, in Vegas, the emphasis seems to be on card play.

Each hand is scored by international matchpoints, or IMPs (pronounced like the mischievous fairy, not sounded out letter by letter). The system is a little involved, but basically boards are scored as they normally would be. Then each pair's result is compared with how everyone else did sitting in the same direction, with the differences between scores converted by a chart into a simple number of IMPs. Essentially, you win IMPs for every pair you beat, and you lose IMPs for every pair that beats you.

Bob Blanchard says, "What we're trying to do here is show the glitzy side of bridge." We are at the cocktail party preceding the Cavendish Invitational Pairs dinner and auction, where, under the light of dangling shaded-lamp chandeliers, men in tuxedos and Nehru jackets mingle with ladies in sparkly dresses. At the shrimp and salmon station, an ice sculpture of a flipping fish slowly drips into a puddle. Around the ballroom, candles flicker atop white-clothed tables that comfortably seat ten. People mill about holding plates of Thai satay skewers or pork spring rolls or colorful salads with crumbles of goat cheese. There is also a pasta station, a cheese station, and a carving station, serving ham, turkey, and prime rib. The air smells rich with garlic and beef. Side tables offer pastries, tiny cakes, candied fruit, and make-your-own sundaes. There is coffee, tea, and—perhaps most important, in terms of the auction—a bustling top-shelf bar.

Blanchard expects tonight's event to draw about 180 people, and he has hired a film crew to shoot footage for a TV promo he plans to send out to what he calls the "game channels." He is the consummate promoter, greeting guests with a hearty handshake as they arrive. As he presses the flesh, he tells me, "There's a camaraderie among bridge players. They're all friends. Some of them have played together, some have married each other's wives. I mean, one of them married my ex-wife—and I'm not the only one. It's a trading world."

In the bridge community, Blanchard is something of an outlaw. He admits he is not a favorite of the ACBL, whom he sued years ago for holding gender-based events. Specifically, he and his then-wife wanted to play in the 1984 men's pairs competition at the national tournament in San Diego. After five years of litigation, the suit was settled—and men's events became open to all.

Blanchard picked up bridge as a math graduate student at New York University. He was deep into chess, but when he got manhandled at a club by a fourteen-year-old girl ("She wore these big goggles—I'll never forget that."), he spent the rest of the afternoon cooling off playing bridge with three friends who needed a fourth. He knew only the rudiments of the game, but he soon took it up day and night. He never finished grad school, not because of bridge, but because "it was time to earn some money." Today he's a successful Manhattan manufacturer and businessman.

Blanchard was on the committee that ran the tournament when it was held at the Cavendish Club. When the club folded in 1991, Blanchard, along with Bob Hamman and John Roberts, an experienced rubber bridge player and one of the original producers of Woodstock (who died in 2001), formed an organization called World Bridge Productions to carry on the tournament. In 1997, they moved the Cavendish to Las Vegas and promoted it vigorously. The auction pool reached more than $1.2 million. Fans could follow the action on the Internet, a cutting-edge feat back then. At this point, a woman in short dark hair and a sequined turquoise dress, who happens to be Lynn Blanchard, Bob's wife, begins listing the casinos at which they have held the event over the past ten years, places such as the Mirage, the Rio, and the MGM Grand. She says, "We had it at the Desert Inn until they blew it up." Bob adds, "I started playing bridge thirty-two years ago, and the game has given me a lot. I would like to give something back. But you can't just donate money—you have to donate an idea. And that's what World Bridge Productions is about."

And so Blanchard doesn't want to talk about himself. He wants to talk about bygone days, "back in the 1930s when bridge was a national game as big as baseball." He says, "It was played at the pinnacle of elegance. Players wore black tie and"—referring to the first world championship match, in 1935—"played at a table in the middle of Madison Square Garden." He is equally focused on the future and believes that the next wave of bridge stars might come from China, Malaysia, and India, where he says "there is a huge middle class playing parlor games." He points out the next world championship Bermuda Bowl will be held in Shanghai in the fall of 2007.

As for the United States, Blanchard expounds a theory he says he shares with José Damiani, the president of the World Bridge Federation, which oversees international competition. Blanchard thinks bridge is in for a one-two boost—first from retiring baby boomers making the switch from golf to bridge, and, second, from an increase of interest in games in general (he points to Scrabble and poker as examples). Despite such optimistic theories, when I ask Blanchard if bridge is dying out, he grabs me by the arm. "Yes, of course, that's why I'm doing this!"

Just what he is doing, in a phrase he often repeats, is promoting bridge from "the top down." In his mind, staging the Cavendish is the opposite of leading a grass-roots effort. It's bridge as aspiration before recreation.

I ask whether the money complicates the game, and Blanchard looks at me as if I'm an idiot or, worse, some kind of purist. Patiently he explains, "When you come out into the hallway between rounds, have you ever seen such energy? You don't see that energy level anywhere—not at a normal bridge tournament. Everybody is going like this . . ." Blanchard chops his hands wildly. "They're saying, 'Oh, what a swing!' The money is key. Can you imagine Tiger Woods sitting around playing for master points?"

I shake my head, but Blanchard is not convinced. He says, "Listen, one year my ex-wife played a $60,000 card. How do you think I felt?" His voice drops. "She just walked by, by the way."

In one corner, there are hugs, handshakes, and high fives for this afternoon's winners, who are glowing. Many stop to congratulate the fortunate foursome's lone female, who smiles and says, "Now I'll have to go buy some things!" While a few diehards can't seem to get into the swing of things—they stand at the party's edge going over the day's hands—no one seems too down. The air is charged with the excitement of money won—and to be won.

If there is a belle of the ball, it is the Pakistani Zia Mahmood, whose team tied for second place. He is probably the most famous bridge professional in the world, known everywhere by only his first name, like some South American soccer star. As an article in a bulletin from this spring's national tournament makes clear, Zia is the kind of player women will travel from Tasmania to Texas to watch play. At sixty, he cuts a dashing figure. In his autobiography, Zia describes a bridge player as "that rare animal, something between an artist and a hustler," and he dresses the part. He arrives at the party wearing a smart paisley jacket, blue shirt, black slacks, loafers, and no socks. His long upswept salt-and-pepper hair is devilishly shaggy around the collar, which on many days—though not today—he flips up. Zia was born into a wealthy Pakistani family and educated in the U.K. He has trotted the globe making a living from cards. According to the *New York Times,* he was the one who played the last hand the night the original Cavendish Club closed—a five-club contract, which he made, naturally.

At the party, a woman in a peach dress breathlessly congratulates Zia's partner in the Cavendish, the British beanpole Andrew Robson, for making a six-diamond contract ("That was some finish!"). Robson, who stands six-foot-six, is a successful player in his forties. Stars like Robson sit at tables marked "reserved" by white placards. I note that of all the tables in the room, Zia's laughs the loudest.

At this point in the party, I am a bit of a social leper, neither high roller nor bridge player. I have spoken to those I know, and I don't want to force my company on them any further. I have three days for that. I take a seat at an empty table and am soon joined by a man who, it becomes appallingly apparent, has come here just to hide out and break wind. While he tries to look innocent, we gain two elderly tablemates, a woman who carries on about the California education system and a man draining a beer from a tall glass. Everyone is eating now. As we feast, the bar does a brisk business in whiskey and gin.

Suddenly the lights dim, and Bob Hamman grabs the mike. He says, "If we're going to indulge in a bit of foolish gambling, we better get started." The audience picks up their programs, long elegant booklets printed on heavy cream-colored stock. The cover lists past Cavendish winners. Inside are the conditions of the contest, plus a short snarky blurb on each of the evening's forty-four pairs.

Bob welcomes the auctioneer to the podium, which is backlit by blue and gold lights and stands next to a large screen. The auctioneer announces, "The rules here are simple: give me everything in your pockets—I'll give you change later."

The rules are indeed pretty simple. Pairs are auctioned off to the highest bidder, who wins money based on how they place. That said, pairs must own at least 10 percent of themselves and by right can buy up to four times that. Meanwhile, if he wishes, the owner may resell shares of his investment to others. Payment is due before the match begins—U.S. dollars only, no third-party checks. Owners of the top-ten finishers receive money from the pool, from 28 percent for first place to 3 percent for tenth. The minimum bid is $12,500. If no one bids on a pair, they are sold to themselves.

Earlier, Lynn Blanchard explained to me why many of the world's best aren't playing with their regular partners. She said the equity would be too high; it would be too expensive for them to buy back a stake in themselves—it wouldn't be worth it. Also, there is the fact that some of the pros can get sure money by agreeing to play with a sponsor, who will foot their expenses and entrance fee. Either way, it's more lucrative to play in a less-practiced partnership and hope to finish in the money.

As for the ones doing the bidding, they run the gamut from deep-pocketed bridge enthusiasts to bands of pro players to spirited gamblers who can't always remember the names of the teams that they've bought. People have come from as far as South Africa to bid on the field, which has an international flavor. Glancing over the program, I see players from Sweden, Israel, Australia, Egypt, Germany, Norway, Hungary, Poland, England, Russia, Denmark, Italy, France, the Netherlands, and even a husband-and-wife team from California, who perhaps will settle the score about playing with your spouse. There are many contenders, but no clear favorites. Last year's winners, the Italian pair Andrea Buratti and Massimo Lanzarotti, are not competing. Their purchasers paid $45,000 for them at auction and picked up $230,152 from the main pool, while the Italians enjoyed a $23,240 bonus from the players' pool, plus whatever percentage they owned of themselves.

Without further ado from the podium, we're off. First up are two New Yorkers who won the event in 2002, and the auction opens with a strong $32,000 bid by a bearded man who keeps the bidding alive up to $42,000, for which they're sold. The auctioneer declares it a bargain, and behind him the number appears on the screen, which keeps a running tally of the pool. It also shows a twelve-second clock that the auctioneer uses to dramatic effect, counting down the seconds before a bid becomes final. The whole transaction takes less than three minutes.

Two pairs later, there is a commotion at the back of the room. All eyes turn to see two scantily clad showgirls in short sarongs strut through the door holding silver platters piled with cash. With two security goons in tow, they weave their way through the crowd and reach the stage, where they set the money at the auctioneer's feet. This is just a little Vegas razzle-dazzle on the part of Bob Blanchard. Apparently, the platters hold a million dollars, which is what the auction hopes to bring in. (Later, I will find Blanchard and ask if the money is real, to which he replies, "Would you expect any less?") I can't help but notice the crowd takes this pretty well in stride; maybe this kind of thing happens a lot to some people.

Bart Bramley, one of the players I met in Bob Hamman's office in Dallas, sits down with me. He is competing with Barry Rigal, a bridge journalist who is also writing a book about the game. Bart was at the second ever Cavendish Invitational in New York in 1976 and has played in the event some twenty times, including every year since the tournament moved to Vegas. As we watch the bidding, he tells me which pairs he thinks are underpriced. It's good inside scoop, but unless I make a dash for those trays, I won't be bidding anytime soon.

The audience is enjoying itself, and the auctioneer has to keep calling for quiet. He booms from the podium, "All the noise seems to be coming from where Bob Hamman is." Eventually the auctioneer gets Hamman to take over the mike and sell a pair or two—in an effort to silence him. This year, Hamman is playing with his nineteen-year-old office wunderkind, Justin Lall. The bidding on them opens at $13,000. At $16,000, the auctioneer pleads for more action, saying, "Come on—$12,500 on Bob and the rest on the kid." Despite his efforts, they sell for $17,000.

Still, the money flies freely. Some bidders stand, some sit, some bid while walking and chatting with a woman, others stare intently into their programs. One man bids from the carving station. When Zia enters the auction—with a graceful offhand wave—those at his table smile at him in unison.

Halfway through the evening, the Calcutta pool stands at $474,500—just a little off track to break $1 million. As the pairs fly off the block, I overhear a lot of wheeling and dealing. One man in a silver mane buttonholes his buddy at the bar and says, "Hey, help me out—wanna give five percent for your Florida pals?" The friend replies, "Naw, I can't. Not those guys." In the background, discussing the prospects of another pair, the auctioneer cries, "These two are worth nineteen thousand dollars playing with your shoe!"

About three quarters through the program, there is a respectful hush as the man with the mike says, "Now I am about to auction off one of the three best pairs in the room." It is Zia Mahmood and Andrew Robson, whom the auctioneer calls, "arguably the most dangerous pair in the world." The bidding begins at $32,000 and immediately starts climbing as hands fly up around the room: $34,000 . . . $36,000 . . . $38,000 . . . With each new bid, the auctioneer voices his approval and the crowd gets louder. "Forty thousand? Yes!" "Forty-one? Yes!" "Yes—forty-two! Forty-three! Forty-four! Yes! Yes! Yes!" The wave finally crests and Zia and Andrew are sold for $48,000 to a well-known mathematician turned horse-handicapper turned bridge champion, who reportedly has won more than a million dollars betting on sports. The crowd goes wild.

After such excitement comes the predictable lull. Many people head to the bar. In time, the bidding picks back up, but it soon becomes clear that the pool won't reach the million-dollar mark. After the final duo—two Italians, one of whom is a world champ—goes for a strong $42,000, the final number on the screen reads $821,000. The auctioneer tries to put a brave face on it, pointing to the money-laden trays and saying, "That means we have an extra couple of thousand up here—please help yourself."

While the new owners go to settle up at a table, Bob Blanchard tells me, "I'm a bit disappointed, but okay." Two years ago the auction raised almost $1.4 million. Tonight it fell fairly short, with the average price around $18,659 a pair. He says, "We knew we were going to be a little light this year, because two of our big bidders couldn't make it. In fact, we usually know within twenty thousand dollars what we'll get—just by knowing the field." Leave it to a bridge player to take all the suspense out of an auction.

In the grand Estancia ballroom, the first round is ready to begin. Six gilded chandeliers burn brightly overhead. A table of snacks stretches along one side, and I am happy to see that even at the highest level, tastes don't run any healthier than they do at my club back in New York. There are cookies, brownies, and pretzels in burnished silver bowls, as well as piles of bagels, fruits, nuts, candy bars, and bags of chips. Coffee and tea are served from large urns, while bottles of soft drinks stand in tight phalanxes in long trays of ice. Around the room, clear plastic prisms of cold water rest on black-clothed tables.

The ballroom is divided into booths by green hanging curtains that, when drawn shut, give the room the look of a very ritzy polling station. In each booth, four players sit at a table covered in green felt. A lacquered wooden "screen" divides the table along the diagonal, making it so that a player can only see one adjacent opponent. On the other side of the screen, one's partner is hidden. Cut into the bottom of the divider is a low rectangular swinging door that is raised after the auction, allowing everyone to see the cards on the table.

The purpose of the screens is simple—to keep players honest. With so much on the line, ultra-competitive bridge has evolved into a curious mix of ethics and etiquette. Cheating is a constant specter, though there are varied levels of deviousness. On one hand, players are encouraged to bring the full power of their faculties to bear on the match; on the other, not all information is fair game. If your opponent hesitates, you may read into it what you may (and play accordingly), but by no means are you permitted to exploit a hitch in your partner's play, or fake such indecision yourself. Few games ask a player to play knowingly (and wordlessly) against his best interests—such self-policing requires equal parts vigilance and honor. The most egregious cheating, however, involves collusion between partners. It takes an expert to spot a good cheat, but it can be done, usually by noticing a pattern of counterintuitive but lucky leads, of risky moves that never backfire, of slight hiccups and off-tempo play (imponderable pauses when the choice should be clear, quick discards in the face of uncertainty)—and, in general, insights of such preternatural brilliance that it seems as if the partners are able to see through the backs of each other's cards.

One reason that last year's Cavendish winners, the Italians Buratti and Lanzarotti, are not present in Vegas is that about a month after their victory, they were accused of cheating at the European Championships in the Canary Islands. After putting down his hand as dummy, Lanzarotti peeked at his left-hand opponent's cards, then signaled to Buratti that the player held three trumps by crossing his arms and pointing three fingers at the man. The Italian dummy employed this not-so-cagey code not once, but three times while his partner pondered his play. For their efforts, the Italians were booted from the tournament and banned from playing together ever again by the Italian Bridge Federation. They were also expelled from the ACBL.

Unfortunately, the history of cheating at bridge is long and inglorious. At least some of the methods have been more inventive. A brief tour of international bridge scandals, by nationality: at the 1957 European Championships, two Austrians were found to be telegraphing their aces by various signs, including the orientation of the cards in their hands. In 1960, a French duo was accused of employing the devilishly cunning (and devilishly simple) *l'ascenseur* (or "elevator") method of cheating— the strength of a partner's hand was determined by how high he held it. In Buenos Aires in 1965, a top British team was found to be using the position of their fingers on the back of the cards to signal their number of hearts. Ten years later, two Italians were found to be playing footsie under the table, tapping out a code upon each other's feet. A year later, the Italian team was embroiled in another scandal, this one involving the suspicious angling of cigarettes and cigars and the clicking of a lighter.

The bridge community responded with stringent remedies. In 1974, the Swedish-made bidding box was accepted in international competition; bids were now made silently by placing pre-printed cards on the table, thereby discouraging vocal cues. A year later, upright screens were introduced that hid partners from each other, allowing them to fidget and make faces free of suspicion. The success of such anti-cheating measures has been dramatic. All but five of the world-champion teams before 1976 have been suspected of foul play. After the screens went up—and were extended to the floor—every winning team has been considered above reproach.

When the ballroom is full and all the curtains closed, a man announces the start of the round. A hush settles over the room; the only sounds are the distant music piped in from the hall and the sporadic clacking of bidding cards being shoved back into their boxes. During the auction, any explanations or alerts between opponents must be made and responded to in writing—the bidding and play are to occur in complete silence.

Twenty-five minutes later, eighty-eight bridge players spill out into the hall. They carry jackets, cushions, and boxes of Kleenex. Once outside, they talk and curse and kid around with the aggressive energy of teens butting heads at the mall. They're friendly, but it feels like a rumble could break out at any point. The air resounds with a smattering of Polish, Italian, French, and English. Zia, who wears loose white pants, dark glasses, tan slip-on shoes, and a beige knee-length tunic, shouts across the crowd to Justin Lall, "Tell me I've already won the money I bet on you!"

There's a mad rush to smoke, and not everyone makes it to the designated area. Some head through the nearest fire exit; others just light up where they stand. Vegas is clearly a smoker's town. Here at the Green Valley Ranch there are even ashtrays in the men's room—both at the urinals and in the stalls.

At the Cavendish, the dress seems to run along the lines of business casual, with a majority in sport coats, though the gamut runs from a dapper white suit (with white shoes) to a lone unapologetic pair of jean shorts. The tumult in the hall is reaching fever pitch as players gleefully rehash hands. At this point, every pair is in the hunt, and I witness two forty-year-old men in blazers reach out and thump knuckles in victory.

Everyone seems to be telling or listening to a story except for the large man who stands alone in the corner, patting his belly. A ring has gathered around a short hyperkinetic man in khakis and big white sneakers who is clearly in the middle of a whopper; he drops to his knees to deliver the kicker: "And the jack of spades took the trick!" His cronies go nuts.

After some ten frantic minutes (that hardly seem like a break), a man in a dark suit enters the hall and says, "Places, please." Immediately all conversations are dropped as pairs find each other and duck their heads together, all business again, and go into the room. Twenty seconds later, the hall is once again silent. As if on cue, a cool clutch of skinny Brazilians in their twenties waltz by in low-slung jeans, tight shirts, chic caps, designer shades, and tattoos, probably heading to the bar, oblivious to the fierce mental feats going on behind closed doors.

This pattern will continue between rounds for the next three days, with bridge players erupting forth every twenty-five minutes, like some frenzied Old Faithful, to clog the halls and confound casino guests. It soon becomes good sport watching harried tourists try to shove their way through the crowd, crying "Excuse me, excuse me!" as they bowl over bridge players who take no offense—or rather, no notice.

The awards are posted in the playing room. This year, the owner of the first-place pair receives $193,236, while the winners themselves get $21,560 from the players' pool. The rest of the prize money is spread out among the top ten, with the owner of tenth place getting $20,704 (and his players $2,310). There are also awards for winning each session that range from

$2,500 to $12,000. In short, there are lots of ways to end up in the money.

As I am trying to study the angles, Lynn Blanchard grabs me and gives me a quick lesson on how to kibitz a pro. She whispers, "Sit directly behind a player, say nothing, don't move, show no expression—and only look at one hand!" With that, she parts one of the green curtains and shoves me into a seat behind Jeff Meckstroth, whose son, Rob, I met in Gatlinburg and who last night was called "one of the greatest players in the world." He who doesn't even look at me.

Next to him sits opponent Seymon Deutsch, an elderly, wealthy Texas retailer. I am so scared to look in Deutsch's direction—lest I see his cards and set off an incident—that after the match I am unable to even say if he wears glasses. Without a word to any of the four kibitzers sitting inches away, the players settle in and get going.

The swinging door in the screen is lowered for the auction. Meckstroth and Deutsch place their bids on a black plastic tray that slides back and forth under the door, which has a little white skirt. All is quiet except for the faint rattle of an AC vent high overhead. At one point, Meckstroth makes some scribbles on a white notepad and shows them to Deutsch, presumably alerting him to a bid. Once the auction is over and the opening lead is down, the door is swiveled into its open position where it is held by a little magnet. Now we see the cards on the table.

Meckstroth is playing with Bob Blanchard, a headless portion of whom I spy through the doggy door. Blanchard leans forward when he plays, with his hands almost always on the table. He is a consummate games player, and I am curious to see him in action. Last night he told me he and his gambling buddies used to play everything from Hold'em to Risk for money.

On my side of the table, Meckstroth, a big bearded man in a blazer and polo shirt, exhibits a surfeit of pent-up energy. He declares the first two hands while fidgeting in his seat, tapping his fingers, and shuffling his feet. At times he goes completely still, lost in thought—I can't fathom what is holding him up, but, given his reputation, I imagine he's processing the game at its very deepest level. Every time Blanchard tosses down the dummy, Meckstroth mumbles, "Thanks," in a low gravely voice.

It turns out Deutsch is playing with the legendary Paul Soloway, Bob Hamman's usual partner. Soloway seems very much at ease as he pours a cola into a glass. I am sitting hairs away from some of the top minds in the game—people whose every move is chronicled in newspapers, magazines, and online—and, once the round is over, I will hardly remember a card they played. Twenty-five minutes fly by when there is so much at stake—not so much for the players (okay, the money would be nice) but for nervous kibitzers hell-bent to only stare at one hand. I don't know these men, and I fear having one of those hellacious bridge tempers unleashed on me. My neck is getting sore and my stone face threatens to crack. I begin to sweat at the pressure. Time seems to break down in the little green room; one board is over in a blink while another hinges on a card poised to fall for what seems like an eternity—before Meckstroth goes down. These guys play at a wholly different tempo than the tournament players I've seen in Kansas City and Gatlinburg, who seem to decide on a line of play and stick to it come hell or high water. Here there is an odd halting rhythm to the game, full of deep pauses at peculiar moments, while the masters try to peer into the mysteries of the hand. At the end of the round, the bridge players hit the snacks on their way into the hall.

For the next round, I decide to sit in on the great Zia Mahmood. He and Andrew Robson will be competing against past Cavendish winners Robert Levin and Steve Weinstein, making this a match between two of the top three most expensive pairs. There is a combined $90,000 riding on these four guys.

As I enter the booth, a figure slips in behind me. It is none other than Zia. I take a seat over his shoulder. We are the only two in the booth, and—breaking the unwritten code—he smiles at me. In the hall, I had seen Zia frowning and gesticulating at

Andrew. Now he is the model of consideration. Then Andrew comes in and, perhaps finishing an earlier conversation, says, "I should have doubled."

A few other well-dressed kibitzers straggle in. Many are keeping an eye on Zia and Andrew this year; they seem to be favored to win it, at least based on their top price at auction. The cult of personality that is Zia's is such that when he—a dedicated night owl—decides to go to bed early, it is written up in the daily bulletin as a newsworthy item, one that might possibly affect the outcome of the match.

Zia is considered to be more of a brilliant gambler than a pure technician. He achieves his remarkable results by not always playing the percentages but by taking risks, acting on instinct, and making impossibly devious plays. Even in terms of his table manners, Zia handles his cards with flair. He has large hands with long thumbs, and he holds his sorted cards very tightly together, a hairbreadth apart, affording just a peek at the values and making for a very trim package in his hand. During play, he suavely flops his cards down on the felt; when he's thinking, he'll pick up a stray card from his pile of tricks and lightly flick it in the air in little half spins. Zia plays so quickly that I'm sure I'm not learning much in the way of theory, but I certainly am picking up a few cool tricks to impress the gals at the club. My favorite is the way these guys throw down the dummy with such effortless, offhand ease, the momentum of the toss splaying each suit attractively across the felt.

Zia's screen-side opponent is Steve Weinstein, a short man in an orange T-shirt, jeans, and loafers with no socks. When play begins, Weinstein kicks off his loafers and crosses his legs, his bare toes making an interesting contrast to Zia's soft leather shoes. The two players joke around a little during the round, and at one point after cracking particularly wise, Zia smiles to include me. I smile back, his bridge joke having sailed far over my head. But that's the kind of gentleman Zia is. At one point he even angles his hand so that I might better see it.

Zia declares the first board, going down one. On the second, Weinstein claims the contract after the first two tricks. It is the fastest claim I have ever seen. He merely drops his hand to the table and in a literal second—or at most two—everyone is shoving their cards back into the board. Apparently the outcome of the next eleven tricks was so obvious—at a glance—that no one felt the need to say anything.

On the final board, Zia becomes the dummy. All along I have been wondering how much self-awareness Zia, the genteel dreamboat of bridge maidens (and old maids) everywhere, possesses. Earlier I had seen him approach one of the water dispensers that had run out of cups. Many a player before him had selfishly carried over a single cup, but Zia rectified the situation by retrieving a whole stack. What a class act. And yet, it turns out, he likes to play the rascal. After putting down the dummy, Zia stands and declares in a soft British accent, "I'm off to pee." Then, to his partner, he makes—unless my ears deceive me—that old middle school joke: "Do your breast." Zia leaves, and Andrew finishes the hand quickly. With five minutes left in the round, the threesome leave the table.

And so players shuffle in and out round after round. The session is on schedule to finish around three fifteen, after which the pairs will get an hour break before starting up again. There are two sessions today, two tomorrow, and the final on Sunday. The Cavendish is a grueling event.

The schedule can be hard on a spectator, as well. I'm standing in the hall between rounds when a white-haired woman in a chair tells me, "I have to take a break." Her name is Louise, and she wears a stylish white jacket and a bright orange boa. Louise asks if I'm playing or watching. When I say watching, she asks what pairs I have seen. Before I can answer, she says all morning she has been following Geoff Hampson and Eric Rodwell, who have been doing very well. She's not sure whom she'll kibitz this afternoon. That's the way she likes to do it—follow a pair through a full session. She has been coming to the Cavendish for years.

Louise says she has watched Andrew Robson a lot in the past, but today she feels he is "down" and probably wouldn't want her around. ("He would never say it," she whispers, "but I know.") She marvels over a hand she watched him bring home yesterday—that six-diamond contract that so wowed the woman at last night's party. She tells me she played a little bridge herself in her day, and she once beat Zia on a hand (also in diamonds). Another time she finished above Bob Hamman in a game.

A friend of hers in a tan T-shirt comes over to report on the pair he is watching. We all hypothesize about who we think is winning. When the man goes back into the room, Louise tells me in addition to being an accomplished player he is also her weekend houseguest, though she had never laid eyes on him before picking him up at the airport. The two met online playing bridge.

Louise says, "I was a good player once, in New York." For twenty-five years, she worked at a major fashion house. Now she is seventy-six. She moved to town five years ago, after telling herself, "I could go to Florida to die or Las Vegas to live."

Louise's friend checks in again but doesn't stay long. When he walks off, she says, "He likes mingling with the bridge players." She sits in her chair like something of a queen, and I am more than impressed when a player stops by to tell her what table he'll be at next.

The first session is over, and people mill about awaiting the results. Justin Lall comes up behind me drinking a large soda. He and Hamman are at about minus 400, which he says "feels about right." He goes on to explain some of the hands and how they were unlucky. He tells me they are not in the top fourteen, but hope is hardly lost.

When the crowd clears, I look at the scores. After the first session, none of my horses are doing too well. Out of forty-four pairs, Bob Blanchard and Jeff Meckstroth are twenty-fifth, Bob Hamman and Justin Lall are thirty-third, and Zia and Andrew

Robson are fifth from the bottom. The players have an hour for lunch. I walk into the casino to check out the food court, and I am surprised to see Zia standing alone at the back of the line for Panda Express.

A quick bite and a few unprofitable pulls of the slot machine later, I'm back in the playing area for the start of the second session. Yesterday Bob Hamman introduced me to Gavin Wolpert, the Canadian half of the "hot young couple" I had tried to track down in Gatlinburg. Gavin was in the hall talking hockey and eating pizza with his Cavendish partner and fellow Canadian junior star, Vincent Demuy. When Bob walked up, they began discussing the NBA playoffs. Wolpert and Demuy seem like friendly fresh-faced guys, and they're currently in fifth place, though I wonder if their youth is perhaps starting to show when, as the round is about to start, they're nowhere to be seen. Friends frantically start calling their room. One quips, "I hope they don't think it's over!" By now the directors are walking the hall, calling out their names. Suddenly, there they are, rushing down the corridor, sodas in hand. They dash into the room with sheepish grins as the doors are closed.

For this round, I slip into a seat behind Justin Lall. He and Bob are sitting East-West against a pair somewhat similar in makeup—a grizzled veteran playing with a much younger whiz. The veterans sit on the same side of the table, and for the first two rounds of bidding the youths talk poker, specifically how they're doing in Vegas and the differences between the live and the online game. Lall seems pretty calm for a teen playing for almost $200,000.

Through the screen, I can see Bob playing cards willy-nilly from his unsorted hand. Outside I had heard kibitzers complaining that it's impossible for the average person to keep track of what he has. I smile when I see that Lall's hand is only lightly sorted, perhaps something he learned at the office. Afterward, Lall says to me, "Keep watching us, please. You're our good-luck charm. That was our best round yet."

I oblige, following them for another few rounds. It's fascinating to be in the booths, which from the snack table seem so tranquil. On this side of the curtain is a maelstrom of nervous energy: card flipping, leg bouncing, hand tapping, convention-card fiddling, and unspecified pointing into space. Removed from their surroundings, some of these guys would look like they had the DTs.

Outside the room, one name is on many lips in many different tongues: Zia, Zia, Zia. I am eager to interview him, but I know better than to approach him during a match. He and Andrew continue to struggle, and they spend their breaks in deep discussion down the hall. On the last round of the night, they come up against Bob and Justin. I'm still sitting behind Lall. On the other side of the table, I spy Louise and her friend kibitzing Zia. Apparently she feels Andrew is up to handling spectators now. Justin plays the first hand, then Andrew, then Zia. At times, while thinking, Andrew holds his head in his hands. It is a short round, as he claims the second board after trick one.

Then play is over for the day. It turns out my teams fared better this round. Blanchard and Meckstroth are now fourteenth, Hamman and Lall are twenty-third, and Zia and Robson have clawed their way out of the basement to thirty-sixth.

The talk around the room seems to be about a quick dinner and then going to bed. Bob Hamman is preparing to lead a crowd to a nearby Italian place. As for the Italians, they want sushi. Many players head for the food court, though more than a few don't make it that far, getting caught up in the slots.

I can imagine the players are looking to blow off steam. I've watched ten hours of bridge today, and I'm exhausted. Sadly, I have little fun to look forward to. I'll go back to the strip, hole up in my room, and stay up typing my notes. I realize that I have yet to visit the hotel pool. I keep the drapes drawn at all hours, like the Howard Hughes of the Tropicana.

On my way out, I see Lall and say, "You did well today." He corrects me with "We did average," which might be true, statistically speaking, but so much for encouragement. Justin doesn't seem to need it. He's having the time of his life. He says, "This is it for me. I mean, you play at sectionals for money. You play here, in a field like this, for the beauty of the game." The irony, of course, is that there's a ton of money on the line, but I don't point that out. He's already telling me again how a few big boards can really swing the scores. Just then, Bob Hamman saunters over. Justin says, "Bob, tomorrow we make our move."

The next day, on my way from the strip to the tournament, I draw another chatty cabbie. This one is German, and he says, "I play poker, not bridge, for plenty of years, man. Five, six years ago, the casinos were closing the poker rooms. Now, any casino worth a shit has its own poker room. Maybe one day they have bridge, too." He says Las Vegas is still a boomtown—there's plenty of room for everybody. Then he launches into a long and essentially unintelligible grievance against Circuit City and its rebate department in which he uses the term "jerk fart" numerous times to refer to certain members of the store's customer service team.

Outside the Estancia ballroom, players lounge about. Checking the clock, one pair decides to go out to the car and listen to some music. There is no sign of Zia, and while I doubt he's still in bed—today we're getting an afternoon start—I know from his book that he likes to sleep as late as possible, sometimes right up until the match. One player stands alone in a corner, taking imaginary golf swings.

Off to one side I see the world-class player Eric Rodwell, who with his partner Geoff Hampson is currently in first place, sitting quietly in a chair reading a book. I try to peek at the cover but my view is blocked. I'm dying to know what he's reading; I saw him carrying the book around yesterday, too. I assume it's a tome on bridge esoterica. Rodwell, whose regular partner is Jeff Meckstroth, is a renowned theoretician. He reminds me of "Iceman," the unflappable flyboy from the movie *Top Gun*. While other people psych themselves up with lucky tunes and goofy golfing tics, the leader of the pack is reading a book.

By now, some players are showing a little wear. The Cavendish might be an upscale tournament, but bridge pros have their limits, and I notice a lot of rumpled clothing. Robson has been sporting the same blue shirt and red pants for a few days now. The Canadian kids are in well-worn hoodies. Even Zia is dressed down in a canary yellow fleece. When three teenage girls in tank tops and lip gloss walk by a particularly gamey player, the leader holds her sides and whispers back in a high help-me voice, "Ew, groooss."

Louise again wears white, this time with a purple boa. She says her plan is to keep kibitzing the leaders, Hampson and Rodwell, and she invites me along. Hampson is a thin Canadian thirty-something who competes internationally for the United States. Rodwell wears a short-sleeved tropical silk shirt that is open to reveal a gold chain. By nature, he seems an unassuming fellow, but he's a big guy, and with his dark hair and mustache he gives off a certain smooth Tom Selleck air—except that his beige boat shoes are untied.

When Louise and I watch them play a Hungarian pair, I finally catch a glimpse of Rodwell's reading, which is stashed under his chair. All I can see is the title—*Game of Shadows*—and my mind begins to reel. It must be some deeply abstract text on the mental shadowboxing of bidding, most likely involving the use of covert CIA mind-control tactics. Back at the Tropicana, I look up the title online; it turns out it's about Barry Bonds and the recent baseball steroid scandals.

According to Louise, Rodwell and Hampson annihilate the Hungarians. I note she is not as timid around bridge stars as I am. She is a fearless kibitzer, barging into any booth at any time regardless of who's playing. She tells me, "They're really not allowed to say no. They can ban one person from watching them for the whole tournament, but that's it." That sounds a little fishy, but later that night I look up the rules, and she's right.

I also notice in today's bulletin there is a picture of her from the auction. Naturally, she is sitting at Zia's table.

Despite the fact that Zia and Andrew are hovering low in the ranks, their booth overflows with kibitzers who jealously guard their seats between rounds. There is no room for us, so Louise and I visit the snack table, as Louise has a thing for the cheese. Upon seeing a man scooping up nuts with his fingers, she says to me, "Bridge players can be very disgusting." Later, she takes it upon herself to tidy up one of the booths—throwing away scraps of paper and empty cups—before the players arrive.

The rounds wear on, and one session stretches into two. After flitting around for a while, Louise again makes us lie in wait for her leaders, Hampson and Rodwell. They are playing the Canadian kids, and the match has been moved to one of the three so-called Vugraph rooms. I am now seeing the other side of the Vugraph, that Internet broadcast Zeus first showed me at the club. Thus Louise and I find ourselves in a special booth where, perched high on a stool so he can see both sides of the table, a man sits in front of a laptop. He enters every bid and every play into the computer. For years, the Cavendish tournament has been broadcast on the Vugraph, which is always live and always free and carries quite a schedule. In the days leading up to the tournament, bridge buffs could catch Polish Premier League games from Warsaw, the Eighth Torneo Bolivariano taking place in Lima, the Scottish Cup Finals from Dundee, and the German Team Championship in Kassel. When all the Cavendish excitement is over, diehard fans can take consolation in the upcoming District Knockout Teams broadcast from Tokyo, Japan.

Hampson and Rodwell take on the young Canadians in their usual cold-blooded style, though I notice Rodwell does have a slight nervous habit of fanning his cards open and closed, most often when he's declarer. After a few more rounds of steady devastation, I begin to feel like a fair-weather fan, so I bid Louise adieu and check on Hamman and Lall.

They are matched up against two crafty-looking middle-aged guys in chinos and running shoes. This time I sit behind Bob, who kindly sorts his hand for me. He declares the first two boards, and I get a close look at his style. When the bidding is over, he waits for the lead with his hands in his lap, his cards piled neatly on the table. When the dummy hits, he stares at it for a long while, formulating his attack. Remarkably, he does all this without reviewing his hand. Those thirteen cards are already stored away in what seems to be a human computer. Bob sits motionless, and all I hear is rhythmic nostril breathing, one-two, one-two. It reminds me of what he said in Dallas about perfectly conserving his energy. Even his speech becomes clipped. When Jeff Meckstroth, standing outside after the round, starts to say something, Bob cuts him off with one word—"Obliterated."

With two rounds to go in the fourth session, it's 10:20 P.M. Outside, the casino is in full Saturday-night swing. Inside, we are on a bridge Bataan death march. Between rounds, I watch a man ritualistically tap a garbage can with his foot, and I wonder if I'm witnessing an outbreak of low-level OCD. By now, Louise has taken to calling me "Eddie." It grows too late for her; she can't follow the hands anymore, and she says she is going to close her eyes for a bit. I leave her with half a cup of coffee in a chair in the hall and go in to watch Zia and Andrew for the last round.

They are competing against two Poles, one of whom is a ringer for Bob Dylan. Zia is feeling squirrelly from the start. He pretends to throw a card at Andrew, and they give each other a lot of good-natured grief. By now, the fan club has diminished to three other kibitzers, all of whom laugh heartily at the jokes. Then, on the last hand, things get a little dark. Zia gets angry at Andrew for something, it's not clear what—either for defending poorly or not bidding something at auction. He drops his cards to the table, conceding the hand, and Andrew ducks his head under the screen and says, "What?" We clear the booth to leave them to talk. Up until that round, they were having a big session. In short time, I see them laughing again, and I hear Andrew say, "It's just a question of style."

Unfortunately, Bob and Justin are not so quick to bounce back. Bob walks by with a hangdog look. They will post the lowest score of the field for that round. It's eleven thirty and the session is over. Players crowd the halls; some have found drinks. When the results go up, a crowd rushes the wall. A few people hang back playing it cool, "Iceman" among them.

Overall, with one session to go, Hampson and Rodwell are still in the lead. Bob Blanchard and Jeff Meckstroth are twenty-seventh, with Zia and Andrew two spots behind them. As for Bob and Justin, in one ill-fated day, they have dropped from "average" to third-to-last place.

The bridge players check their scores and scatter, losing themselves among the Green Valley guests. At one end of the hall, the casino is hopping with hopefuls dropping dollar after dollar amid a cacophony of bells, whistles, and electronic beeps. At the other end, the nightclub is blasting the Cure. Along a velvet rope, girls in artfully distressed designer jeans teeter on high heels and a vodka buzz, clutching the arms of guys in dark shirts with expensive dyed hair and subtle nose rings. The limos and Lexuses roll up outside, spilling forth parties of people swigging half-empty bottles of Tanqueray and Grey Goose.

I jump into a cab, and the driver asks me the same question Louise first did, whether I'm playing or watching. I say watching. In the distance we can see the light of the Luxor hotel pyramid piercing the sky, and I wonder who would want to stay in a tomb. The cabbie tells me, "That's good, brother. You can learn a lot by just watching. This town is built up by the losers." As he says that, the clock strikes midnight, and somewhere either the bridge players go to bed or they don't.

On Sunday, the temperature tops one hundred degrees. The final session starts at noon, like a showdown in a western. At the Green Valley Ranch, I see many happy mothers pulling slots beside their children and grandchildren, and it reminds me to call my mom. It's Mother's Day. I wonder how many bridge players will remember to do the same.

Today Louise approaches me in a yellow boa, and off we go to watch Hampson and Rodwell. On our way in, one of her previously favored players gives her a hard time for abandoning him. When he's gone, she says his booth had grown too crowded for her taste. We seem to be the only ones faithfully following the leaders. At the Cavendish, kibitzers stick to their own favorites, no matter the score.

The leaders sit against the field's only all-female pair, two nicely dressed middle-aged women who are both named Jill. I notice Hampson has developed a case of sewing-machine leg, perhaps a sign he knows he's closing in on the money.

Next, I convince Louise to follow me to the Vugraph room to watch Zia for a round. He and Andrew are essentially out of the race, but they're having a good time. Zia makes snide asides to the Vugraph operator ("Here's a hand for the fans!") and heckles his opponents ("Is that the best lead you've got?"). When Andrew, as declarer, takes a bold finesse, Zia says, "That's why they call him big-balls Robson." Then he notices Louise and smiles.

Louise is tickled. With still half of the session to go, she sighs, "It's a shame it's over." She goes back to her favorites, and I seek out Blanchard and Meckstroth, who, when I find them, are apologizing to each other. They're not in the top ten, but they remain focused on the prize.

On the second to last round, Hampson and Rodwell are sitting against two men in blazers, one of whom has a fat cigar poking out of his front pocket. He asks Rodwell, "Are you nervous?" to which Iceman merely responds, "Nervous?" The guy presses on. "Do I make you nervous?" Rodwell ignores him.

At one point, an opponent doubles Rodwell's one no-trump opening. When the bidding tray comes back from the other side of the screen, Rodwell asks the cigar aficionado for an explanation. The man writes, "Meckwell," then whispers, "Do you know it?" Finally, a joke I get. "Meckwell" is shorthand for a convention used to intervene against no-trump bidding; it's named for the men who play it—Jeff Meckstroth and his usual partner, Eric Rodwell.

When the men in blazers get up, I notice they carry their wallets in their front pants pockets, which looks a little odd. I guess when you spend as much time on your keister as these guys—and your wallet is as fat—carrying your cash in your back pocket might give you a serious hunchback.

For the finale, Hampson and Rodwell are in the Vugraph room. One of their opponents, a man in a brown sweater and khakis, is agitated by something that happened last round. During the bidding, he ducks his head under the screen and asks his partner if they should have called the director. Hampson snaps, "Either way, you shouldn't be talking about it now."

The first hand is a tortuously bid five diamonds, in which Hampson goes down two. He and Rodwell defend the next two boards. Because of the slow start, this match is the last still being played. The noise building outside the ballroom is a roar that can't be shushed, try as the directors might. The mood in our booth is intense, all concentration and no smiles. At four thirty the final hand of the 2006 Cavendish is over and the possible winners exit the playing area.

There is to be a closing barbecue by the pool, but no one is heading there yet because some preliminary scores were posted during the last round—and they're somewhat surprising. With three boards to go, Hampson and Rodwell had fallen to second place. No one is going anywhere until the final results are in, and so for one last time bridge players crowd the hall, jostling, talking, and smoking.

Louise sidles up and says, "My Geoff got knocked down." It turns out he and Rodwell had a disastrous session, coming in near the bottom. She says, "It's just a game," but she seems down. We watch Zia walk by. Thinking of the picture in the bulletin, I ask Louise how she knows Zia. She says she has seen him play over the years, but she wouldn't say she knows him. "You can't make friends with these people. They don't care about you. They'll walk right by. They're oblivious."

Right then, the results go up, and the place goes nuts. Hampson and Rodwell indeed have finished in second place. Hampson looks upset, while a woman kisses Rodwell, who manages to smile. They were well in the lead from the second session onward, but after a dismal final day, it was the story of the tortoise and the hare, as they were overtaken by the second-place team, who managed to stay in the hunt by posting three final above-average scores. Still, Hampson and Rodwell's owner wins $124,223 on his $32,000 investment, and they will receive $13,860 from players' pool.

Across the room, a man sings, "We're in the money" and hugs a woman by his side. One owner walks around with a computer printout of the teams he bought, consulting the awards chart as he tallies up his winnings. Bob Hamman is standing with Zia and laughing at something he said.

The winners are a Dutch pair, Huub Bertens and Ton Bakkeren. It is their first time at the Cavendish, and they are something of a dark horse. They sold for a mere $14,000 despite the fact that they had won a European pairs championship.

None of my pairs finish in the money—or even higher than middle of the pack. Bob Blanchard and Jeff Meckstroth come in twenty-fifth, while Bob Hamman and Justin Lall finish thirty-sixth. Three places below them, or sixth from the bottom, are Zia and Andrew, though they don't seem to care. When Bob Hamman walks by I ask, "Bob, are you tired?" He says, "Not particularly."

Out in the desert heat, sun-soaked hotel guests amble past a wooden door leading to a small, secluded pool ringed by palm trees and a hedgerow marked by a sign saying "Private Function." Inside, bartenders with buzz cuts and sunglasses busy themselves while bridge players with drinks pore over hand records, recounting a litany of victories and defeats they will no doubt revisit again and again in the months to come. They chuckle and shout and slap each other on the back. From speakers overhead, Bob Marley booms, "Let's get together and feel all right . . ."

Around the deck of the pool sit mod orange- and red-striped chairs. Misters are spraying down above us to alleviate the heat, though they only serve to make it humid as hell. Of everyone, only Zia doesn't sweat. In a tan suit with a scarlet handkerchief peeking from his breast pocket, he looks as graceful as ever—even in defeat—telling a friend, "We played like shit, but I swam, I won chips at the casino, and I had a great time."

Blue sky shines through thin scrims hanging above us. The late-afternoon sun slices through the awning to cast long, noir-ish shadows on the white concrete floor. There are white umbrellas and a brown wooden bar. Some of the more adventurous bridge players lounge on beds by the rectangular pool into which a sheet of water pours, casting attractive ripples.

There is a carving station serving slabs of rare corned beef, plus Brie pastries, fajitas, chips and salsa, cold penne pasta salad, and seasonal fruits and berries. A cake is brought out and the crowd sings "Happy Birthday" to a blushing Meckstroth, who is turning fifty. For a world-class player, he looks a little uncomfortable in the spotlight.

Now that it's all over, Louise seems depressed. "I'm not good at working a room," she says. "I'm going home to relax." She and her friend walk out as Bob Blanchard introduces the winning Dutch duo to great applause. He makes a speech thanking the organizers and hotel staff. Everyone claps as he introduces the other winners, though not all conversations cease, some players still insisting on rehashing old hands. Bob Marley sings on, "Every little thing gonna be all right . . ."

Someone seems to have set the misters on overdrive, and they create a sort of horror-film effect, with bridge players lumbering in and out of the fog. On the other side of the pool, Bob Blanchard's camera crew is shooting more interviews for his promo. By the carving station, Bart Bramley (who finished thirty-second) tells me, "Well, we didn't do well, but you can't beat this," taking in the pool scene with one expansive gesture.

I catch up with Justin Lall at the bar and ask for a summation. He says, "It was a great opportunity to play with Bob. My hope was to win, but we got unlucky. I didn't play my best; I'm kind of disappointed—and I'm really tired."

I try to cheer him up by reminding him that, at nineteen, he was the youngest player in the event. One day, I say, he'll be running this tournament. Justin perks up. "That's my goal!" he says. "I want to be the next Bob Hamman. One day I want people to say, 'Oh, you're playing with Justin Lall.'"

After a while, the winners head out. On their way to the door, everyone stops to congratulate them. Over the sound system, Van Halen implores us to "Jump," but the party seems to be winding down. The half-eaten birthday cake now declares, "appy hday eff!" I am approached by a Canadian TV crew filming a documentary on the Canadian kids, who finished twenty-eighth. The producer and his cameraman have been following them around for a year and a half, and they tell me they've grown tired of the company of bridge players. They say they haven't found them to be a very forthcoming bunch. The cameraman compares bridge conversations to Klingon—a kind of secret code you learn just to prove to others that you can.

The producer asks to interview me, though I insist I'm no expert. As we're talking, a tipsy young fan named Justine wanders over to see what we're doing. It turns out she caddied last year at the Cavendish, which was a great deal ("They pay more than all the other tournaments!"). This year, by chance, she is working at Green Valley Ranch, so she got to watch a lot of the action. I ask her what kind of hotel guests bridge players make. She squeals, "The worst! They're pigs! Some hotels don't ever let them come back." Looking around, she whispers into the camera, "And they're soooo arrogant." Then she smiles. "But these guys get a lot of money to play bridge. What a totally envious life!"

A few days later, sitting in the garden of his nineteenth-century townhouse on a quiet block of New York's Upper West Side, Bob Blanchard puts the same sentiment another way. He says, "There's a real feeling of accomplishment that comes with being rewarded with money. It gives players more esteem in the eyes of other people. But bridge players are unique. They lead normal walks of life, and then they go to a tournament and everything disappears. Time goes away. Watches get turned off. They're only playing bridge. It's a unique world for that reason. We have everyone from Supreme Court judges to actors to basketball players to opera singers to high achievers in all walks of life who just want to play bridge. Now there is no other game in the world where that is true. Where do you have a championship tennis player who is also CEO of a company? Where do you have a world-class golfer who is also a federal judge? I don't know too many poker players who are at that level."

Blanchard lights a cigarette. The tournament is over, but he can't stop promoting. "The time is ripe for bridge," he says. "About a month ago, I was at a business meeting in Florida that coincided with the nationals in Dallas. It was Sunday morning, and I was sitting by the pool. I open the *New York Times*, and there it is on the front page looking me in the face—dominoes. Dominoes are being taken up by ESPN2. Dominoes! Now that's not to say dominoes isn't a wonderful game, but it's nothing compared to bridge. So I got on the telephone and started calling people at nationals, saying, 'What the screw is going on?'"

Blanchard takes a long drag and slowly exhales. "Two weeks ago, before we left for the tournament, I was sitting in this garden with the other Cavendish organizers, and I stood up and said, 'Guys, we've got to make this work.'"

CHAPTER ELEVEN

London Bridge Isn't Falling Down, But It Might Come Second to Fishing, Part I

London, England, May 2006

Midway through my Vegas vacation, I begin to feel a need to broaden my horizons, get in touch with the roots of the game, and so I book a flight to London, the town that gave Americans whist—and thereby bridge. Nothing seems daunting when considered within the bowels of the Tropicana, but before boarding my flight in New York, I remember the words of the immortal P. G. Wodehouse: "A city like New York makes the new arrival feel at home in half an hour, but London is a specialist in . . . the Distant Stare. You have to buy London's good-will." That is unfortunate, as it is the world's third-most expensive city. Still, this will not be my first visit—and my wife will be coming along—and I believe the British are not without their peculiar brilliance: room-temperature pints, pay toilets at bus stops, and the BBC comedy *The Office.* On the other hand, I am puzzled by the large "Look Left" and "Look Right" pedestrian signs at street crossings—do the Brits need reminders that they drive on the wrong side of the road, too?

A week after the Cavendish, I catch up with Zia at another

food court, though this time it's called a Food Hall and it's on the ground floor of Harrods, the famed 157-year-old London department store. Our meeting has had an air of improvisation, more a casual encounter than an actual interview, despite a number of increasingly anal e-mails from me, some alluding to the fact that I'm flying across five time zones to meet him and it would be a shame if by chance we didn't connect.

I spoke to Zia yesterday, as I was heading to the airport. I caught him on his cell, and after I identified myself, the polite British voice on the other end said, "Ah, Edward. I'm just hitting a shot in a golf tournament. Can you call me in two minutes?"

After another day and another call, I am sitting in a busy café in one of Harrods' black-and-white Edwardian-tiled food halls, where you can buy quail eggs, Krispy Kremes, and chocolate towers in the shape of Big Ben. I am rumpled and jet-lagged, having arrived almost straight from an overnight flight. Zia, naturally, is dressed impeccably in a cream blazer, yellow button-down, black undershirt, and faintly tinted black-rim glasses. He is kind to see me on what I imagine is a busy afternoon. He leaves tomorrow for Pakistan, where he will receive a medal from the president—"for something or other, I don't know what," he lies, with becoming modesty. (It turns out President Musharraf is devoted to the game. He plays a strong-club system, and in Islamabad he will ask Zia to partner with him against two of his top-ranking generals.)

Zia tries to order plain toast to go with his tea, but the waitress can't do something that simple. And so the most popular bridge player on the planet resigns himself to tea without toast, as I sip a cappuccino and settle in to hear him explain—in a most mellow British accent by way of Pakistan—his thoughts on the game past, present, and future. Suddenly it hits me that I have become one of those little old ladies who will cross an ocean just to sit at the feet of the master.

Typical for Zia, the story begins with a girl. "I learned to play bridge when I was twenty-one," he remembers with a smile. "I didn't have any idea what the game was, but I found the only way I could meet a girl I was trying to meet was through a bridge party. In Pakistan, girls weren't allowed out on dates, so I had to pretend to be a bridge player so I could get to know her. So I went to the bridge party, and I got stricken by the bridge bug. Now it's almost forty years later—and I'm sixty and still stricken."

Zia admits to having an addictive personality—"When I like things I go all the way"—but his devotion to the game goes beyond mere addiction. He describes a life in bridge as a campaign of small successes in the face of overwhelming defeat, a life to be envied, he insists with great cheer: "Bridge is so impossible to conquer that the fact that you occasionally win little battles is your excitement. The frustration of screwing up and the aggravation of not being able to be more than limitedly good—that gives you incentive. It's like a passion, an emotion. It's slightly illogical, but it's very much consuming."

Beyond having a brilliant technical mind for bridge, Zia is known as an irrepressible card player with a gambler's flair for crafty games of cat and mouse and bold counterintuitive plays that pay off in the end. If Eric Rodwell is the cool calculating "Iceman" in my oversimplified *Top Gun* pantheon, then Zia undoubtedly is "Maverick," full of flash and genius and derring-do—not to mention the one who always gets the girl.

Zia cut his teeth playing rubber bridge, first in Pakistan for small stakes with his friends, then in London clubs with greater sums on the line. Soon he was banned from a club—for winning too much. (He remembers, "I used to say, 'Look, I haven't paid my rent yet. Do you mind paying my rent today?'") He is an enthusiastic gambler, though he says, "I'm not dumb. I don't play roulette for high stakes. For me, bridge is a calculated gamble. I don't mind if there are very good players against me—I've got an edge."

Zia is a zealous proponent of rubber bridge. He agrees with Bob Hamman that the money game is the best way to learn to play—a trial by fire—though the number of top competitors who grew up playing for stakes is dwindling. Zia finds high-level duplicate competitions a bit sterile, whereas making the most of a rotating cast of rubber bridge partners takes a certain elasticity of character and creativity of vision—never mind the ability to suffer great financial swings without a break in confidence. He claims to play bridge in five different ways, depending on the level of his opponent.

Zia takes a sip of tea, before adding a final caveat. "Also, you obviously don't play the same bridge game against a pretty girl as an ugly girl." Then, realizing he might sound a bit impolitic, he corrects himself. "Or perhaps let's say against a pretty girl and an ugly man."

And just like that, we're back on the subject of women. For decades, the bridge world knew Zia as the debonair Pakistani playboy, with his well-tailored suits (never jeans), suave accent, and elegant manners. Forget "Maverick"—a James Bond for the bridge set would be a more apt analogy. It is a role he sometimes seems to cultivate. This is a man who, in his autobiography, writes that meeting a certain bombshell on the Côte d'Azur was like "picking up a ten-card suit for the first time—a mixture of fantasy fulfilled and the surge of wild expectation." He tells me, "You know, it is much more interesting to seduce a woman on the bridge table. You seduce her by playing flamboyantly and excitingly." These days, however, Zia is a married man—he and his wife of five years have two sons on whom he dotes—and so he hastens to add, "And by seducing, I don't mean making her jump into bed with you, but just so she says, 'Wow, what a guy you are.' That's an ego boost we all play bridge for."

So far, at the tournaments I've been to, I've seen precious little seduction going on—especially at the serious tables. (As Zia puts it in that same book, "Cricketers and footballers might need a bodyguard to keep girls out of their rooms; bridge players need one to bring them in.") In fact, many of the vices traditionally associated with card play are noticeably absent. Zia happens to be one of the few big-time players who admits to having the occasional drink between sessions. "Well, I may not have a glass of wine during the last round of the final of the world championship, but apart from that . . ." He smiles. "First of all, if I have a bottle of wine, I'm still about three times better than the next guy who hasn't had a drink. And for me to go into training and starve myself to play—I don't think it's worth it. At serious tournaments, sure, I agree you shouldn't have wine and you should eat light and all this, but hey, if I did that I would be working in the corporate sector—I wouldn't be a bloody bridge player."

Such an attitude seems like a throwback to decades past, before the playing areas went smoke-free and big-time bridge was played with cigars, booze, and groupies at the table. Surprisingly, Zia's favorite bridge memory has nothing to do with a beautiful woman or a high-stakes game, but a match he played in 1981, when he led an underdog Pakistani team to the finals of the world championships in Port Chester, New York. It was Pakistan's first international outing representing the newly created zone of Central Asia, and the world was shocked to see the newcomers mount a charge from second-to-last place to secure a berth in the final, which they led at midpoint before eventually losing to the United States.

Zia remembers, "We didn't expect to do anything, and the world certainly thought we wouldn't." In fact, one Pakistani player had to purchase a new return ticket, since he originally had scheduled to fly home during the semifinal round. Zia admits such pessimism was hardly unfounded. "I'm not saying we did it because of our merit; you know, we fluked our way into a situation that we couldn't believe. Our guys didn't know any methods; we were playing basic, basic bridge, which we had picked up from books. We didn't know keycard Blackwood or anything that today a beginner knows. We were just playing momma-poppa bridge." It was a true Cinderella story and America's introduction to the magic of Zia Mahmood, for while he was a fixture in the London rubber bridge clubs, he was relatively unknown in the States.

But Zia does not typically dwell on the past—he has too many opinions and ideas for the future. Like the United States, England is in the grips of a poker craze, with ads for gaming Web sites on its double-decker buses and shows on TV—to the detriment of bridge. Zia says, "Bridge is not in jeopardy of dying out, but it's certainly in jeopardy of becoming very particular and specialized, which is a bad thing. You have to have the ability to say what we are doing is not working. It's working at some levels, yes; we have our cadre of top bridge players, but the game is not growing as it should, it's not catching on as it should, the youth is not coming into bridge as we'd like it to—so we're doing something wrong. Now what are we going to do to change it?

"To me, it's a mixture of marketability. Poker is being marketed very well. Bridge has never been marketed properly—ever. You need someone who says, 'Let's make this game what it can be.' You've got to have money. That's what makes the Cavendish so great. Have charity matches. Have Omar Sharif playing Bill Gates for a million dollars going to starving children in Africa. You've got to change it up. Have a match of the top bridge players against the top poker players where they play bridge and then they play poker. Let's see which mind sport is the greatest. Have chess players involved, I don't care. But let's try to make waves, make excitement, as opposed to just present what we're presenting, which is not working."

Zia's ideas strike at the roots of bridge, and for such an august ambassador of the game, he reveals himself to be surprisingly radical. "I think bridge needs lateral thinking," he says. "There's a game called cricket you might not know much about. When I came along, cricket spectatorship was falling by the wayside. Then came an extravagant and colorful Australian multimillionaire named Kerry Packer. He lured away the top cricketers in the world with huge sums of money and devised a new format called the one-day cricket, where everybody had to get in and out by one day. You had a limited amount of time to make runs, and because you had a limited amount of time you had to score as many runs as possible so the whole game became more exciting. In bridge, you should do the same thing. Let a grand slam pay five times more—then everybody tries bidding grand slams. Let doubled contracts be more fateful for the loser and more profitable for the winner. Do the same for redoubles. It's the doubles and redoubles and grand slams that excite viewers—make them sexier! As the scoring is now, it's graded very nobly. Let those noble penalties be played at the top-level game. But if you want excitement, change the rules!"

Zia's revolution would extend beyond scoring into bidding. Top-level bidding has become so artificial—and complicated—that the majority of social bridge players (let alone those who don't play the game) can't follow along. What bridge has gained in science, it has lost in spectator appeal. Furthermore, Zia feels for him to have so many weapons at his disposal when playing against weaker players is, as he says, "rather a bullying effort."

Zia's remedy for this is the conventionless tournament. No coded bidding, no sophisticated systems—just straightforward auctions and old-fashioned card play. If a player could not do without an artificial agreement in his arsenal, he would have to pay for the right to use it—in points. Zia says, "I think a lot of good players use conventions as crutches. If there were no conventions and everybody sat equally, now you would just have to use good judgment—and that's when real abilities come out."

Such a move would not be the only difference in format. If bridge is to approach poker in terms of television airtime, then significant changes must be made. "You have to have a very simple form of bridge, probably a form of individual bridge, where players are playing for themselves," he says. "That becomes much easier to sell. Have an individual event where there's an element of luck and an element of skill and competitors play head-on matches until they get down to the last table standing. Like a poker tournament, they keep playing for stakes until one guy remains. A formula like that has never really been tried. But you must have large prizes. If you have huge amounts of money, you'll get your public watching because they want to see a guy screw up a million dollars on one hand. That's very marketable."

And then there's the philosophy behind the typical American tournament, which essentially offers players a marathon chance to glut themselves on bridge. Zia prefers the more leisurely French style, with a few hours of bridge played in a luxurious locale. He says, "If I ever brought my family to an American bridge tournament, my wife and children would say, 'Those are bridge players?' and run away. They'd ask, 'This is your whole life?' and they'd be frightened."

As it should now be abundantly clear, it's easy to get Zia talking; he has so many ideas and makes his points so compellingly, it's a wonder no one has picked up on them. But for all his candor and charm, they remain just ideas—there is no televised conventionless tournament, no leisurely international event in luxurious Palm Beach. As if to explain the mystery, Zia sighs and sits back in his chair. He says, "The thing about bridge is the players, as a whole, are well meaning but lazy. They don't do anything. And the vested interest in the management of bridge is particularly uninterested in things—they're usually bureaucrats who want to maintain their traditions and live their usual lives. They're not motivated. The bridge players seem to be well motivated, but, look, what do I do? I talk, I play, then I go off to a golf game or home to my family. I don't really go to meetings to work out all these things."

But what about the other movers and shakers of the game? Zia says, "The bridge world is full of interesting guys. A lot of them are idiots, a lot of them are, you know, autistic—deformed mentally. They're complete nuts. They wouldn't even fit into the trailer of a movie of life. But when it comes to bridge, suddenly they're flowers. Guys who look like cabbages turn into beautiful flowers when they start talking about bridge."

This is something I have noticed about certain bridge players, which—to be fair—is exacerbated by the fact that I'm usually showing up on their turf alone, overcaffeinated, and carrying a notebook. Still, many of them are incapable of functioning in the most basic social situations. They can't carry on a casual conversation, meet new people, stand in line, deal with life. But sit them at a bridge table, where the interaction is governed by a proscribed set of rules, a protocol they enjoy, a social language that they speak, and they're incredibly fluent—capable of flights of articulation and nuance that would be impossible for them in the real world.

I mention this and Zia laughs. "They're dysfunctional," he says. "So many bridge players, you put them in a car, they can't sit, you put them at the dinner table, they can't eat, you send them some directions, they don't know how to get anywhere— they're totally lost in the world. They're really hopeless. But at a bridge table they're incredibly competent. Then you take businessmen who are exceptionally bright and successful and charming and wonderful and you sit them at a bridge table and they lose their strength. They wither and look to this other guy—the bridge player."

He continues. "I'll tell you a story. These four bridge players—three pros and a very wealthy guy—are playing bridge in a club in London many years ago. They play all night and between them the pros win about £3,000 from this guy. At the end of the evening, it was raining, and the pros started walking home, all three sharing one umbrella, while the rich guy was being driven home by his chauffeur in the back of his Rolls-Royce. As he passes them, one of the pros smiles and says to the others, 'There goes the mug.'"

It's a funny story from a guy who refuses to teach his children bridge. Zia says what others pros have said, that he's reluctant to have his sons suffer the addiction of their father. "Because it's not a road to choose as a career," he tells me. "It's the most wonderful hobby in the world, but as a career I would never recommend it. Unless they change the business."

Up next for Zia is a tournament in Verona, Italy, called the World Bridge Championships, which, in the complicated system of international competition, is held every four years and is not the same event that Zia led his pack of unproven Pakistanis to near-victory in 1981. That event is rightfully called the World Team Championships, or more colloquially, the Bermuda Bowl; it now takes place every odd-numbered year.

The Verona tournament will be a transnational event, meaning pairs and teams can be made up of mixed nationalities. In many ways, the eyes of the world will be on Zia. He has won many major European tournaments and holds countless national titles in the States. Last year he was the ACBL Player of the Year, meaning he won the most master points in top-rated national events. It was his fourth time to win the award. This year, the ACBL has named him the Honorary Member of the Year, which—beyond the obvious honor—means he won't have to pay dues for the rest of his life. (In 2007, he will be inducted into the ACBL Hall of Fame.) In 1999, Zia even took on the top seven computer bridge programs in the world and won. For many years he had a standing £1 million bet that no computer could beat him. But while his accolades are many, Zia has never won a major world title. He came close at the last World Bridge Championships in Montreal in 2002, when he and his partner, Michael Rosenberg, lost the pairs event on the very last hand—an incident Zia calls "annoying." The duo won't be competing together again this year, as Zia says Rosenberg "got a better financial offer." Instead, Zia will be playing with Andrew Robson, adding with a wry smile, "with whom I did so wonderfully at the Cavendish." Zia also will be competing in the mixed event with Jill Meyers (a wine-drinking buddy) and in a team event with a combination of Americans and Poles.

But while the world holds its breath, Zia remains cool. Ask him about Verona and he says, "I love it—I see all my friends, we discuss, we play, sometimes we do well, sometimes we do badly. The only downside is I'll be away from my family for too long. Apart from that, it's a great holiday."

Few professional players would describe a heated international contest as a holiday, but that's just Zia. He seems to enjoy bridge at all levels in all situations with all kinds of people. He even plays with his in-laws when he and his wife go for a visit, which is a bit like having Michael Jordan marry into your family and take part in your post-Thanksgiving pickup game.

Of all the pros I've seen, Zia seems to have the best time. He says, "I know we did terribly at the Cavendish, but half an hour later I was out having a drink and playing poker or going out to a café—it totally doesn't last. Still, I know people who feel very . . ." He begins to compare his outlook to one of his partners', though which partner he's talking about—Robson, Rosenberg, or even someone else—is perhaps intentionally left a little unclear. He says, "The difference between my partner and me, we'll be leading a match by a hundred IMPs, and he'll get a two-diamond contract, where there's like one point at stake, and he'll take twenty minutes to play it, because he says, 'That's the way I am.' And I say, 'Forget it!' I'd like to play that hand and give the opponents five tricks so they feel happy. What do I care? Our attitude is so different. I want to win and go to the next thing. I don't want to squeeze the last drop out in a situation, because once I've won, I've won. And that's also why when I lose, I can be very up about it."

I mention that he and Robson seemed pretty up in Las Vegas, and Zia continues, "I get turned on in bridge from things other people notice, the little oddities. In the Cavendish, I defended a hand that made no difference, that was totally unsuccessful—we didn't win any points—but I knew that I did something that nobody else would think of. It was a very good play. And I know I came in last and all that, but the play remains in my mind.

"If I can lose and do one thing of great beauty, that turns me on. If I can win and play like a schmuck, then I feel terrible. It's performing to a level that excites myself—and maybe three or four other people with whom I can share that excitement.

Some people think the things I do are stupid, but some might say, 'Wow, that was a great thing.'"

Neil Mendoza is gushing. "I've become completely addicted to this club, the Portland Club," he says. "It is the best, best, best thing in the whole world. There's nothing like it. It's only rubber bridge. It's only men. There are only about a hundred members."

We sit at a blond wood table in an airy conference room in a decidedly new-media kind of office on a busy street off bustling Piccadilly Circus: modish leather chairs, lots of open space, translucent paneling, and Pop art on the walls. We are in the headquarters of Forward, a custom magazine publishing business that Mendoza cofounded in 1986 and sold in 2001 for more than £40 million. He says, "Oddly, I can still hang out here, but I have no job, no role, no title—nothing. I'm a freelance business guy." Mendoza, forty-six, owns or serves on the board of several companies, one of which is Hammer Films, the venerable British horror house that delivered such titles as *The Quatermass Xperiment* (1955) and *Dracula A.D. 1972* (1972).

He says, "I love clubs," and cites his membership in the hallowed Garrick Club—founded in 1831 for gentlemen of the arts and stage on the idea that "it would be better that ten unobjectionable men should be excluded than one terrible bore should be admitted"—as proof that he is willing to venture beyond the Portland.

But clearly the point of such a club—and indeed all clubs, on some level—is exclusion. Mendoza says of the Portland, "The thing I used to find about bridge is that I would end up in these clubs with people I wouldn't normally want to hang out with—whereas at this club I'm very comfortable. It's such a convivial atmosphere."

I have to take his word for it. We are not meeting at the Portland Club, nor will I ever set foot inside it, because, as Mendoza says, "They are a private lot." He assures me, "It's nothing sinister; it's just that it's a little cozy sanctuary, and they don't want or need any publicity." Cozy is a word Mendoza will use again and again to describe his beloved club, which conjures for me images of distinctively Wodehousian comforts. I see society idlers sunk into plush chairs, some recuperating from last night's fancy-dress ball while others are set to sally forth on some silly upper-crust hijinks. Such is my cheerfully outdated stereotype of the English clubman that I would not be surprised to hear Mendoza spin a yarn about pinching a bobby's helmet on a hellacious Boat Race Night bender.

But Mendoza puts me straight: the Portland Club is about bridge. Zia had told me, "London rubber bridge is very much dying, but the Portland is flourishing"—though perhaps a better word might be abiding, as the club has been in existence since 1825, when the gentlemen of the Stratford Club (established 1816) regrouped themselves to purge their ranks of one unwelcome member.

The Portland is often said to be the oldest bridge club in the land. In 1894, Lord Brougham, just back from Cairo, presented to the club a newfangled variation on whist that he had encountered abroad. The game was called bridge, and it was an unrefined version of the modern contract bridge we play today. A year later the Portland Club composed the first official laws of bridge, and its card committee has remained an international arbiter of the game ever since.

At the Portland they play a peculiar game—a fact the members take pride in. Mendoza is a friend of a friend of a friend; before coming to town, I contacted him to ask about the London bridge scene. In an e-mail, he disavowed any knowledge of such a scene, writing—with amusing understatement—"I just play at an all-male club called the Portland Club, which invented the rules of bridge and still plays very old-fashioned cards by not allowing any conventions." I had heard about this quaint and curious wrinkle: no conventions allowed. In some ways, it's the way Zia dreams of playing, only taken to the extreme. At the Portland, even the most modest modern advances in artificial bidding are thrown out the window. Members must play the game of their forefathers.

Mendoza outlines the policy, which is simple and strict: "No conventions. Everything you say is supposed to mean exactly that. No-trump means no-trump—and it's a weak no-trump. You can only bid a suit if you have four cards in it. You can't cue bid a suit or say two clubs for Stayman. If you bid clubs, you mean clubs. No negative doubles—they're not allowed. You can't do Blackwood and ask for aces." When I look a little doubtful, he adds, "Still, you regularly get to the six level."

If there seems to be a latent conflict between the desire to draw up a formal set of laws while at the same time insisting the game be kept simple, I suspect the impulse is tied more to notions of purity than playability. Conventions are inherently radical; they buck at the status quo. Anyone can invent one. They rise up, the brainchild of some player—be he hustler, highbrow, or hack—and compete for credibility at the table, living and dying in good democratic (or perhaps Darwinistic) fashion, as they're tested match after match. If the conventions are foolish—or wantonly destructive—they disappear or get outlawed. If they provide an edge, they survive and get passed on player to player or even written up—perhaps one day to be known by the name of their visionary inventor. (Or whoever first claims the credit—as I have said, there are several well-known but misattributed conventions in the game.)

And so it is no surprise that, as a regulatory body, the Portland Club is conservative in nature. But to the casual observer of history, an Englishman's distrust for conventions might seem part of his national character. Take, for instance, the Anglo-American bridge match of 1930, at the time touted as the first international bridge contest, but in reality something of a three-ring publicity circus arranged around a grudge match between two big bridge personalities: the colorful Ely Culbertson and a retired British lieutenant colonel named Walter Buller. In short, the match (which was played at the Portland) pitted a more "scientific" American method of bidding against a supposedly more "natural" British system—though Buller probably would have chafed at the idea he was employing anything as formal as a "system." In the early days of bridge, there were those who believed that even the most elementary partnership under-standings were tantamount to cheating. Bids were to be based on loosely defined common sense—nothing else. Prearranged agreements—no matter how transparent they might be—were vulgar and reeked of distasteful American "professionalism." A true gentleman amateur bid from his gut. For all their pains, Buller and his pack of honorable British primitives got steam-rolled by the scientific Americans.

A certain courteous antiprofessionalism lives on at the Port-land. In fact, in his autobiography, Zia goes so far as to say that in a London bridge club "the biggest insult you can pay someone is to call him a professional." And so at the Portland, Mendoza says, "There is never an argument, not one. The game is incred-ibly gentlemanly—deliberately so. If people want to analyze the hands afterward, you would get very upset. They call it 'king-x-x-ing'—you know, when people discuss a hand they go, 'I was holding king-x-x . . .' Here they say, 'No king-x-x-ing!'" Fur-thermore, while professional players are occasionally admitted as guests, they may never become members. As one social player is said to have sniffed about a pro who aspired to join, "I don't mind subsidizing his racehorses—but I won't pay his rent."

Thus over the years the Portland has welcomed only the noblest of gentry. As of the mid-1940s, a gentleman had to be in his fourth decade and earning at least £10,000 annually to be considered for membership. Famous Portland men include author Ian Fleming, who played his cards at the club, though reportedly with less bravado than his dashing character 007. (Fleming partly based Blades, a club in *Moonraker* in which Bond wins £15,000 at the bridge table on a crafty grand slam, on the Portland.) More recently, the club has displayed a sport-ing sense of democracy. The Portland hosts the annual Lords vs. Commons bridge match, a thirty-two-year series between the houses of parliament that is all tied up.

The club has inhabited a number of locations. Today, the Portland rents a section of the esteemed Savile Club (established 1868), whose members have included Darwin, Yeats, Wells, and Kipling. ("It's like a club within a club," notes Mendoza with enthusiasm.) The Portland offers a daytime and an evening game and holds celebrated Monday-night dinners in a gilded grand ballroom. The stakes at the table—while described by Zia as "very small"—seem high enough to subsidize those pesky stable fees. In a night it is possible to lose upward of £1,000. The game was even bigger in the past. Mendoza says, "The other day I was looking in the minutes book at entries from during the war. They played for much higher stakes then, hundreds of pounds, which in the forties would be the equivalent of tens of thousands of pounds. It was really big stuff. I saw they had to impose a rule that you couldn't play cards after five in the morning."

But who, exactly, shuffles his cards these days at the Portland? Zia, who Mendoza says "gets invited along regularly because people love playing with him," told me. "It's very hard to get into; it's a nice group of people who all come from a certain social level."

Today one still becomes a member in the time-honored way: be brought along as a guest by a well-regarded regular, be friendly but not pushy, and make sure to meet as many people as possible—if one man is against you, you won't be let in. Mendoza joined the Portland five years ago, and he speaks of his conversion into a bridge-playing clubman with evangelical fervor.

He begins, "I picked up bridge after college. The impetus was completely social; it was about hanging out with people. You see, London is quite different from America. When you leave university, everyone comes to London. There is no other city to go to. In America, my take on it is that you graduate your Ivy League school and you disperse to a dozen cities across America. Over here, everyone's in London, and you haven't got kids because you've just come down, and you want to hang out. So you have parties, and bridge is an excuse to drink and smoke and eat without the additional burden of having to make conversation with people."

He remembers the time fondly. "When we were kids first out of school, the best, best thing was to go to someone's house, have loads to drink, and stay up playing bridge. I even had friends who, after their huge country wedding, went off in the car while we followed them to their house and then played bridge until five in the morning. On their wedding night! It was like, 'Thank God this wedding is over so we can get down to playing cards.'"

As his game improved, Mendoza graduated into duplicate matches at regular bridge clubs. He says, "I went through a period of playing duplicate, which was exciting, I suppose, up to a point. And then I stopped liking the people anymore; I didn't like hanging out at those places."

At the Portland, he says, members are more sportsmen than nutty neurotics. He says, "The Portland world is different because it comes from more of a club gambling scene. It comes from the old history of clubs in this country. This is prepoker, when guys went to clubs and played whist for crazy money. Today, at the Portland, the second there aren't enough guys to make up proper foursomes for bridge, the leftover people start playing backgammon and betting on it: gamble, gamble, gamble. They flip between bridge, backgammon, horseracing, and golf."

Mendoza smiles and assures me again, "There is nothing like this club. I'm completely sold on it. And maybe it's not really bridge; maybe it's a different kind of existence. But life's too short to try to be expert at something."

CHAPTER TWELVE

London Bridge Isn't Falling Down, But It Might Come Second to Fishing, Part II

London, England, May 2006

The Andrew Robson Bridge Club, owned and operated by Zia's partner at the Cavendish, is on a quaint and quiet street in southwest London, with a fish-and-chips shop across the way and a tube station down the block. As you walk through the door, the bar is on your left, with shelves stacked with wine and a bartender at the ready. She will pour you a glass of beer, or invite you to help yourself to coffee and tea served in blocky white mugs. There are paintings, many of them for sale, ranging from Impressionist pastures to more modern dreamscapes, plus one large graduated color field that dominates a wall. Cushy chairs sit around green felt–covered tables topped here and there by the club magazine, an attractive publication that might slip easily into a purse. This issue is filled with pictures of smiling clubgoers, bridge tips, and advertisements for upcoming club outings such as the summer jaunt to St. Moritz and the winter ski trip in the Alps. A bulletin board lists last week's session leaders next to a poster advertising Thursday afternoon games of "gentle duplicate." There is a collection of bridge books for browsing or sale. The windows are cracked to let in cool air, and one of two overhead fans lazily spins. The wood-planked floor is dotted with rugs, while the back portion of the room is elevated one step and surrounded by a low white railing. The lighting is cheerful and bright and conducive to card play, but with none of the clinical fluorescence that can flatten the mood in big clubs. Step into the Andrew Robson Bridge Club on an overcast midweek afternoon, and you can't help but register that without a doubt this place is—to borrow a word from Neil Mendoza—cozy.

The front room is empty but for three or four people, one chatting quietly on a cell phone. I am greeted warmly by one of the managers, who offers me a beer. I consider calling Tina to tell her I've found us a new club. The manager says Andrew is still in the back teaching a class, and as he tells me this a door opens across the room to emit the faint—and surprising—sound of applause. Most classes I've witnessed end in confusion, not clapping, but soon fifteen or so chipper students stream out of the back. They're mainly in their forties, with a handful of thirty-somethings, the men in blazers and sweaters and the women in pants and heels. Either it's me, the unseasonable chill in the air, or the picturesque persuasions of old London itself, but the people who emerge seem to glow with good Dickensian cheer. It's like a nice holiday party just spilled into the room. Some students head to the bar to have one for the road, as the bartender busily begins uncorking chilled bottles of white. It seems to have been a class on bidding; I now hear, over drinks, the familiar patter of bridge-speak.

On a wicker table in front of me a fat, well-thumbed copy of *The Official Encyclopedia of Bridge* rests next to a stack of flyers for a show by "the Jimi Hendrix of acoustic guitar"—not the first sign that this place attracts something of a younger crowd. I wander over to a table displaying the latest in a series of instructive booklets by Andrew Robson. On the back is stamped a quote by Omar Sharif: "No one else has the capacity to explain bridge more clearly than Andrew."

As I'm reading this, Andrew appears and invites me into the back classroom. He wears a green-and-blue-checked short-sleeve shirt, red pants, and hiking boots, which he props up on a chair as he stretches out his full six-foot-six-inch frame and lets out a contented sigh. Tonight is Beginner Night at the club, and we have about an hour before the next class begins.

Robson seems relaxed for such a busy man. At forty-two, he has been a world-class player for a surprisingly long time; he looks younger than his years, with a shock of hair and coolly casual clothes (sometimes rumpled, always untucked). In 1989, he won the World Youth Championships. Two years later, no longer a junior player, he captured a European title. In a few weeks, he is looking forward to competing with Zia in the World Pairs championship in Verona, because—as he says—"We really have a shot." But first he's off to Morocco to play rubber bridge with a multimillionaire and his high-rolling cronies, who came to him looking for private instruction.

Andrew also writes a daily bridge column in *The Times* and a weekly one in *Country Life* magazine, and last fall he published a book on how to avoid common mistakes at the table. Moreover, he is something of an adventurer, though his outdoor activities have been curtailed since, as he puts it, he "nearly copped it" in a 2001 hill-walking accident that sent him sliding down an icy chute over a hundred-foot cliff. Andrew spent months in a wheelchair, and while he can no longer run, he now enjoys mountain biking. "Out of the frying pan and into the fire," he says with a grin. He is married with two daughters, five and four. The secret? He snorts and says, "You've just got to bend time."

Of course, Andrew also owns a wildly popular bridge club, which he founded in 1995—"against my better judgment"—above a Chelsea pub called "The Goat in Boots" because, as he says, "There was a huge need for a nice place for people to play bridge." Three and a half years later, the club had overrun its digs and moved to its current location. Technically, the club is only for members, but visitors are always welcome and joining up is a snap—you can download a form off the Web site, and dues are included in the price of beginner courses. Today a little more than a hundred people a night will drop by for a variety of games and lessons, and the club now boasts some two thousand members.

Andrew believes the club's success has to do with its overriding philosophy of providing a fun, light, social atmosphere. But if heads remain cool, that's not to say the action at the table doesn't ever get a little heated. To the many hats Andrew wears—player, owner, teacher, writer—you could certainly add part-time matchmaker. He says the club is responsible for at least ten marriages. He remembers, "One Thursday night, another guy named Andrew said, 'I want a partner.' You can always come here and get matched up with a partner. So I was just going to put him with someone who was free, but then this woman, Lucinda, rings up, and I start thinking to myself, 'Oh, that would be fun.' But she's very late, and meanwhile Andrew keeps asking, 'Why haven't you put me with someone?' I had to keep telling him, 'Relax, I have a plan for you.' Finally in walks this girl, and they play together, and I don't really hear anymore about it. Then three years later I get the wedding invitation!"

Scratch a British bridge player, it seems, and you'll find a student of Andrew's. As former pupil Neil Mendoza, tells me, "Andrew Robson is the most loved teacher in all of London."

As I can attest, we know-nothing newbies are notoriously difficult to teach. Andrew seems to relish the challenge. He says, "I'll get a class of beginners in here—they've never played before—and beginners is beginners is beginners. So I'll start off by saying, 'This is a pack of cards. Here's an ace, a king, a queen. There are four suits, and the person sitting opposite you, that's your partner—smile at them. You're on the same team.' Otherwise, how do you start? Why should they know what a trick is? Maybe they've played hearts before on their mobile phone, but maybe they haven't. You got to keep it simple, you got to keep it light. We take things pretty slowly. I give them nice colored sheets, and they sort of blossom. I've taught, you know, thousands and thousands of people to play bridge over the years."

But what fun can a world-class player get out of wrangling rank beginners? Robson tells me, "I love to see my students get pleasure out of the game. Many of them I know in truth aren't going to become terribly competent players. But that really isn't the point. I know it's going to enhance their lives. They're going to make new friends; it's going to keep their minds active and give them pleasure. And for me, that's a lot."

When Andrew was about ten he learned to play from his parents, who were social players. Now they are students at his club. In fact, they are coming tonight for an intermediate class. Andrew says, "I don't find I'm quite as patient with them as I am with others; though I am very protective—I want them to have a nice time." He remembers what first fascinated him about bridge was the play of the cards, "the logic of how they all fall together and how you can make extra tricks out of seemingly nothing."

The allure continues, as Robson remains the kind of player who loves "to grind out the overtricks." Thus he is drawn to duplicate bridge over the less precise money game, where it's more a matter of making—or defeating—the contract. In fact, many rubber clubs don't score overtricks, which vastly speeds up the game—thereby increasing the number of hands (and money) that can be won and lost in a session. Andrew thinks rubber bridge is on its way out, but—unlike Zia—he sees that as no great loss to the game. He says, "Let's face it, people do not particularly like to gamble with their bridge. Bridge is a partnership game; it's not a game you have to play for money like poker. In fact, I think more and more people who like the money edge are moving into poker. I don't think there will be much money bridge in the decades to come."

Although he enjoys playing at the Cavendish, he points out that even there the stakes can "create a little bit of awkwardness." He tells a story from a few years ago, when he was playing against an Egyptian pair on whom his partner had bet a lot of money. When it was Andrew's turn to bid, he found himself in a bit of a spot. He says, "We weren't in contention at that point, but they were. I knew what I wanted to bid—and what was likely to be the winning decision. I also knew it was going to cost my partner tens of thousands of dollars. So what was I supposed to do? I didn't want to do anything. But in the end, I did the honest thing and made the bridge bid—and I cost my partner fifty thousand dollars."

And what is it like to play with his current partner, who draws kibitzers like flies? I ask Andrew if he's ever been mobbed by besotted bridge biddies. He laughs. "Well, we always get a little bit of support," he says. "Zia is a fantastic partner. We're great friends; playing with him is lovely. In Vegas, we were hardly dropping a trick, making as many tricks as declarer and on defense as we could, and yet doing very poorly because our bidding was a bit errant. We're both used to being the drivers within our partnerships, and you don't want to have two drivers."

With its "uniquely social ambiance," the Andrew Robson Bridge Club is known to draw a younger, hipper crop of players, partly because it caters to beginners and partly because the emphasis is on having a good time. Its more accomplished members range from actors (Susan Hampshire, David Rintoul) to members of parliament (Michael Mates).

Robson points out that it's not just his club, but "in England there are quite a lot of famous people, people in the public eye, who play bridge." Through my reading, I know Nobel laureate Harold Pinter is a player, as is Sting. But Andrew names some more youthful Brits like Damon Albarn, lead singer of the band Blur and now the man behind the cartoon supergroup Gorillaz, as well as the gods of British alt rock, Radiohead. In 1993, band member Colin Greenwood reportedly told a reporter from a now-defunct New York newspaper, "There's more pressure playing a four diamond contract than playing in front of two thousand people."

In fact, both bands, Blur and Radiohead, have been reported to play a rubber or two on the tour bus between shows. The latter band, jokes Andrew, might even be his most enduring claim to fame. He says, "Radiohead went to my old school, actually, Thommy Yorke and the boys. They all play. They're slightly younger than me, but I set up the bridge club in school, so it could well have been that it was still there when they were there. So maybe I sort of indirectly taught Radiohead."

All kidding aside, bridge in Britain is facing the same serious challenge that it is in the United States. The demographics of the game have changed—even at Andrew's club. Five years ago, standing before a class of twenty-five beginners, he would be the oldest in the room. Now, at forty-two, he's often one of the youngest. He blames, of course, poker.

Andrew says he has witnessed a parallel bridge boom that seems to be offsetting the loss, as early retirees begin to pick up the game. In fact, he believes overall participation might be on the rise. He says, "People are living to be a lot older, and all this research has come out about how playing bridge uniquely halts the slowing-down processes. So now you're getting all these early retiree couples in their fifties and sixties starting to play or improving their bridge. It's an explosion, in fact—and I think it's to be lauded."

Thus Robson remains confident about bridge. As of 2000, 1.2 million Britons played the game, making it only second to fishing among popular pastimes. By now, Andrew hopes bridge might be on top—though I'm not sure that's exactly the kind of endorsement that will cause ripples worldwide. England is notoriously wonky in its tastes. Bridge might be huge, but so are televised darts and sheepdog trials. Night after night, I was bowled over to turn on the set in my hotel—in a country that has famously few TV stations—and see *Murder, She Wrote* living on in heavy rotation. Just when I thought this might be a fluke, an endlessly cultured friend dropped the name Jessica Fletcher over lunch, making me nearly choke on my chow mein.

At Andrew's invitation, I decide to stick around and sit in on tonight's class, which starts at six forty-five. It's called "Next

Step," and Andrew says it is "basically one step up from beginner." He outlines his lesson plan: "It's a one-and-a-half-hour class. I'll probably lead them through some practical-based learning for about half the time, and then they'll play with some supervision for the second half. Then I'll encourage them to come out and play in the club afterward in our beginner game, so they can make a night of it if they want to."

With that, Andrew busies himself preparing for class. Students have started trickling in through the front door, stashing their coats and umbrellas before bellying up to the bar. By the time I get there, there is a bit of a queue. In front of me, two women make off with two glasses and a bottle of wine and head for the classroom. I get a beer and follow them, taking a seat at the back of the room. There is a large whiteboard in front, nearly a dozen paintings on the wall, and eight or so tables covered in red and green felt that already have filled up. The students greet each other with cheery chirps of "Hey, luv!" and "Helloooo!" They're mainly in their fashionable forties and fifties. A teenager in a black T-shirt walks in, but he doesn't stay long.

Andrew tells people, "Come and join us wherever you fancy," while a few students ask questions about Las Vegas. I have yet to single out his parents, but a man in a beige blazer hands him a tiny pink cotton shirt and announces, "Your nightie, sir." Andrew looks at me and says sotto voce, "Brother-in-law."

Class commences with a review of when to open one no-trump, which in the British bidding system is a much weaker bid showing only twelve to fourteen points. Andrew has his students lay two hands across the table from each other and go over the auction. I notice the cards bear the stamp "Andrew Robson Bridge Club."

With the review finished, Andrew launches into tonight's lesson, which is called "Finding Fits." True to his word, multi-colored handouts begin circulating the room. Soon he has the group caught up in the familiar call and response of the spirited bridge evangelist.

Andrew: "Look at the hand. Do we have enough points for game?"

Crowd (weakly): "Yes . . ."

Andrew (unsatisfied): "Yes?"

Hallelujah (with vigor): "Yes!"

Andrew's explanations are clear and his examples are simple, though he refrains from batting down wrong answers with the iron fist of bridge "rules." He's like the cool dad who knows when to treat his teen like a grown-up; he's firm in his pronouncements ("two hearts is *the* bid!") but leaves a little room for wiggling—and admits things won't always be so simple. After the bidding, he goes over the play, demonstrating whether the contract will make. He's friendly, funny, and engaging, often getting a little excited over the lesson himself ("My partner is going to love this queen!"). He gives the group a few hands to bid on their own while he wanders the room, watching, talking, and dipping his tall frame to toy with the cards on the table.

From my smug seat, I can't help but marvel at this flock of beginners. Oh, for Tina and a few friendly hours of rubber—we could have cleaned out the lot. That's why it's amazing to see one of Britain's bridge greats, a man capable of unraveling treacherous tangles of logic, lean over again and again to explain—with patience and humor—how to count up to twelve. Forget the trials of a three-day tournament—how many top pros could last three minutes in this room?

Suddenly I'm no longer safe at the back of the class. It's time to play, and I'm approached by a young instructor named Richard, who carries a glass of red wine. He asks me to fill in at a table that's short a player, which is how I come to meet Francesca, a blonde twenty-something in a salmon cashmere sweater and a colorful scarf. She apologizes up front for any mistakes she might make; she came late to class and, as she sips her white wine, claims she's still in "work mode." Francesca says she enjoys the lessons, which she received as a gift from her "mum," but her progress has been stifled somewhat by the fact that she keeps skipping class and "going out drinking."

We are matched against a pair in their thirties whose names I don't catch: Monica, as I'll call her, and her new acquaintance of the evening, Fred. I tried to pay close attention to the lesson, but I'm worried about bidding in the unfamiliar British system known as Acol (named for the road on which it was developed). One no-trump isn't the only bid that's different. Here, opening a suit on the two level (i.e., beginning at two hearts) shows a strong hand with plenty of potential to make tricks, whereas in New York that bid would be preemptive and weak (but promising plenty of hearts).

Somehow I manage to muddle through, perhaps partly because the game is so relaxed. In fact, my Manhattan-honed playing posture—crouched over the cards, brow furiously furrowed—is laughably out of place under the warm lights here. I'm sitting like some psychotic, a killjoy counting cards, while Fred is blithely trumping tricks he has already won, gladly on his way to going down in two diamonds. Indeed, Francesca and I set him pretty terribly, but Fred is more interested in Monica, the woman across the table, whom he asks if she plans to stick around for supervised play. When class is over, I see them take seats opposite each other in the game in the big room. It occurs to me that in New York bridge clubs the drink of choice overwhelmingly is coffee, while here it's wine, which perhaps explains why we're jittery and they're getting married.

At the end of class, Fred and Monica aren't the only ones who decide to make a night of it. One jolly old chap with a nose that almost matches the purple of his sweater corrals a gaggle of women into seats at a table. A thirty-something in a spangly pink top makes it all the way to the front door but then doubles back, preferring the warm and dry club to the soft spring drizzle that's now falling outside. There are about twelve tables already full at the front of the room, and again the bar is hopping, as players mix and mingle on the way to their seats. On one side of the room a lovely buffet is being set up for the supervised players: grilled chicken, avocado salad, potatoes, and such, with white plates and silverware stacked at the ready.

As the rest of Robson's students scatter out into the night, they bid him farewell and wish him luck in Verona. Stopping at the door, one lady calls back, "Do us proud, Andrew, do us proud," as the would-be world champ moves methodically around the room, gathering empty glasses and getting ready for the next class.

At perhaps the opposite end of the spectrum from the friendly and forgiving Andrew Robson Bridge Club is TGR's, the London club known these days as the place for rubber bridge. Susanna Gross, the literary editor of *The Mail on Sunday* and bridge columnist for *The Spectator* magazine, says, "I'm scared of almost everybody at TGR's. At its best, it's the most exciting club in the world. But we behave like children in a playground. I've had rows, terrible rows, and I've witnessed terrible things. Tempers flare up. Punches have been thrown among the men, and among the women there's the screaming, the tears, the insults. I've seen tables overthrown. Rubber bridge is a different game than tournament bridge. Most of the top bridge players don't play for money, by the way. They either don't have the money or they don't have the balls. And you need balls to play rubber bridge—you really need them."

I'm enjoying this ball-busting bravado from Susanna, who, at thirty-seven, has fair skin, a ponytail, and is visibly pregnant. We are meeting in the lobby coffee shop of her newspaper's Kensington office, where an unfailingly polite security guard has taken a scrunched-faced photo of me and printed it askew on an ID badge that misspells my name. I feel a little self-conscious because the picture is so bad it looks like I was mugging on purpose. Susanna talks very fast and today she's somewhat frazzled; the woman at the counter kindly suggests a decaf cappuccino. Susanna and her husband have been house hunting, with poor results so far, and this afternoon they expect to hear whether the bid they made on a property was accepted. They would like to be settled before the baby boy arrives in September.

When it comes to London bridge, it seems all roads lead to Susanna. I have heard of her from a number of people on both sides of the Atlantic, all of whom say she's plugged into the scene.

Susanna has promised to take me to TGR's to witness the afternoon game. Like everyone else in London, Susanna seems smitten with her club. She tells me, "At TGR's, you get all the great players. You're making high-level decisions and gambling for money; your heart pitter-patters, and your bladder is bursting because you can't bear to leave the table to go to the loo. There's so much adrenaline involved, you can get addicted to the rush—then life without bridge can seem terribly dull."

Susanna started playing bridge in university, when some friends needed a fourth. That started her down the slippery slope—call it a rake's progress—from social player to club punter. "I'm very competitive," she says, "and I've never minded what people are like in a bridge club. I would say in most clubs people are pretty awful. And yet I'd rather spend my time with awful people at the bridge table, because nonetheless we're united in our passion for bridge. Really, I can spend longer with them than I can with great friends I much prefer as people."

Despite her fervor, Susanna admits she is on the scene but not entirely of it. She might pal around and even play with top masters, but her game is not nearly as sophisticated as theirs. She says, "In my judgment, I'm a baby beginner—and I read bridge books in bed most nights! The people I play with are experts; they're in another league. It's a totally different game yet again. I'm a different player in theory than I am in practice. I read a lot, I know a lot, but I do idiotic things at the table. It's a bit like learning to drive a car in theory and then finding yourself driving down a high-speed motorway. You can't keep it all in your head at one time."

Because of bridge, Susanna lives something of a roller-coaster existence. She says, "I live and breathe this game. The rare occasions I do something clever, I'm buoyed up for weeks. And if something bad happens, I think about it in the middle of the night. I have to sort of do therapy on myself, make myself relive the moment until I stop squirming."

The attraction, as she sees it, is somewhat counterintuitive, a public exorcism of humiliation and pride. "For years my boyfriends were all grand masters. My pillow talk was, 'What would you bid with this hand? And what would you bid with that hand?' Bridge alone was enough to glue several relationships, because we could have endlessly fascinating conversations about bridge."

Lately, kicking the habit has become something of a concern, as Susanna recently got married—to a non-bridge player. She says, "When we started our relationship it was problematic, because I didn't see the point of not playing. He had this absurd idea that I'd want to spend some time with him on weekends. I was so used to playing every Saturday and Sunday that we used to argue about it. I couldn't accept I had to give up one of these days for the marriage. I said, 'What do you want to do—bloody walk in the park or go to a museum?' How boring. I could be gambling, you know, in a basement on a sunny afternoon."

I remember a column Susanna once wrote about a conversation she had over dinner with Bob Hamman. She was surprised to learn he couldn't tell her the year he got married or his manner of proposal, but he could recall hands—to the card—he held decades ago. These days Susanna seems all too aware of the romantic deficiencies of the bridge fanatic. She lets slip that she found time on her honeymoon to memorize forty pages of bridge notes in preparation for a tournament.

But the idea of cutting back on bridge is not what depresses Susanna. It's the thought of the game disappearing altogether. She says, "If bridge got phased out, I would feel as sad as I would if people stopped being interested in oil painting. It would be as if a certain type of music had just vanished."

She raises the specter of poker. "All the professional bridge players I know are either moving into poker or wish they had played poker," she says. "That's where the money is—and the skill is so much lower. As a game, bridge is much more evolved. The top poker players of today are probably equivalent to the top bridge players fifty years ago. It would be almost impossible now to catch up with the top bridge players in a short amount of time, but the top bridge players can catch up quite quickly with the top poker players."

But like Andrew Robson, she does not think all hope is lost. She hearkens back to the days of Ely Culbertson, when "a match between the Brits and the Americans was traffic-stopping excitement. All it would take is for, you know, Robbie Williams to start playing bridge fanatically. It would just take one cool public figure or film—or maybe even book!—to change that all around."

Part of her passion stems from the fact that in recent years the big game at TGR's has suffered a lull. In London, stakes are set at a certain number of pounds "per hundred"—meaning the difference in scores divided by one hundred, a figure that is then somewhat confusingly referred to as a "point." Thus if you thrashed your opponents one afternoon by three thousand on the score sheet, that would constitute a "thirty-point win." If you're playing £15 a point, you're walking off with £450.

Susanna says, "Seven or eight years ago, you'd have your little old ladies in the back room who'd been playing for a pound all their life, and then you have Bob Hamman, Zia Mahmood, and all the English internationals playing for one hundred pounds a point. And of course there would be all the people they needed to get their money from, the nonprofessionals, what you Americans call 'pigeons' and we Brits call 'bunnies.'"

Playing £100 a point is sizable stakes, making a rubber often worth well over £1,000. Now the big game at TGR's seems to hover between £30 and £50, and Susanna is at something of a loss to explain why.

As for Susanna, the big game was never her thing. Instead she has staked a place for herself at the £15 tables, where players usually win or lose a few hundred pounds in an afternoon. It took her a while to get to that level. She recalls, "I started off at a club called St. John's Wood, playing for twenty p and going out with the manager. And then the manager decamped to TGR's, and so I jumped ship. And I went up to two pounds, five pounds, and ten pounds, and now I've found my ceiling with fifteen pounds, which is an amount at which I'm not likely to win, but I'm not likely to lose too much, either."

That is the game we are off to go see. Susanna warns me that the club might be slow. Zia is out of town, as is the Swede Gunnar Hallberg, one of Zia's rubber-playing friends who won this year's Vanderbilt Cup. It's also the Friday of Bank Holiday weekend, and much of London's smart set has left town. For instance, Janet de Botton, who usually plays in the £15 game, won't be at the club. While Britain has far fewer bridge sponsors than the States, de Botton is one of the few multimillionaire die-hards willing to finance a pro team.

Before we can go to the club, Susanna asks if we can pop over to Marks & Spencer to pick up her supper. She apologizes profusely, but I'm happy to visit one of the upscale supermarkets where you can get things like precious little bags of perfectly diced organic cucumber bits to toss into your salad.

While we're wandering the store, Susanna shows me a hand that someone sent her from the Portland Club involving a pair that—because of a bad bid—missed a cold slam in hearts. It is to be the subject of her next column. Yesterday, when she mentioned the mishap over lunch to her friend Neil Mendoza, he got very red in the face. It turns out he was on the losing end of that deal, and he was chagrined that his sins were about to be made public. Looking at the note, I realize Neil had described the hand to me earlier, admitting, "It was very depressing."

As Susanna zips through the aisles assembling a prepared dinner, she keeps apologizing in advance for her friends at the club. She says, "At TGR's, everybody finds everybody so irritating." I begin to get a little nervous, and I ask if I will be allowed take notes. She says, "They shouldn't mind, but they are a superstitious lot—if they go down in a grand slam they might complain about you."

The most Susanna has won—and lost—in an afternoon is around £1,500 (about $2,800). The last time she was at the club, she decided to play one more round before leaving. In five minutes she had lost £370, which prompts her to look me in the eye and tell me in earnest, "Never play the last rubber of the day."

At TGR's, they play a popular style called Chicago, in which a rubber lasts for four hands. The score from each hand is tallied up, and vulnerability rotates around the table. Overtricks are not scored, which considerably livens the pace. Conventions are kept simple to ease the exchange of partners around the table— when a rubber is over, players cut for new teams. Gamblers have their own lingo, which I had tried to study on the plane over. According to a book on the big game at TGR's, wins and losses are measured in terms of "ponies" (£25), "monkeys" (£500), and "sticks" (£1,000)—though so far I have been too chicken to use any of these terms.

By now it's nearing four o'clock, and we're running late for the game. Susanna says in her more dedicated days she would play from two thirty to eight. When I raise an eyebrow, she says in spite of her two jobs—editor and columnist—"I really don't work very hard." Since she has been pregnant, however, she has lost some of her stamina, and today she really only wants to play for an hour and a half.

Groceries in hand, we hop into a black London cab and soon we're speeding along famous Hyde Park. I am no longer sure what to expect of TGR's. I had read it once held its annual trip at an English manor that a week before had hosted the G8 summit, so originally I had pictured a room full of painfully cool customers swilling martinis and playing for millions. Now after talking to Susanna I anticipate something more along the lines of a pro-wrestling ring.

The cab lets us off in front of an elegant white stone building that faces the park. The entrance, below street level, is marked by a wooden plaque that reads "TGR Bridge Club" next to a picture of a rose. TGR's official name is "The Great Rose," in honor of the club's original director, a beloved British star named Irving Rose, who died in 1996. As we step down the stairs and through the front door, it turns out that TGR's looks like . . . any other bridge club. With its red carpet, yellow walls, green lampshades, fringed felt-draped tables, well-cushioned wooden chairs, and the smell of something good wafting in from the kitchen, it's just another cozy card-players' hobbit hole, with nary a martini or spandex singlet in sight.

We have entered the front room, where the £15 game is already underway. There are three tables, one of which is in play. Two indifferent kibitzers, a man and a woman, sit at opposite corners of the room reading. A player greets Susanna with, "Hey, Floozy, you're in next." At each place at the table sits a bidding box and a small marble-topped pedestal for holding drinks and cell phones. There are two decks of cards—one red, one blue—with TGR's stamped on the back. At the end of the rubber, the person who cuts the high card not only chooses his or her chair, but which deck to use first. An unoccupied backgammon table stands off to the side. English hunt scenes and photos from black-tie club dinners hang haphazardly on the walls. It doesn't take long before the trash talking starts, as both men and women begin to tease Susanna about her weight. When she is offered a seat to watch the end of the rubber, she tells them, "Oh, I don't care to watch you lot," before explaining to me, "Bad habits, you know."

After a few minutes one of the players gets up to leave, and Susanna cuts into the game. She asks the group brightly, "Are we goulashing today?"

To play a "goulash"—or "ghoulie," as it is affectionately known—is a way of artificially upping the stakes on a hand. If the final contract does not exceed a rather humdrum one no-trump, the deal is scrapped, and players sort their hands into suits and pile their cards in the middle of the table. The unshuffled deck is then cut and redealt to each player in bunches of five, five, and three—thus stacking the odds that each person will get an unusual number of cards in the same suit. Such wonky distributions tend to be biddable to big contracts, which lead to dramatic results. Thus "goulashing" is insurance against an afternoon of what bridge players scornfully call "flat hands," when the cards tend to fall equally—and tediously—around the table. A goulash is the gambler's best friend, providing jerry-rigged excitement, volatility, and of course more money on the line. Bidding one is an art in itself. As Neil Mendoza told me, "In a goulash, you regularly end up in seven going down because the other person would have made five or six—and it's better to sacrifice. It changes the whole nature of the game. By pushing the bidding beyond the no-trump, you're saying the game is on. By keeping the bidding below one no-trump, you're encouraging a goulash, which encourages big swings."

Thus goulashing is a means of spinning low-scoring deals into gold, and it is one of the many ways the rubber game forgoes the precision of duplicate. Unfamiliar (or just plain poor) partnerships, less-scientific bidding, the luck of the draw, and the added pressure of playing for stakes all make for a messier—and some would say livelier—game. I am looking forward to an afternoon of studying this elusive (and endangered) bridge beast. In many ways, it's the antithesis of the game I've been learning to play. It's not about making the correct bid or percentage play based purely on cold logic. In all my classes, I have never once been instructed to study my opponents to decipher their "tells."

Furthermore, gone is the democratic comfort of duplicate, the constant consolation that if your side loses a big hand to your opponents, your real opponents—the other pairs sitting in your direction at the other tables—are having to make do with the same unfavorable cards. In rubber bridge, luck reenters the equation; no matter your skill, if you don't get good cards, you'll have a hard time making much money. On average, a good punter can win about three points an hour off less-skilled tablemates. In more evenly matched games, the proceeds are even less. Thus if you are going to make a living at rubber bridge, the odds favor playing for the highest stakes you can afford as often as you can.

But sometimes even the biggest games must be protected from predators. Zia, a man who remembers rubbers played for £300 or £400 a point, is one of the few players ever to be banned from the big game at TGR's. It wasn't for any impropriety, but simply because if left to his own devices he would empty even the deepest pockets in the club. When reminded of this, Zia frowned and told me, "It was very unfair." There was a time when the most he could play for was £50 a point, though now that the highest stakes have fallen to about that amount, he again enjoys free reign.

As Susanna predicted, the club is quiet today, with many players already on holiday. There is only one £15 table, as opposed to the usual three, and while the cards are dealt, the regulars take turns mocking people who are not there. We sip tea or soda, and Susanna says to me, "It's a shame Zia is not here. There'd be champagne for all!"

Susanna is the youngest at the table by at least a decade. She is playing with a big friendly forty- or fifty-something in glasses, a man whose gregariousness quickly shows itself to be a not-so-subtle form of goading. He seems to enjoy discussing the finer points of each hand—especially one he just won—and so for that I'll label him the Professor. Sitting next to him is a stylish Persian woman of a certain age—we'll call her Bangles, as she sports several shiny silver bracelets. She is partnered with the droll gray-haired Oldest Member, a man whose silk red shirt unbuttons surprisingly southward as the afternoon progresses, so that by nightfall it is nearly open to his navel.

The play gets off to a very quick pace. On the first hand, the Oldest Member claims nine tricks after two rounds of play, causing Susanna to mutter, "Bloody lucky." The next hand is no better; she half jokes, "I'm never playing this game again." While no one wears a tux or sips a martini, these people play their cards like cool cats. They sit back in their chairs and toss them into the ring with a discreet flick of the wrist, piling up the pasteboards with remarkable precision and no small amount of flair. It's a minor point, but they seem to fling the cards in one of three ways: one, the standard lazy lob, which gets the job done; two, with a high, early release that will send, say, an ace spinning in a somewhat pretentious parabola (rubbing it in); or, finally and most feisty, three, coming up low from beneath the table and skimming the card a hair above the felt so that it slides to a stop atop the neat center pile. In about ten minutes, the Oldest Member and Bangles have won the first rubber by ten points, putting them up by £150.

Susanna says she is distracted, worrying over that bid on the house. Her husband could call anytime with news, and, as she tells the group, "My baby needs a home." Susanna's husband has never met her club friends, and in the cab over she said she would have to introduce me right away before they got confused. Now seeing her with the group, I am surprised by this detail; this bunch clearly knows each other well—perhaps too well—like a big dysfunctional family. They make fun of the Oldest Member, who only knows how to turn off his cell phone by removing the battery; they say he's become "wimpy" in his old age. I am amused by the nonstop patter and the snatches of songs sung while others are thinking—clearly meant to annoy. They talk about their opponents as if they are no longer in the room ("I wonder why she did that?"). After a card is played, someone says, "So it's like that?"—only to receive the curt confirmation, "Could be."

Not all taunts are reserved for one's opponents. After one of his more philosophical postmortems, the Professor muses, "But I have to do with the partner I got," prompting Bangles to snap, "Oh, shut up." There is also an amusing interpartnership ritual that I've come to enjoy. After the auction, while one opponent ponders the opening lead, the dummy often offers to exchange hands with the declarer, just for a peek. This is considered a huge no-no in duplicate. Here the swap sometimes is accepted and sometimes not—and in the latter case usually with a little boast based on the bidding: "I know what you have."

Minor arguments erupt, like when the Professor goes down in three no-trump, and he complains to his partner about a bad bid. She fires right back, but the bickering stops in spite of itself the minute new cards hit the table. Everyone has a cell phone out, though the room complains in unison when one goes off. In general, the group seems to dispense with the usual pleasantries. The Oldest Member sneezes, and no one says, "Bless you." A woman enters the room with, "Hello, all!"—only to be ignored. Apparently yesterday someone accused an effectively blind man of peeping at her cards.

One older woman does gain the group's attention, but only for her trespass. She wanders in from a table in the hazy back room, a cigarette dangling from her lips, and the players are quick to point out that the front room is nonsmoking.

As play continues, the Professor exhibits some curious bidding behavior that I had observed at the Cavendish. When his turn comes in the auction, he begins to mouth a mute conversation with himself while making what I could only describe as one-handed orchestral motions—his wrist curling around and around—as he tilts his head to the side and stares into the felt. It's an oddly elegant tic, as if he's listening to the music of the cards as he runs through the bids. Meanwhile, he might slightly shake a leg or torque his torso, his full body in the game.

Another rubber is over, and this time Susanna wins by seven points, or £105. It ends with a goulash in which the bidding jumps from one spade to four hearts, only to end in five spades (down one). Despite her disclaimer, Susanna doesn't seem overly worried about the house. Periodically her phone bleeps to signal a message, making her glance over and silence it. I'm impressed by the number of bleeps going unheeded while she focuses on the game.

By now, I am experiencing serious time dilation, a phenomenon well known in bridge clubs. I'm surprised to find I've been here an hour. I've watched a good deal of hands, because—without overtricks—many are chucked in after the first card. (Sometimes only a good lead can stop a contract from making.) Susanna and the Oldest Member lose £15 on a rubber decided by only one point, after which she walks over to the window and returns one of her messages. It's someone from work with a question about a review. I hear Susanna say, "Listen, I'm in the middle of a thing. Can you deal with it yourself?"

Bangles orders white wine from the waitstaff, two young women wearing aprons. With half the glass under her belt, she begins to bid a little more boldly, jumping to a risky three no-trump against Susanna and the Professor—but making it in style. Soon the rubber is over, and Susanna has lost another £150. At that moment, she reads a message off her still-bleeping phone, and says to the group in a tone that's part explanation and part need for affirmation, "We just won the bid for the house, and my husband's jumping off the walls to celebrate—and I can't take his calls because I'm at bridge." Finally a few hands later, when she becomes the dummy, Susanna steps outside to call her husband back.

When the rubber is over, the girls have won £30 off the boys. The Oldest Member orders a fruit salad, and Susanna starts cracking jokes, surely relieved about the house. At this point the game's only other kibitzer, a smartly dressed woman in white, sneezes for the umpteenth time today. As with all the others, this sneeze goes unnoticed.

The mood in the room lifts for a while, but then Susanna finds herself playing in five clubs doubled, after some overbidding by the Oldest Member. She plays it beautifully, however, and makes the contract—causing Bangles to snap at the Professor, who she feels made a poor lead. I notice whenever the

Professor loses a hand, he is quick to silence the table talk with a businesslike, "Okay, next case."

At six, some of the afternoon games in the back begin breaking up. At our table, I have noticed the players keeping track of their wins and losses on a long white heavy-stock scorecard. At the front of the club hangs a small wooden house about the size of a mailbox. Players slip their cards into it on their way out the door, briefly gathering to discuss plans for the long weekend, which for many seem to involve being back at the club. A man asks a woman, "See you tomorrow?" and she answers coyly, "Oh, you never can tell."

The Oldest Member seems cranky, and he and Bangles get into a row over bidding, having lost a rubber by a point. When he finally drops the matter, she takes out her ire on a drowsy kibitzer who has slipped unnoticed into a seat by the backgammon table. After barking him awake, she tells me, "He never plays—he just sleeps in that chair and brings me bad luck." Perhaps to reverse her fortune, Bangles buys the room a drink, and I remind myself it's probably not wise to peep at a drinking woman's cards.

What wine she has had and will have—as one more becomes a few—certainly hasn't affected her game. After one hand, the Oldest Member tells her she "played it like Paganini," which needles the Professor, so the Oldest Member keeps saying it.

And so the game goes on well into the night, as Susanna stays long past her allotted hour and a half. It grows later and later, and somewhere in London my wife goes hungry waiting for me. After my time in Las Vegas, this feels very familiar, as hand follows hand, and last drinks pile up. When new cards are dealt, four palms hit the table, fingers splayed like spiders doing push-ups, greedily gathering their cards into a pile. It's hard not to think of those little old ladies playing predawn slots at the Tropicana, with each pull half-holding their breath to hear sirens going off. In the bridge club, when luck strikes it comes as thirteen huge cards, a lay-down slam or the like, but the ritual compulsions seem one and the same.

Bangles and the Oldest Member appear to be getting the run of the cards, and after one £330 loss, Susanna takes time out to compliment herself on being a gracious loser. She sighs and says, "After the bid we made on this house, it's all a drop in the bucket." At the end of the night, Susanna will sum up the session as "a quiet day with some of the nicer players," who, she assures me, "were on their best behavior." Her remarks will seem all the more charitable knowing she has finished down some £700—roughly $1,300. Standing outside, she'll say, "Well, you sure are expensive," and manage a smile.

But for now it still seems Susanna has a chance, as the girls are in for six spades, and there's a shot it will make. Unfortunately Bangles has miscounted her suit, and after a trick or two the Oldest Member breaks the bad news. He holds the ace and a queen, and the girls are going down one. Thus the evening wears on. The same jokes are made over and over, repeated by rote, more of a comfortable habit than an attempt at good humor ("Don't worry, I'll lead your suit next week.").

Everyone but Susanna orders another glass of wine. The rubbers fly by. Players win £45, £60, £120 off each other. At one point the Oldest Member gets stuck in a tough four-heart contract. Pondering his cards, he says, "If I had any sense, I'd go home," and then he plays on into the night.

CHAPTER THIRTEEN

East Side Story

Gail Greenberg tells me, "I've always lived in the City—born and bred." The capital C that comes through clearly in her voice broadcasts Greenberg's hometown louder than her soft accent, because only for New Yorkers is there just one city worth mentioning. We are sitting on Manhattan's Upper East Side in an empty classroom in Greenberg's club, Honors, which is the largest bridge club in the country.

Greenberg is something of a legend. She is a five-time world champion who has not missed a national tournament since 1964. When reminded of that, she says, "Other people might have had some reason for missing a national now and then, but not me." She is a Grand Life Master, which means she has more than ten thousand master points. She has raised her daughter and two sons to be experts. Greenberg herself didn't pick up the game until her teens, when she walked into—what else—a national tournament in 1956.

New York is a bridge town. The city has a handful of public clubs, ranging from the Culbertson, a small-time neighborhood club in Greenwich Village (whose Web site boasts more pictures of babies than bridge), to the competitive East Eighty-seventh Street club run by bridge star Bjorn Fallenius and his wife, Kathy, that by agreement uses the historic Cavendish name. The Manhattan Bridge Club reigns on the West Side, while the Regency quietly goes about its business half a block east of the park.

And then there is Honors, which many Manhattan bridge fanatics discuss the same way as one would the Death Star, with a mix of fear and awe. The club is a behemoth, every year recording the highest table count in the country. On a typical day, Honors will host more than 225 players, many of whom play five times a week. In 1999, the *New York Times* reported the club had 19,600 tables in play—or more than fifty-three a day, if Honors were open all 365 days—making it the second-largest club in the world, after one in Stockholm.

Running a New York club is a competitive business, and in many ways Honors sets the bar. The food goes beyond the usual tuna and egg salads, and a few nights a week the club offers a hot dinner of chicken l'orange, pot roast, pasta, pierogies, roasted new potatoes, and such. The club has a TV lounge, a library, a soft-serve yogurt machine, and gift shop. Honors was founded in a townhouse in 1993 with the intention to be a cut above the dingier clubs.

As the little club grew, it moved to a building on East Fifty-seventh Street—right across the street from what was then the country's largest bridge club, the Beverly, which had been struggling in the two years since its venerable owner, Jim Becker, passed away. It was a bold move and set off something of a scandal. The newspapers cried feud and reported the beginning of a bridge club death match, with both businesses offering freebies and cutting prices to keep bodies in the seats. Making matters more awkward, the proprietors of the Beverly asked a good friend of the former owner to step in to help revive business. That friend happened to be Bob Blanchard, who at the time was going through a divorce with Gail Greenberg's daughter. Bob remembers, "That was a scene and a half. We could look into each other's windows!" Two years later, the Beverly moved to a location on Central Park South, before folding itself into the Manhattan Bridge Club in 2000.

Explaining how club owners do business, Zeus tells me, "You need to remember that all the people who own the clubs play games—and they play to win." Indeed, many owners feel the pressure of trying to keep pace with Greenberg; it is a constant game of one-upmanship. When Honors began offering wine on Friday night, it sent ripples through the club world. As Zeus says, "If one club puts out a spread, we all have to keep up—it's hard." As if to prove his point, later in the summer the Culbertson closes its doors, leaving downtown Manhattan without a club of its own.

Greenberg tells me, "I can't imagine the clubs not being competitive. But I'm not on bad terms with any of the owners. Obviously, I'm happy when people come here rather than there, but I wouldn't say there is any bad blood."

New York is unique in its ability to support a number of big clubs, but Greenberg claims even a giant like Honors seldom breaks even at the end of the year. The rent is astronomical, and the card fees can only go so high. She praises her partners, who don't look on the venture as a business investment, but as something that profits the city's bridge players.

For years Honors was in the Galleria high-rise on East Fifty-seventh Street. Over the summer of 2006, it moved one block up to East Fifty-eighth. Greenberg has taken on two new partners, Claire Alpert and Scott Levine. I meet her at the new building, where—despite ongoing renovations—games and classes are underway. I ask when work will be completed and Greenberg laughs. "The way it's going, it'll be when I'm in a wheelchair and unable to appreciate it."

I have caught Greenberg between her morning class and the afternoon duplicate. When I arrive, she is busy saying good-bye to her students and taking phone calls. She is a bit of a rock star, and players hover reverentially around her, waiting to put questions to the master. I hear her tell one supplicant, "I tend to lead very aggressively against low-level contracts," before she brushes him away and sits down with me.

I ask if there is a similarity between running a club and playing winning bridge. She thinks for a moment. "No, I don't think so. I think somebody with a good business sense might have done better than I did." It seems a funny thing to hear from the club owner with the best attendance in the country. "All I can say is that for many years, when I was busy going to all of the major events and playing in the world championships, that was my primary focus. When I decided not to play nearly as much, I needed a new challenge. I'm not the type of person who wants to sit in a rocking chair. So the new challenge became playing to some extent, teaching—as I've been doing for the last thirty years—and operating a club." Obviously it is a direction she has enjoyed. In 2000, she started a club with her sister in Westchester, New York. It, too, is booming.

As we are forced to move out of the classroom to make room for an overflow of duplicate players, I ask Greenberg if she is concerned about the future. I know a Scrabble group meets at Honors, and lately the club has been offering poker lessons. She says, "I'm not worried. Other games might be more trendy, but bridge is everlasting."

It takes me a while to get up the nerve to play at Honors. When in town, I have been playing with Tina as much as I can, usually twice a week at the Manhattan Bridge Club for three to four hours. She calls more frequently, leaving messages that begin, "Edward, this is Tina—bridge," before launching into her reason for calling, usually to confirm a game. In general, however, I have to call her. Tina is almost pathologically afraid of intruding. Whether we play is up to my schedule, because she says, "You have a life. You know us little old ladies, we're just marking time." The irony, of course, is that she keeps busier than I do.

We have improved a lot, though our defense still could use work. Tina has a bad habit of leading aces that are best saved for later, and sometimes I try to do something too clever by half. I am always eager to show off whatever skills I've picked up on the road, even if it's just a new way to flick the cards. We are toughening up. One opponent tells me, "Tina is so quiet and gentle, but when she pounces it hurts!"

Tina is a practical gal. Some days she arrives carrying empty grocery bags because her favorite store in the neighborhood is having a sale on spinach; on others she's off to buy a bottle of wine she read about in the *Wall Street Journal.* One afternoon she is picking up a friend from the hospital. When I say that's nice of her, she says, "Well, one hand washes the other." I wonder if she has any family in town. She remains reluctant to talk about herself, though once when I mention I play soccer on weekends, she tells me about the team at her grammar school in New Jersey. "Everyone was very poor," she says, and when the ball wore out they had a social to raise money for a new one. "It was the Depression," she says, "and it was very depressed."

While Tina still goes to Tommy's class—and we see Ranko and Kathy on weekends—we decide to make a foray to Honors to test the waters. On Wednesday mornings they hold a short "duplicate and discussion" game that begins with a lesson and ends with a review of the hands.

Tina has already taken a lesson with Gail Greenberg, after which she came back bursting with news. The women at Honors fascinate her, she says. They wear sable coats and give away pairs of $500 shoes. One woman told her she had never done laundry in her life, which prompted her partner to tell everyone she received a live-in maid as a wedding present. In general, Tina is a reporter's best friend, always asking politely probing questions in the most charming manner. She's so genuinely interested she always gets an answer, despite that, as she admits, she can be somewhat nosy.

The first time I visit Honors it is still at its old address in the Galleria. It is on the same street as the Manhattan Bridge Club but on the other side of town, and the contrast between the clubs is as simple as that between the Upper East and Upper West sides, at the feet of which the two clubs stand. The Upper West Side is lovely, but on the Upper East even the subway musicians dress up for work. In the coming months, as I exit the station at Sixty-third and Lexington, I will see what looks to be a well-shod soccer dad playing classical violin for coins. He wears imported leather shoes, dress pants with a nice belt, and a sweater with a small logo; he looks like he put his hedge fund on hold for the day and popped down from Darien.

Bright and early one Wednesday I meet Tina at Honors. The night before I dreamed of bridge, either the result of nerves or too many late-night bouts against my computerized nemesis, the Bridge Baron. When I see her outside the club, Tina is in something of a state. She says she has something to tell me, but she doesn't have the words to say it in English. She blurts out a sentence in Italian and asks me if I understand. I don't speak Italian. Basically, she's worried she's going to "reflect badly on me," a laughable concept I try to assure her. I remind her it's just a game, but Tina won't listen. As we walk through the door, she says, "I hope I don't disgrace you." So much for her confidence.

On the sixth floor, in a room with wallpaper stenciled with spades, hearts, diamonds, and clubs, Tina and I sit down at a table. The East-West seats are in high demand, because those pairs don't have to keep score. We hold firm as latecomer after latecomer asks if we want to switch. "We're all guppies," confides one woman, though they don't look like guppies to me. When I walk in, an older woman with frighteningly plump lips and long heavy earrings—whose face must be the masterwork of a platoon of plastic surgeons—says voraciously, "Oh, our first gentleman." When she learns I'm a writer, she says, "You're not doing an exposé on all of us ladies sitting here instead of working, are you?" There is an uncomfortable silence.

The classroom holds seven tables of players, plus a sidebar of coffee and tea. Here we use real cups and saucers. The windows look out across the atrium onto the club's main room. Our teacher, Joe Byrnes, gives a lesson on defensive signals—how to tell your partner your attitude, count, and suit preference by playing certain cards. Joe is a pleasant "punny" guy who barks out the lesson in a friendly New York accent. When giving an example, he asks us to name our favorite suit. A woman in back shouts, "Diamonds!" and everybody laughs.

One of our first opponents is an elderly woman in a blazer and a big red hat. It's unclear whether she is a member of the Red Hat Society or just fashion forward. She reveals she gets up every morning and does "thirty minutes of Denise Austin" before walking to the club. Her chatting relaxes Tina, and we play three pretty good hands.

At the next table we face two gum-chomping socialites, one of whom carries a big rhinestone purse and sports high boots with multicolored laces. After playing two similar contracts in a row, I tell the table I am growing sick of diamonds. As if she thought it up herself, Shoelace chirps, "I'm never sick of diamonds!"

Two ladies draped head to toe in pink warn us never to come Thursday morning. "That's when the barracudas come out," one of them says. "They're dressed to the nines and play six days a week. They sit down and don't even say hello. For these ladies, bridge is their life." On a recent Thursday, one of the Pink Ladies brought a hard-of-hearing partner. She says the opponents took advantage of her friend and stole an extra trick. "Oh, they're terrible," the other one says.

All this talk of barracudas and guppies reminds me of reading groups in grade school, when we were divided into—no joke—sharks and minnows based on our ability to follow along with Dick and Jane. It occurs to me that perhaps bridge is the revenge of those more mathematically inclined minnows.

On closer inspection, the difference between Honors and the Manhattan Bridge Club can be summed up in two words: purses and perfume. Here the handbags that slump over the side tables are a luxurious lot: Birkin bags, Prada purses, and totes by Louis Vuitton, plus various more hip but no less expensive downtown models with dyed hides stretched into unnatural shapes. As for the perfumes, I feel like I'm choking in the garden of olfactory delights. With each new opponent comes a brave new scent— exotic, distinct, and beyond a doubt rich.

After the game is over, Joe passes out diagrams of six of the hands and explains how to defend them. When he is finished, we check out our score. I thought we might have done well, as we nailed the hands Joe covered in the lesson, but I never dreamed we would come in first in our flight. We are pleased with ourselves and our new .2 of a master point. Tina says, "I'm going to wear those points on my chest!" After someone makes the third—and final—joke about how much they love diamonds, we break for lunch.

Lunch is included in the $10 card fee, which is cheap given that a regular lesson at Honors costs $25. As Joe collects the money, one of the women says, "This is the best deal in town." "Hush!" says someone at another table. "They'll hear you and raise the rates." I doubt they will do so—this is no accident. It's a savvy move on Gail's part to cultivate a crop of beginners.

As I expected, lunch is somewhat more refined. There are the usual salads and sandwiches, plus real plates, free soft drinks, and a bowl of red Jell-O. We eat in the main room, which is beginning to fill up in anticipation of the afternoon game. As we navigate the buffet, I overhear two men talking behind me: "I said I'm not going to give you ten thousand dollars without a presentation."

We find a table toward the back. The cool kids, I notice, seem to take the seats by the window. In a minute, Red Hat and her partner ask to join us for lunch. They are old hands at "duplicate and discussion," but they didn't enjoy it today; they thought some people were "pushy." It turns out Red Hat was the admissions director of a swank private school. Her granddaughter is about to marry into a prominent political family. She and her partner become our usual lunch buddies.

Despite minor moments of angst—such as what Tina calls our "coatroom shame," when I have to hang our jackets in a sea of cashmere and fur—we enjoy our morning games. We also accumulate fractions of master points.

Honors is a comfortable club, with *Saturday Evening Post* covers and trophies along the halls, and Tina continues to find the people of anthropological interest. When we sign in, she nods at the Park and Fifth Avenue addresses, and one day we both get our first glimpse of a black AmEx card. As summer nears, it is not unusual to hear people discussing their plans: "Where are you going this year?" "A month's safari in Tanzania." "Oh, that sounds nice. Maybe we'll do that next year."

Honors remains the kind of place where you can sit down with strangers and be treated to a lunch-long discussion of the lineage, profession, and real estate holdings of various Rockefellers, living and dead. That is not to say every conversation is civil. One guppy tells us someone threw a pencil at her and accused her partner of cheating. A day later the two of them remain scandalized.

One morning, playing against a socialite mother-and-daughter pair, I hear the younger thirty-something sneer, ludicrously, "Two no-trump is for *peasants*. I always bid three." I give praise to the swift and severe gods of bridge justice when we set them by one, but I'm not sure the lesson sinks in. Other than this woman, I am the only player who's not over the hill. One kind grandmother tells me, "I always remember your name, because you're the only young man in the room."

When we're not lunching with Red Hat, we meet some interesting people. One day we share a table with a woman and her bridge pro. He is an Israeli national champion looking for his first U.S. title. His client, who is paying to play with him this afternoon, is a product of Honors. She began in the beginner classes, and while she has only been playing four years, she says she can't do anything halfway. She estimates between fifteen and twenty players in the afternoon game will be competing with a hired gun. Usually, she says, that works well for everyone. If there is time, the pro might give a short lesson at the table, even explain to the opponents where they went wrong. She thinks that's great, though not everyone agrees. She says, "Some people don't let their pros talk at all."

Despite his client's enthusiasm, the Israeli champ doesn't look like he has much to say. He keeps his iPod on the table and leaves one earbud in. The other dangles precariously close to his cottage cheese. Only when prompted by her does he mumble at us newbies. Otherwise, he stirs his food and looks bored. In a few days the two of them are off to a week-long tournament.

Tina is now playing four times a week. When I miss a class, she brings me a photocopy of the handout. We continue to split time between Honors and the Manhattan Bridge Club, despite the fact that after Honors relocates to Fifty-eighth Street it stops serving lunch. The new building doesn't seem as nice as the old one, though the elevators are faster, and the instructors promise that once the fourteenth floor is finished we'll be in for a treat.

I'm not sure how long I can wait. The people in our class at Honors begin to drive me crazy. I used to think it charming to watch them vie for the teacher's attention; few of them like to be out of the spotlight for long. But in time it grows tiresome to have to listen to pointless recaps of how the hand played out at their table, even though it has no relevance whatsoever to the lesson. They find everything they do endlessly interesting. Worst of all, the group is growing incredibly snippy—myself included, obviously—which makes for an unpleasant morning. Our class-mates seize on each other's mistakes—even minor ones, like making an insufficient bid (say bidding only one club over one no-trump, when it's obvious the person meant to bid two)—and they treat every infraction like a personal affront. A simple apology is never enough. They can be insufferably rude to Tina, who gets flustered when she's nervous. It's maddeningly unfair. They cannot abide the errors of others, yet they seem to have no problem making plenty of their own. I feel myself sinking to their level. Telling myself it is in Tina's defense, I become an insufferable know-it-all. When a particularly rude woman fails to follow suit, I relish the chance to put her in line. And so Tina and I find ourselves migrating back to the more mellow Man-hattan Bridge Club, where Tina tells stories about the woman who has two full-time live-in nannies, one for each child.

CHAPTER FOURTEEN

The Battles of Gettysburg

Gettysburg, Pennsylvania, July 2006
Gettysburg is a quaint and charming south-central Pennsylvania town with a population that hovers around 7,500, though locals note that without the 2,500 college students who tend to keep to the northwest quadrant of town, it really is a much smaller place. Of course Gettysburg also happens to have been the site of the bloodiest battle of the Civil War, a three-day conflict that left some 51,000 Confederate and Union soldiers dead, wounded, or missing. And that brings tourists.

But once you get past the abundance of minivans, out-of-state license plates, and grimly determined sightseers lugging books and sweaty kids, Gettysburg is something else altogether. Walking the town square at dusk, when the Civil War reenactors begin to blend with the ghost tours—which now number in the double digits—it becomes hard to tell if someone's costume is supposed to be historical, spooky, or just plain weird. Squint your eyes and what you see might surprise you: a 100 percent genuine American small town.

What does all this have to do with bridge? Gettysburg is the kind of place where people sit on the side porch and watch fireflies rise up from the lawn like green fire. They eat local sweet corn in summer and apples in the fall. They put on carnivals with fried foods and 4-H contests. They hold fairs where they exhibit old-timey farm machines, bob for apples, and win goldfish by plopping Ping-Pong balls into fishbowls—and enact count-less other wonderful homespun clichés. It is beautiful country, and the great tourist magnet that rings Gettysburg—the battle-field national park—has in fact preserved some of its small-town charm, as it has limited the amount of physical expansion that can take place. Gettysburg seems to be one of the few places in Amer-ica where they are tearing down car dealerships because they're unattractive when viewed from a historically significant ridge.

So it seems reasonable to come here looking for a vestige of the quintessential quaint bridge game—the game as it has been played socially between husband and wives, among a ladies' club, or at the local Y for years and years and years. I am curious to see whether community bridge has suffered the aches and pains of the national game's decline, whether modernity has intruded on my small-town stereotype.

Of course, I am incredibly biased: Gettysburg was the scene of many a childhood summertime idyll. My grandmother lived and played bridge there, and the drawers of her house are still filled with all kinds of curious bridge knickknacks: bidding book-lets, scoring pads, and countless decks of colorful cards—some monogrammed, others in Art Deco boxes, and still others from old airlines and country clubs. I know that sounds like a pretty weak link, but in the end, despite all the hand-wringing and propaganda to the contrary, if you're writing a book about pop-ular bridge in America, you're writing about grandparents. The aging of the bridge population is an inescapable fact. But—as Jeff Bayone pointed out to me when I started this journey—not because the game is inherently suited to the retirement crowd, but because they belong to the generation that learned to play when both they and bridge were young and in something of their heyday. Thus for every young hotshot wanting to turn pro, or every crafty punter hustling in a rubber bridge club, or every master-point-mad neurotic playing duplicate seven days a week, there is an older person playing the game they got hooked on decades ago, a game they picked up with the idea that they would always have something to do with another couple, or pass the time on a train, or keep them up late during college.

In my research for this book, I frequently have been mistaken for someone else's grandson. And for every old man at the club who tells me it's been nice to sit for a spell with a young person, for every afternoon whiled away at the table playing with another person's grandparent—I can't help but feel a pang of guilt and wonder who is playing with mine. My father's parents—my Gettysburg grandparents—are gone (though their house remains in the family), and my mother's parents never played bridge, but I can't escape the feeling that somehow they all figure into the story.

And so it seems "fitting and proper," to borrow a phrase from President Lincoln, to come to Gettysburg. Even more so on this of all weekends, the Fourth of July, when the nation supposedly sets aside its squabbles and unites under the banner of barbecue, firecrackers, and patriotic parades, a holiday itself that harkens back to small-town ideals. Thus with the corn, as they say, "knee-high by the Fourth of July," I took a short detour to see what bridge in Gettysburg is really all about.

In the life of a small town, there are small scandals and big ones. Independence Day coincides with the anniversary of the battle, which raged the first three days in July, and this week everyone is talking about the postponement of this year's reenactment. Recent heavy rains have prematurely washed out the celebration, called "Three Days of Destiny," to be held on a farm just north of town. The event's organizers have rescheduled for the following weekend, which also happens to be "Bike Week." Thus three thousand impeccably costumed Civil War nuts (and the attendant eight thousand spectators a day) are set to collide with twenty thousand motorcycle maniacs about to descend on the borough. People are predicting something of a perfect storm, and everyone is upset at the poor timing: townspeople, reenactors, bikers, and beleaguered hotel managers, who now face one impossibly overbooked weekend instead of two consecutive sellouts. Later in the week, I'll see a house with a sign in the window offering rooms to rent.

The major town crisis has been occupying headlines for more than a year. It centers on the proposal to build a casino in Gettysburg. After Pennsylvania passed a law that would allow for slot machines to be installed in parts of the state—mainly at racetracks, but also in a handful of newly built casinos—an investment group petitioned to build a slots parlor just outside Gettysburg. The $300 million casino resort would boast three thousand slots and a thirty-thousand-square-foot spa. A local wealthy philanthropist—and owner of the Harley-Davidson dealership—is now leading the charge.

Slots are seemingly the small potatoes of gambling (all those cute bells and whistles—they're like video games for adults!), until you learn that Americans feed five times as much money into one-armed bandits as they spend to go to the movies. Thus the casino is big business, and it has sparked a big battle for Gettysburg. There are Web sites and counter Web sites, rallies and meetings; the articles and editorials have progressed beyond the *Gettysburg Times* to the *New York Times* and the *Washington Post*. All over town, yard signs have cropped up, both No and Pro casino. There have been reports of both sides swiping signs. Gambling in Gettysburg has hardly aroused such complicated feelings since Civil War soldiers buried their playing cards before stepping onto the field.

Over the phone, Mrs. Jean Hartman tells me, "In this town, if you want a social life, you need to join a church and you need to join a bridge club." During her eighty-three years, she has belonged to many clubs, past and present, and we are trying to find a time to talk. Sundays are no good, as she has church in the morning and dinner at her son's house, but she believes, "Monday might suit." She then gives me directions to what she calls the "downsized apartment in which I'm living quite contentedly," a litany of local landmarks made slightly irrelevant by the existence of online driving directions—which, to be fair, never would have ended with "the one with the rocker on the porch."

Come Monday afternoon, on a short block off one of the old roads leading out of town—roads simply known by the name of the next burg they lead to—I pull up to a white-columned red-brick building with candles in the windows and, indeed, that solitary seat.

Mrs. Hartman's apartment is the one with the wreath on the door. When I walk in, she greets me with the apology, "I'm sorry my hands are cold—I've been washing strawberries." And there, on the dining room table, arranged on a tiny plate, are four plump berries in danger of being lost amid a bountiful spread: cheese and crackers, sliced apple, cashews, mints, and cookies of all kinds daintily displayed, including some in a fancy tin, about which she says, "Those are sugar cookies I only give to my special people."

She wears cream-colored pants, a white floral-print blouse, and a necklace of pink stones; she has a warm face, white hair, and glasses. After we fill our blue china teacups and pile our plates with goodies from the table, we move to the living room, where she settles into an armchair and says, "Now watch this." She claps her hands twice, and the lamp behind her springs to life. She gives me a big grin. There is a writing desk at the window, with a white wool shawl draped over the chair, and many pictures in frames—one here of a great-grandchild, another there in old black-and-white. I sink into a floral-print chair, and we pass a pleasant afternoon over the soft ticktocks of various clocks.

She moved here in 1949 with her husband, who was fresh out of law school after three and a half years in the Army. She raised two boys in Gettysburg and taught elementary school for fifteen years. At the end of our conversation, Mrs. Hartman will pass me a sheaf of paper, eight single-spaced pages of notes written up in a teacher's neat cursive, which she calls her "bridge reminiscences." I quote from them here:

"My husband played cards—bridge, poker, etc.—in college. I learned when we were first married, being 'taught' by other already seasoned players. I cried a lot! That was 1943.

"When we came to Gettysburg, we came to my husband's hometown. It wasn't that I found Gettysburg unfriendly, but bridge was a way to get to know the community. My husband had a lot of relatives who were older and played hearts and pinochle, but several of his high school classmates (gals) were kind enough to take me under their wing. I 'subbed' in their bridge clubs willingly. I was getting to know young people.

"In the war years, wives had formed sewing circles. Bridge clubs were an extension. Bridge became a social experience. Parties were hosted in the ballroom of the Gettysburg Hotel. It was special to be invited as a young lawyer's wife—new—and also quite intimidating. We wore hats and gloves to many of the functions. The older more experienced ladies might even criticize your play out loud! It was, though, my very best way to learn to know the people in my husband's hometown. All ages taught me about the generations and the roots of the town."

She had grown up in Shippensburg, some thirty miles down the road, and met Gene, her husband, at a dance pavilion halfway between there and Gettysburg. It was August 1940, the summer after high school. Both were there with someone else. She knew his date, and the couples exchanged dances. A month later he knocked on her door at what was then called Shippensburg College. "I didn't recognize him at first," she says, "but soon we started dating, and that was that. We danced all our life."

In one corner of her apartment stands a memory table for her "dear sweet husband," who passed away six years ago. She points to a picture of him and says, "We were married fifty-six and a half years, and we went together for three and a half, so you do the math. That is my life." She recalls, "I didn't know many people when we moved here, but Gene was an active youth, president of his high school class and that kind of thing. So his friends became my friends, and I just loved that."

When her husband was stationed in Harrisburg, one of his Army buddies would come over once a week for an evening of cards and Mrs. Hartman's spaghetti, which was "about all we could afford." The three of them studied a bridge book lent by a friend. When I ask her why she persisted in learning the game—especially as the weak link in an already tricky threesome—she tells me, "I'm not a 'now' woman. I grew up in a home where my father was the last word, the king of the roost, a wonderful, wonderful person. That's the way I grew up. I won't say I'm subservient, and neither was my mother, but Father was the main person in the family. There was respect. And when I was married that's exactly the way I was. I would do anything for my husband. I was just that type of person; I just had that type of love. I don't mean to get weepy here, but if Gene was going to fish, I was going to learn to go fishing with him. If Gene was going to play golf, I would learn to play golf. And he wanted me to. He loved the competitiveness of bridge, poker, gin rummy, and I played all of them."

Anticipating a follow-up question, she adds, "I don't know that we can say out loud that bridge is more genteel than poker," though she does have an amusing story about that. Her husband used to have a regular poker game with his friends at a still-existing local restaurant. Mrs. Hartman says she sees all the poker on TV and thinks, "It sure is a different era." When her husband's group wanted to meet, they would run a notice in the town paper to alert the members—but when they first started the group, no one knew how to word the announcement. A lawyer and his buddies spending the afternoon playing cards might strike some as unsavory, and thus was born a certain "Literary and Walking Club" that periodically would announce it would be meeting that week.

Mrs. Hartman says, "If you asked ten people in Gettysburg if Jeannie Hartman takes bridge more serious than anybody in Gettysburg, they'd say, 'No . . . but she plays decently.' Which I do." Her brother-in-law was a man who took the game seriously, and she shows me a library of bridge books she fell heir to, the titles marching through the history of modern bridge theory: Culbertson's *Contract Bridge Self-Teacher* (with a picture of the teacher promising "All you need is this book and a pencil") next to an edition of *Goren's Bridge Complete* alongside a book called *Card Play Technique, Or the Art of Being Lucky.* Mrs. Hartman modestly points out, "I'm not saying I've really read all these entirely," though I notice some of the Culbertson drills are filled in.

While Mrs. Hartman reads a syndicated bridge column in the paper every day, I am reminded that for the most part small-town bridge exists beyond the standardizing influence of the ACBL. There are no sanctioned clubs, no master points, no one reading the *Bridge Bulletin.* In such places, remnants of bygone bidding systems and quirky local customs can sometimes live on.

But even without the ACBL, small towns have their own ways of keeping the game in line. When Mrs. Hartman moved to Gettysburg, she tried to import a whimsical rule she had played in Shippensburg. "We made up a rule that if you dealt three times and everybody passed, everybody took a hundred points. Well, right away the big bridge players in the community told me, 'Jean, that doesn't work in Adams County.'"

"In general," she says, "Gettysburg plays social bridge, though there are some groups that play duplicate. I have played duplicate, but not for twenty-some years." She does have some friends who play over the Internet, but she says, "I'm one of these people who think it's good for you to get out."

I know of Mrs. Hartman's bridge playing because her husband shared a law office with my grandfather, who was his preceptor. I hope she might be able to tell me something about my grandmother's bridge habits that I can't glean from the artifacts in the house. Some of the scorecards are filled in, but there are no names. I wonder how she played, how she bid. She died while I was in college, long before I ever showed any interest in the game, when I was only just beginning to know her as an adult.

One of my favorite pictures of her is a long black-and-white photo of the Yale Law School class of 1935. There are rows and rows of sober men in dark suits arranged before an impressive ivy-draped building, and there, in the second row on the right, the only woman in the frame, wearing a brilliant white frock, is my grinning grandmother. In many ways it is an iconic shot: she was a fearless world traveler. She was of the generation that dressed for dinner and packed the kids off to summer camp at age six for a now-startling eight weeks. She was wonderful to her grandchildren, sending us poems and letters sprinkled with foreign phrases; she and I never played bridge, obviously, but I remember a marathon session of gin when the power went out one night.

Mrs. Hartman tells me my grandmother was known to be a lovely, intelligent person, and yet, much to my surprise, Mrs. Hartman never played with her, nor set foot in her house. She doesn't even know who attended my grandmother's bridge parties, which says a lot, I suppose, about how big small towns can be.

Mrs. Hartman details for me the bridge groups she participated in over the years. The first bridge club she belonged to in Gettysburg met Monday evenings, and it was one she helped form. There were two doctors' wives and two lawyers' wives, and they came up with a plan. She says, "On Mondays our husbands went to a service club, Lions or Rotary, that served them supper. So we, mommies all, decided we could cook less, get a bath, dress up, go play bridge, and the dads would come home well fed and babysit. Never mind *Monday Night Football*, because we didn't even have a TV until 1950." Soon the group added a fifth, so that the hostess could serve and sit out, or sub in if someone's child was sick. To this day, Mrs. Hartman's Monday bridge club endures, though she is the last of the original members still playing in the game.

There was also a two-table Tuesday evening group, but when she was teaching she found it to be too much. The Thursday group played an afternoon game, and met beforehand for lunch. Mrs. Hartman remembers, "We got out our best bib and tucker for that. We even decided to have sherry. I'm not particularly a drinker—and none of the other girls were, either—but we just decided that might be fun."

The Wednesday group is still going strong and meeting twice a month. She says, "Some of the restaurants in Adams County allow you—if you buy lunch, rather than just dessert—to stay and play bridge. They set up water and coffee and so on." And so this group meets at the Holiday Inn, with everyone taking turns as hostess. On Wednesday the women play for money. Everyone puts in fifty cents, and the winner takes $2.00. Monday is a money game, too, and this past month Mrs. Hartman made $4.00.

Then there's her "birthday group," which meets once a month for lunch in a restaurant of the celebrant's choosing. She says, "That started out as twelve people, of course, but now, bless their hearts, we're down to six or seven." Every time someone goes down in a contract, she puts a penny in the "penny pot," which becomes the low prize. At the start of the game everyone puts "a quarter on the corner," which the day's big winner gets to collect.

And on weekends, Mrs. Hartman used to play in her husband-and-wife bridge club, which, taken with her Monday bunch, "has been my network, my nucleus of friends my entire life in Gettysburg." The four couples started gathering together in 1949 or 1950. Most of the men grew up in town, while the women, she says, "were from Shippensburg or New Jersey or someplace else"—a small slip that suggests in the geography of a small town, down the road might as well be in the next state. She says, "For years, we met once a month in our homes. We even became known as the 'International Bridge Club,' because we decided to do some traveling as well. We went to Canada, and when we came home, we called ourselves 'international.'"

With so many games going on day and night, I'm surprised to hear there's one club she didn't participate in. But there is, and she thinks it's important that I know of its existence. It's called the Hospital Bridge Club, and Mrs. Hartman believes it was started around 1946 by the wife of a surgeon. Today it's not all doctors' wives, and it remains a sizable game—three or four tables, perhaps, in a town where most groups only have two. The women meet in the restaurant or country club of the hostess's choosing. Mrs. Hartman says, "It is the most prestigious game in town, and I don't say that bitterly. I never belonged, I was never asked to belong, and that doesn't bother me. But that is the kind of thing that means a lot. I know some people who were just wildly excited when they were asked to join. And how it has worked in many cases, truthfully, is that somebody passed away, and there is a vacancy. I mean, you have to have four to a table, and quite often a mother-in-law suggests a name, or whatever."

I guess I shouldn't be surprised that there are politics in small-town bridge, I say, but Mrs. Hartman stops me. She says, "That's one word. That's not a good word. Let's not use it. Like in any other town, there are just certain names that are outstanding names in the community. That's all there is to it. I don't know whether people put those attachments to names nowadays, but there was an era when they did. And if you were a friend of someone of one of those names, it was pretty special to you. If you were that type of person."

But what about the next generation—where do they play? She says, "If we have a young group playing bridge in Gettysburg, I am not aware of it." She is surprised by the fact that the game isn't being picked up by "the young marrieds." She says, "That's how we started out. I don't know the reasons, other than that everybody's busy. But we were busy. I think it's a cop-out when young people today say they can't do what their parents did because they're working. We worked! I taught school. I raised two boys. It's choice; it's priorities. To learn to play bridge you have to take time. And I think that's another benefit. It sits you down. I'm just a little bit worried that people don't take time just to sit down and talk. Or be silent even and think."

Which is why Mrs. Hartman thinks it's a game tailor-made for marriage. She seems disappointed when I tell her my wife has no interest in learning. She says, "Do you know why I like bridge? Because it's about a couple. Teamwork. I don't think of poker or pinochle as being about that. Same for hearts or canasta. I think that's important, if we're getting into psychology here. You know, you don't need to pick it apart—bridge is fun, after all—but I think teamwork is important."

Much of Mrs. Hartman's bridge playing was with other women, and they taught her plenty, too, often on subjects that had little to do with the game, at least on the surface. "Being a young bride coming to Gettysburg, I learned a lot from my elders," she says. "One woman came up to me one week and said, 'Jean, if you haven't learned anything about the game, please learn to be a better hostess. I don't see any excuse to run out of ice.' Well, that just hit me right between the eyes. That's something I've never forgotten."

The times she has been unable to play, because of her health or her husband's, she finds she misses it terribly. She says, "I have given up golf, because of age, and I've given up tennis. But I can still go and play with my bridge club. They're your network, your close friends. Hopefully I give as much as I take, but they're around in a crisis. I used to kid my sister, who lived in Harrisburg, and say I see my beautician and my bridge players more than I see my sister."

These days, Mrs. Hartman only plays about once a week. As she knocks on a wooden side table, she says, "You're talking to me at my age when I'm slowing down, but I'm stubborn and I still do all my own stuff"—meaning she balances her checkbook, keeps up her correspondence, hosts her bridge club in her home, and drives a car (though not at night). Every day she is up at seven, though she avoids early-bird bridge clubs: "I taught school and I raised children, and now I like my morning."

In general, however, she is up for a game. She subs frequently in other bridge clubs, which makes for interesting comparisons.

She has one friend who schedules all her doctor's appointments on Monday mornings or afternoons, because she doesn't know any groups that play that day, and she always wants to be available as a stand-in.

Mrs. Hartman smiles. She says, "You know, in your senior years, it's a pleasant afternoon. I think bridge is just serious enough for me. Magazines tell us to stretch our minds, and of course we should. Now you can get silly and brush your teeth with your left hand instead of your right or do a crossword puzzle and you're stretching your mind. But with bridge you're stretching your mind with somebody. You're trying to think what they're thinking. There are also rules, and I believe in rules. I'm a disciplinarian—I was a teacher. And bridge has rules, and you can't stretch them too far. And I think I like that. I think I like that in anything. It's how I was brought up."

In her reminiscences, Mrs. Hartman touches on this, encapsulating the rationale behind a lifetime of bridge in two simple sentences. She writes, "I personally feel you must have a friend and a passion. You must feel needed, you must learn to follow a rule, and you must have some fun."

If Mrs. Hartman evokes certain Eisenhower-era social mores, then perhaps it is no coincidence that Gettysburg was once the home of America's most bridge-obsessed president, General Dwight D. Eisenhower, who used the farm he bought in 1950 as a retreat before retiring there for good once he was no longer in office.

Ike loved bridge, and the Supreme Allied Commander played to unwind while awaiting news from Normandy and North Africa. He was even said to have picked his subordinates based on their skill at the table, tapping General Alfred Maximilian Gruenther to be his deputy at NATO because—as the story goes—he was a far better player than the other man up for the job.

Perusing Eisenhower's presidential papers, bridge pops up a fair amount. The general excelled at the game, which he describes in suitably militaristic terms. Of one card-playing campaign—conducted while on vacation in Georgia—he writes, "At the moment the Thomasville battle rages, with inconclusive results." Later, in another dispatch from the same front, he concludes a letter to Gruenther, his longtime bridge partner, "I am annoyed. I am looking for revenge. I expect help."

One official document finds him appointing a friend, "Professor and Instructor in the Laws, Rules, Techniques, and Skullduggery of Bridge." And on November 2, 1956, days before his reelection—and while in the midst of an international crisis over the Suez Canal—Eisenhower writes to Gruenther, "Life gets more difficult by the minute. I really could use a good bridge game." He ends the letter, "I have heard many people say a fellow would go crazy doing nothing. But I think a life of raising prize cattle, going shooting two or three times a year, fishing in the summer, and interspersing the whole thing with some golf and bridge—and whenever I felt like talking or writing, doing it with abandon and with no sense of responsibility whatsoever—maybe such a life wouldn't be so bad."

In many ways that is the life Ike lived in Gettysburg. Many residents still have stories about letting the president play through on the golf course at the Gettysburg Country Club, or bumping into Mamie at Faber's Drugstore or the A&P supermarket. Mrs. Hartman remembers one time her family was on the links when they spotted Ike's unmistakable fringed-top cart. The president was playing with the club pro, who was a friend of the Hartmans'. When Eisenhower knocked his ball into a ditch near the hole the family was playing, he drove up in his cart and, in the words of Mrs. Hartman, got out—"like the delightful politician that he was"—and said, "Well, Mrs. Hartman, what club do you think I should use?" Mrs. Hartman told me, "At that moment I thought my boys would just die."

And so one afternoon I find myself standing at the Gettysburg Visitor Center parking lot next to a sign of Ike's smiling face. I am waiting for a shuttle to the Eisenhower Farm, which has been designated a national historic site. In 1950, Ike and Mamie bought the 189-acre farm with grand westerly views to be their retirement home after the war, but then presidential politics intervened, and they couldn't live there full time until 1961. Remarkably, it was the first home the couple ever owned.

At the farm the shuttle is met by a perky Park Ranger in an impossibly stiff-brimmed hat. He gives the group a brief tour, and from him we learn the president shot skeet with his Secret Service detail, painted canvases on the porch, and putted around on his putting green, a gift from the PGA that came complete with a sand trap. He also raised prize-winning Black Angus show cows, and upon arriving at the farm any visiting dignitary—be he Khrushchev or Nehru—first had to endure a golf-cart tour of the general's cattle operations.

The remodeled farmhouse has eight bedrooms and nine baths. The grounds include a wrought-iron windmill and flagpole, as well as a greenhouse, rose garden, teahouse, and brick barbecue on which I imagine many an Angus ended up. The steps off the back porch are adorned with a pair of green rubber doormats, one lettered in white "President Eisenhower" and the other "First Lady." The garage holds a Jeep, some golf carts, and a custom Crosley runabout with a fringed top in which Ike chauffeured Churchill and de Gaulle and blew a horn that went "moo."

When entertaining, Ike eschewed the house's formal living room, piled high with gifts of state, and preferred to conduct his diplomacy over cards or drinks in the modest sunroom with sliding glass doors that everyone called "the porch." There the Eisenhowers had a TV, and Mamie watched her soaps and Ike watched his westerns. The president also liked to sit at an easel and dabble with oil paint, and while he didn't think much of his skill, his wife hung his works all over the house. In the dining room sits well-polished proof of Ike's long interest in cards: a silver tea service that the young Army major bought for his wife one piece at a time with his winnings from poker.

At one side of the house stands a remarkably small and simple office where Eisenhower worked while recovering from a heart attack in 1955 (when the farm served as his temporary White House) and in which, in 1960, he got word of the Soviet U2 crisis. Next door is the wooden-floored den where Ike played his bridge. It is a dark, cozy room with lamps covered in fishing flies, leather chairs, tall bookshelves, and a fireplace topped by a Civil War musket.

Ike and Mamie rarely played cards together as partners, a fact they cited as one of the secrets to their long marriage. Mamie played a little bridge, but she was not as competitive as her husband, who reportedly was less than diplomatic when it came to scolding a partner for a bad bid.

Mamie preferred canasta and one of its variants called Bolivia. And along with the president's monogrammed pilsner glass, fishing pole, putter, and golf shoes—plus a smattering of Mamie's hats—the Eisenhower Farm museum holds many of the first lady's Bolivia score sheets. It is in the museum that I stumble upon a treasure trove of Eisenhower bridge supplies.

There is a bridge set from *Columbine,* then the presidential airplane: a gold box covered with green felt that holds two decks of cards, one navy, one turquoise, both monogrammed and sporting the name of the plane and the presidential seal. Also on display are less-imposing cards for use on the farm, a handsome gilded-edge deck with pale blue backs reading "D.D.E." Next to those hangs a pad of tear-off score sheets clasped by a brass monogrammed holder.

I would like to stay and linger, maybe check out the show barn or see in what else the Eisenhower *esprit de bridge* lives on, but I have to get going: I promised my night to a more pressing bunch of bridge-aholics.

Half a block off the town square, on a humid fifth of July, the Blue Parrot Bistro bridge group is set to convene around six-ish. At the front of the restaurant, within a napkin's throw of the long wooden bar, two empty tables are set with cards, pens, pads, and plastic signs that read "Reserved." Shaded lamps dangle above the tables, their silver-bottomed bulbs casting a mellow light. Bebop plays over the speakers. A small neon parrot glows demurely beside the mirror-lined bar. The tables at the windows are full of early diners. A chalkboard on the wall proclaims, "Welcome, Bikers, 2006," above a roaring motorcycle drawn in prim pastels, though I sort of doubt too many road warriors will stop in for a baked Brie puff pastry when a joint just outside of town is advertising a $10 pig roast. There is a mute TV high in one corner and a sign at the bar that says NO CIGAR SMOKING.

The bistro is on a historic block—in 1850, an oyster parlor stood on the site—and the Blue Parrot has the air of a jazzy old saloon. The floors are wood. Thick beams run across the ceiling. An overhead fan spins despite the air-conditioning, which is cranked. When the first player walks in and sees me sitting at one of the reserved tables, she says, "You're the first new face in years!"

Every Wednesday night at the Blue Parrot for the past ten to fifteen years, a group of spirited baby boomers has been playing what they call bistro bridge. It's a pickup game that usually attracts two to three tables. It's a lively bunch, as Holly Giles, the Parrot's sixty-something proprietress points out: "Because we're in a bar situation, we think we're pretty funny." The group originally started out as a book club, which after seven or eight years had run its course. I ask Holly what led to the invention of bistro bridge, and she swirls a few ice cubes floating in what looks like a giant glass of sangria before saying with a snort, "Because I had no business Wednesday nights!"

Holly pads around the bar in flip-flops, greeting diners and hugging the barflies. She is trying to square things away so she can settle down to bridge, but I manage to get a few answers out of her. Her mother, a Life Master, taught her the rudiments of the game, but growing up Holly refused to play with her because she was too serious. When Holly was thirty-two she returned to bridge and found it didn't have to be so unpleasantly uptight.

More than once over the course of the evening, I'll hear her shrug off the concerns of the cards—be they hers or another's—with the cheery refrain, "Oh well, that's bar bridge."

If, as a watering hole, the Blue Parrot "caters to locals"—as one regular puts it—then bistro bridge might best be said to cater to movers and shakers. Holly is on the Gettysburg Borough Council, the town's ten-member governing body, and she points out the sharks in the bunch, one of whom wears shorts and a yellow T-shirt that says "Bermuda" and happens to be the past president and current chairman of the board of the bank. Holly says he started out as a "lurker"; not part of the original group, he often could be caught standing on the street peering at the hands through the glass, waiting to be invited to play. Now the game, of course, is open to all.

Holly takes a seat at the banker's table, which is rounded out by a local lawyer and his wife, who is the information systems manager at the bank. The banker's wife, Carolyn, takes a seat at my table, which is now full. My partner is Sharon, a peppy community-college biology teacher who wears glasses and has short hair. She scares me a little when she announces she usually plays "strong twos and weak threes"—strong two-bids being outdated relics (popularized by Culbertson and perpetuated by Goren), whose survival out here in the sticks would be laughed at by the snobs in a competitive New York club.

To my left is Susan, a boisterous blond Ph.D., who teaches marketing in the business school at Shippensburg University. Her friendship with Holly goes back thirty years; she lives down the street, and while not a Gettysburg native, she is comfortable describing another couple as being new to town, having "only been here about ten years." Susan's partner is Carolyn, the banker's wife. She says she comes from a card family, and, like the shark that Holly said she was, she makes three overtricks on the first hand.

The drinks around the table go Guinness, vodka tonic, water with lemon, and nothing for me. I'm having a hard enough time trying not to make a faux pas as it is. Every social game seems to have its own idiosyncrasies, and this one is no exception. Here, for example, the dummy lays down the trump suit before the opening lead. My partner asks, "Have you ever seen that done before?" She also clues me in to other points of protocol. In social bridge the team that wins a trick picks it up. (This is different from duplicate, in which players keep their cards separate even after they're played.) At the bistro, when a man and a woman are playing together, the man always gathers up the tricks. If one isn't available to handle the heavy lifting (or is it more a question of impatience?), the cards are kept by the trick-taker's partner, so the winner can lead another card quickly.

At my table, we discuss the health of aging parents, trips recently taken, and the festivities of the Fourth. The women pump me for bridge stories. Some of them seem politely appalled by my tales of Las Vegas. Similar stories of high-stakes London games also flop. In changing the subject, Carolyn tells me there is a group in town that "actually bids with cards, so you can't tell anything by the inflection of your voice." I nod and reflect on my old friend the bidding box. The women seem more impressed that I've used such a device—asking how tall it is, what the cards are like, and so on—than the idea of scantily clad showgirls toting around a million dollars in cash.

By now both the restaurant and bar have become busy, and a pool table sitting under a Tiffany lamp gets its first customers. The jazz is turned up, and Ella scats away while the waitress passes out menus. It's a lot of decisions to juggle at once: what to order, what to bid, what to play. Luckily, the bistro bunch favors more imprecise party-bridge bidding. When I make a slam in hearts that we neglected to bid (and so we don't get the bonus), Sharon cheerfully tells me, "That's why I tend to lie a little about my points!"

While I'm shuffling, a woman in a white T-shirt and khaki shorts walks over; she's one of the regulars, and I happily offer up my place at the table. Free to peruse the menu, I settle on a fried Cajun catfish sandwich served with homemade tartar sauce. I watch a kid with a goatee walk in, settle onto a stool, and say to the bartender, "Oh, it's bridge night," half sneering, half curious. Holly had told me that some diners like to look over players' hands—and even offer advice on a bid—on their way out the door, and sure enough, soon our table has attracted a fan. After watching for a while, she asks, "Do you guys ever play mah-jongg?" It turns out that the bistro is just for bridge, though Susan plays the tile game online.

From my seat on the sideline, I notice another curious quirk. Players line up the tricks they have taken in a variety of ways. It's a matter of personal preference whether to lay them out in a spiral, or left to right like neat little soldiers, or angle them back and forth accordion-style, or even put them end to end like a long sideways snake. With the drinks, the menus, and the wandering tricks, the table gets cluttered fast. When the food begins arriving—first as a breadbasket with butter, olives, and dipping oil with seasoned salt—Sharon tells me, "This is the most difficult part of the night." For the time being, the women set the napkins and silverware off to one side. They discuss the reenactment "disaster," and how they think the tourists should have come to town last weekend anyway to use their already-booked hotel rooms. Now that the bikers and soldiers will be flooding the town, Susan suggests, "This is the weekend we should all stay home."

After a rousing five-club contract is scored by the charming cutthroat Carolyn, we all stop for food. The cards are swept aside to make room for paninis, soups, salads, and my delicious catfish creation. I notice the other table, which sticks mainly to salads, seems more serious in its conversation. I overhear talk of taxes and health care and local Gettysburg politics—topics Holly later will tell me are the usual bridge table fodder. She says, "Most nights we have people here from banking, law, academia, whatever—so we hammer each other about what's going on."

Holly's table, it seems, is also more into its cards. As Sharon puts aside the score sheet, she says, "At this table, we play for

smiley faces," and indeed happy little circles complete the finished columns. "If you sit over there," she says, gesturing to the
other table, "They actually add the scores up. Here, once you've
won, we just stop at a smiley face."

While we eat, we talk our own brand of small-town business.
We discuss the opening of two new movie theaters in town, plus
the renovation of another, and how wonderful it has been to
go from having no movies in town to a multitude of screens.
Carolyn says, "Sometimes you're the only one in the audience!"
Another at our table takes a bleaker view: "And that—mark my
words—is why it will never last."

I steer the conversation back to bridge. Sharon says she
learned to play from the others in a sort of trial by fire. She
recalls, "There were cards, drinks, food, loud music—distractions all around. When I started out I learned to play survival
bridge." Susan and Sharon both play from time to time on the
weekends in marathon sessions they call "breakfast bridge." (It
seems this group never simply plays "bridge.")

At this point, we've finished our meal, and the woman in the
white shirt who took my place offers the best exit line I have
ever heard at the bridge table: "I got to go clean out a barn
before it gets dark." She stands up and walks out the door.

Play resumes with me back in the hot seat. On my first hand
I flop an easy three no-trump contract—because I misplay the
dummy—and Carolyn kindly says, "The nice thing is that here
we learn from each other." The next hand fares a little better
for our side, perhaps because the biology teacher is warming up
to one of her favorite subjects, global warming, apropos of the
Al Gore documentary, *An Inconvenient Truth,* which is playing
at a theater just off the square. At the bistro, no topic seems to
be off the table. Husbands are made fun of, as are ex-husbands
and estranged husbands and even extramarital dalliances. And
so at what I believe to be an opportune moment, I bring up the
real hot-button issue, the casino, in my best offhand way. I had
heard the attendance at bistro bridge suffered a brief dip in April

when the Borough Council—including our host, Holly—voted seven to three to support the casino proposal (citing economic interests). The conversation dies in an instant. I can almost hear crickets, while Sharon and Susan take slow sips from their drinks. In a voice that could get Carolyn a job at the UN, she delivers with perfect neutrality her thoughts on the matter: "Oh." After a beat, we politely move on and bid another hand.

The game breaks up about nine. Sharon has an early morning class to teach, and the bank chairman has a business call to make. The good-byes are short and sweet. Everyone knows they'll see each other around town well before it's time to play again next week. Bistro bridge obviously makes for fast friends. Before the group completely disbands, Susan asks Holly to tell me about what they call "the *West Wing* years," when the show was still on the air and the game ended at eight fifty-five sharp—just enough time to dash upstairs to Holly's place and settle in front of the TV. Holly plops down at our table, a pack of cigarettes now somewhat conspicuously hidden devil-may-care down her shirt, making an amusing outline on her shoulder where it's held in place, one assumes, by her bra strap. She remembers, "The rule was no talking during the show, but at commercials it was yak, yak, yak." Sharon always got stuck with the remote control, because—as they all agreed—she was the only one with "a large enough brain to figure it out." "Boy, they were a tough crowd," Sharon recalls, if she ever was slow to unmute the box after a commercial break.

As her friends stop to say hello to other patrons on their way to the door, Holly tells me, "You know, at the table we often quote our mothers. My mother always said, 'You can have all the drinks and hors d'oeuvres you want, but if you really want to get to know your friends, play bridge.' And finally, after all these years together, we are finally doing it."

Holly heads behind the bar, and a man at the next table leans over and says to me, "These bridge players really are quite a crowd." Susan hears him on her way out the door, and calls back over her shoulder, "Yeah, bistro bridge—it's the hottest thing in town!"

CHAPTER FIFTEEN

Oh, the Sunny Saturdays I Have Missed

Over the summer, I break one of the game's cardinal rules. I begin to keep secrets from my partner. It makes me feel slimy and hypocritical to spend so much time fine-tuning our communication while harboring a half-truth. But it is one I fear will test the very limits of our partnership, lay it all on the table—show us if what we have is meant to be, or if it's just a passing fancy. What I can't tell Tina for now—for fear of sending her into nervous shock—is that I have decided I want us to compete in the summer North American Bridge Championships in July.

There are plenty of reasons for Tina to say no. First, the tournament is in Chicago. Second, despite my nice manners, she has no way to know I don't keep a freezer full of human heads. Third, what chance do we have at a national tournament? For this reason, I keep my dream under wraps, biding my time, waiting to pitch the idea when her confidence is high.

In the meantime, it feels good to come home to the Manhattan Bridge Club—a sentiment unimaginable a year ago. I have been to clubs across the land, and while the Manhattan might lack wine, waiters, and showgirls, I am glad to be back in the only club I know that serves a never-ending supply of doughnut holes.

One day I walk in to find the club buzzing. The excitement is for the Worldwide Bridge Contest, an international duplicate game in which the same hands are played on the same day all over the globe. This Saturday some 5,372 pairs are playing at 252 clubs in thirty-seven countries, including Indonesia, South Africa, Jordan, Syria, Slovenia, Pakistan, South Korea, Germany, Bermuda, and Vanuatu, an island nation partway between Hawaii and Australia. As each club reports its scores, the rankings are updated on the Internet in real time. A duo from Tokyo ends up taking the top prize, followed by pairs from Egypt, Italy, and a club in New Jersey.

That afternoon, Tina and I play in the supervised game, where we have become fixtures. It is not as rigorous as a duplicate session, but we play boards from previous games that still have the score sheets attached, so we know how our performance matches up. The game attracts a regular crowd. We enjoy it because, unlike in the big room, we are free to take our time, chat, and talk a little smack. When Tina trumps a trick that one of the more pedantic players expected to take, he lets out a howl of dismay. With her usual deadpan, she says, "Don't worry, it happens in the best of families," then leads the next trick. The table behind us goes bananas.

Inspired by my time with Zia—and careful study of his book—I realize how focused I have been on making the perfectly correct statistical play. In our Saturday game, I see the same players week after week. I should be paying attention to their quirks—reading them at the table—to gain an edge. Conversely, I am determined to give nothing away. As that same pedantic player, whom I have taken to calling Harold Vanderbilt in my notes, is about to lead through me to the dummy, I make a subtle shift of my cards. He has the ace and the seven of hearts on the board. In my hand I hold the king and the two. At this point he has to guess whether Tina and I each have a heart or if one of us has two. I slip the two to the outside of my hand so I can drop it casually, and—if Harold is watching, as I know he will be—it will appear to be my only heart. Thus he'll peg Tina to hold the king (and only the king) and play his ace to drop it. Doing that will make my hidden king good. While hardly impressive, my little ruse works out, and the instructor, who witnesses it, raises an eyebrow.

Tina plays well, making a six-diamond contract that requires complicated crossruffing between hands. She is in a good mood. It is a golden day for the partnership, and I consider broaching the nationals. Then on the last hand we have a derailment. She bids hearts without holding enough of them, and the instructor tells her she should have settled in no-trump. No-trump has become something of Tina's Achilles' heel—she gets confused about what it means, and she is reluctant to bid it. I decide to hold my tongue about Chicago.

The next time I see Tina, I am determined to bring up the trip. The tournament is drawing near, and I fear I can't wait any longer. When I blurt out my plan, she is both flustered and flattered. Or so she says—I can't tell if she's just being nice. I suggest that she sleep on it and say I can wait for an answer, though the next time we meet I am determined to wear her down. Trouble is, she's in a bit of a slump. She hurt her back opening the windows in her apartment to pull her plants out of the sun, so she's worried about the "physical aspect of the trip." She also doesn't like traveling within the United States; she says it is more of a hassle than traveling abroad. "It sounds tiring," she says of the tournament. "I'll see the nationals next time they come to New York."

In the face of such gloom, I present nothing but support—while at the same time refusing to acknowledge that her answer is final. I know she is like me. If pushed, she'll resist even harder. Nobody can change her mind but herself. I would offer her immortality in print if I thought it would interest her. Ditto for the fact that it's a chance to visit the birthplace of the Wienermobile. As it is, I have nothing to do but wait and see.

And so we enjoy ourselves playing against a competitive married couple new to the Saturday bunch. They're in their late twenties, and they do nothing but fight—all the while trying not to let on that their tempers are flaring. Wearing nothing but smiles, they can hardly remain civil. They shoot terse, pointed questions across the table and shush each other's answers. They are truly a hoot, and my wife enjoys hearing about them when I get home at night.

When I speak to Tina during the week, she is discouraged and glum. She had a tough time at Tommy's class. It was a difficult lecture; Tina tells me, "All the hands were puzzles for declarer where the ace-queen is opposite the ten-something or other and we were supposed to fish out the king." Her back still bothers her, and both Ranko and Kathy were absent. She says, "I'm really in a valley. I feel like all that I've learned is oozing out of my head." I begin to despair. Our chances of going to Chicago are not looking good.

Then out of the blue one bright Wednesday morning, Tina says yes. Fate has conspired to bring about a string of good luck: we had a solid day at Honors (and left with some master points), her back is feeling better (the heating pad worked), and she believes my many assurances that I don't expect her to play for a full week. After I demonstrate what she deems to be adequate knowledge of the airports involved—and again I promise we'll be flying out together—Tina says, "Okay, it will be a lark." I can see she is amused by the notion. When I tell her it is going to be great, she says, "Old ladies don't do this."

Even though I've never seen Tina wear one, I decide I'll have to order T-shirts for the team. Of course I'll give it to her at the last minute, lest it freak her out. I book our tickets online, and when I give her the printout of her ticket confirmation, she makes a funny face. It is her second-ever e-ticket, and she is a little suspicious. Then, despite the fact that the trip is weeks away, she asks if I'm planning to check bags.

To ease Tina's nerves, I tell her I have found us a coach. Every underdog contender has a grizzled veteran cornerman (think Mickey in *Rocky*), and Team Tina is no different. Our old-timer in a wool hat is Jeff Hearn, a playwright and freelance graphic designer who doesn't wear hats and looks younger than his forty-four years. Jeff runs the supervised game at the Manhattan Bridge Club on Saturdays, something he does to raise a little cash in the hope of self-financing one of his scripts. He wouldn't mind starting to play pro, but finding clients is difficult, though he has started giving some private lessons on the side.

Jeff is a good instructor, always keeping us on our toes. He sometimes stacks the boards against us, such as the day he slips one of us the "Mississippi heart hand," a famous con from the days of riverboat gambling—despite having a whopper of a hand that looks cold for a slam in hearts, the most the declarer can take is a measly six tricks. Jeff uses it to illustrate the power of distribution. But while he can be amusing, Jeff tells it like it is. One day I bring a friend to class, and after watching her nervously play a hand, he asks, "Can I be frank?" before letting her know he just witnessed some of the worst play he has seen in a long time. After class he kids her, saying he knew she could take it.

Despite such moments of brutal candor, Jeff is undoubtedly a good guy. He participates in a mentoring program, and his "little brother" shows up on Saturdays, often with his (real) older brother in tow. It is a pleasant sight to see two kids from Bedford-Stuyvesant spending the afternoon playing bridge with a room full of Upper West Siders. The younger brother is getting pretty good. Afterward, Jeff travels an extra hour and a half to get the guys home. I think it is this benevolent streak that leads him to take on the fool's errand that is training hopeless Team Tina.

With Jeff offering pro-bono support, Tina perks up, though she keeps up a fairly constant refrain of "I don't want to shame you." I try to explain that I don't care how we do. I remind her to look upon it as a lark. Then I tell her I'll see her at 5 A.M. for wind sprints and push-ups. I get half a smile. I am sympathetic to her anxiety. Let it never be said that bridge isn't work. Since I started playing I have noticed I perspire at the table; no matter the room temperature, it is a cold, clammy sweat.

Despite the fact that Tina once told me, "I never cram," that is what we do in the weeks before the tournament. We train in earnest, playing for points during the week and going to supervised play on Saturday, where we listen closely to Jeff as he recaps the hands. Through one of our classmates, I find out Tina has been sneaking in an extra session on Thursdays.

After almost Herculean insistence on my part, Tina finally agrees to let me pay for her plane ticket. Ten days before we leave, she relents in an e-mail, though she says she accepts "with muted pleasure: perturbed that I am a triple burden, ignorant of U.S. travel and bridge tournaments and by the cost." She ends the note bravely, "However, you are the captain of this auction, and I will bid accordingly."

In the meantime, we have scoped out a game or two to play in Chicago. The tournament tries hard to seem welcoming to newcomers; there are free lessons and lectures and hospitality receptions. Tina and I shun such pleasantries: our bloodlust is not to be sated by a game sponsored by the AARP. We set our sights on a midweek morning pair game that is stratified by master points.

Happily, we are hitting our stride at the perfect time. A week before we leave, we have our best game ever at Honors. We finish at the top of our flight, and Tina tells me it's the first time she has been wholly comfortable with every bid at the table. The only thing she apologizes for today is that she believes she will have to check luggage. All along I have been telling her I will be doing the same.

While Tina fixates on baggage, I have become obsessed with the hotel. Rooms in downtown Chicago are scarce. The bridge players are not the only ones coming to town. The tournament coincides with the seventh international Gay Games, a sports and cultural festival modeled on the Olympics, with the added attraction of medals for country western dancing. Twelve thousand gay athletes are expected to attend. I searched for hours over the phone and online before booking us rooms at a "historical" (read: run-down) pile on Michigan Avenue. I figure location is the main thing. Plus, these are the only two rooms I can find.

At our last practice session, Tina tells me she's actually looking forward to the trip. It is a brilliant weekend in July, and I am amused to think I have spent some of the sunniest days of the summer hunched over a table on the fourteenth floor of a midtown office building. Every player at the tournament is required to carry a convention card that explains the partnership's bidding system. The "cards" are actually sheets of paper preprinted by the ACBL with a myriad of blanks to fill in and boxes to check that when properly completed explain to your opponents the bids in your arsenal. While I had filled out such cards before, it seems like a good idea to have Jeff go over them with us, both for a review and to ensure our cards are done by the book. Interestingly, in tournament bridge there are certain bids you must flag for your opponents, and Jeff covers those with us. For instance every time you open one no-trump you are supposed to announce your partnership's point range for that bid—in our case, a fairly standard fifteen to seventeen. I can tell going over such formalities is making Tina nervous. We have agreed to keep our bidding simple, and she knows all of this stuff in practice, but it's like freezing up on a pop quiz. Regardless, we have what I feel is a stellar final session. Jeff says that he is sorry he can't come to Chicago, but he'll look for our results online.

When we part ways on the street, Tina asks if I have reconfirmed our flight. I promise to take care of it. Tina is so young of heart that I tend to forget what a big deal this is: an eighty-three-year-old woman going off on a trip across time zones to play in a national tournament of a game she's just learning with a partner who might like to murder little old ladies in their sleep. She is such a sport. For the last time she reminds me that she thinks the whole thing is "goofy."

Ours is a story of David against a field of Goliaths, two friends with a simple system taking on the nation. We hope our straightforward bidding might gain in clarity what others have in comprehensiveness. We are playing with no fancy gadgets or complicated conventions, which I'm counting on to give us the edge that we're comfortable and informed at all times. To my friends I have been joking about the trip, calling it *Easy Rider* meets *Driving Miss Daisy,* which is of course a little unfair. For a book about a social game, I have spent a lot of time alone at tournaments in strange cities, and it seems fitting that on the final leg of my odyssey I'll be playing with a friend.

Tina is so self-effacing that she never really believes me when I tell her she will be in the book. She has no family left. At one point she tells me, "You're the only person in the world who knows this much about me." Indeed, over the past year, I have come to learn things about Tina. I know when her hands are bothering her and she could use help clearing her lunch plate. I know what she thinks of Iraq and the Coca-Cola Company. I know a little of what it must have been like to grow up on a Prohibition farm. I know she worries about checking a bag on a flight. I know she takes her vitamins at lunch, dislikes ice in her seltzer, doesn't celebrate her birthday, and objects to receiving presents. She has a soft spot for Spanish soap operas, but she won't watch TV during the day because she says, "It's like drinking before five." She doesn't like to eat ice cream alone, but when she orders a pineapple sundae at a diner she grins like a kid. When a card doesn't fall her way, she says, "*Caramba.*"

And certainly Tina knows things about me: how I can't shut up when I'm excited, how to tell if I've had a late night, how I'm competitive even when I claim not to be. Good things, bad things—I'm sure she could give you some stories. But after all the early mornings, lazy afternoons, and long nights at the table, I can say I've learned a little about communication, cooperation, and trust—the simplest of lessons—while also gaining a good fun-loving friend. And now we're about to embark on the craziest journey of all.

CHAPTER SIXTEEN

Wild Times in the Windy City, *or* My Travels with Tina

Chicago, Illinois, July 2006

When you're flying across five states with an eighty-three-year-old woman who deeply distrusts domestic travel and—despite your many assurances—is more than a little apprehensive about the trip you've wheedled her into taking, it stands to reason that things will go awry. And indeed our journey starts off on the wrong foot when I wake up the morning of our departure to find that the denizens of our fair city have been running their air conditioners too much in this wretched heat wave and LaGuardia airport has lost power. Tina and I are now bumped to a flight leaving five hours later from JFK. I call Tina to tell her about the rescheduling, and she sounds both disappointed and suspicious. She has already unplugged all her appliances, which is why she missed the news of the blackout. I have more bad tidings: the airline can't confirm our seat assignments on the new flight, so we might not be sitting next to each other. Trying to make the best of it, Tina says she should sit in front of me if possible, because, as a rule, she never leans back in her seat.

Tina prefers to meet at the airport, and when I arrive I find her waiting serenely to check in. It turns out she passed a nice afternoon by plugging in the air conditioner and having a glass of wine with her soup. Because ours is not the only relocated flight, the terminal is a zoo. Then the self-check-in computers go down, and all hell breaks loose. We end up in a long, angry line at the counter, and by the time we're through security, we have only minutes to get to our gate. A large pack of Chicago passengers takes off sprinting before us, and—after slipping on her shoes—Tina gamely quickens the pace.

Of course the gate is in the farthest reaches of the terminal, and while we're hoofing up a broken escalator of positively Andean pitch, I keep glancing at Tina to make sure she's okay. When we plop into the seats at the gate—where they're getting a late start on the boarding—I notice she's a little out of breath. I go off to get her some water, and for the first time it hits me: I am responsible for the well-being and safe return of an octogenarian. Traveling with the elderly is like camping in the wilderness: above all, you want to leave no trace.

From the waiting area, I call the hotel to confirm our now-late arrival. Clearly I have taken on some of Tina's travel neuroses, as this is the second time I've checked on our reservation, and I am still worried about the hotel. I just pray there are no roaches.

On board, we can't get seats together. The plane is packed, and everyone is in a hurry because we're running late. Tina has been given an aisle, and I'm in the middle one row back, but as I follow her down the cabin, she falls on the sword and takes my seat between two hefty ladies—leaving me the aisle. I feel like a heel, taking charity from a senior, but she's insistent, saying I'm too tall to squeeze into the middle. While we're sitting on the tarmac for the next hour—because of congested air traffic—I look back and try to smile.

Finally the flight leaves two hours late. Tina is a trooper, and I hear her cheerfully discussing the politics of Wal-Mart with her seatmate, who is munching from a bag of pistachios. When the woman falls asleep, Tina spends the remainder of the flight staring straight ahead.

We land in Chicago at dusk on a warm summer night. We get

in a cab and hit strangely heavy traffic for this time of night, but as we crawl toward downtown, fireworks start going off over Lake Michigan, and I begin to think our luck has changed. It seems an auspicious welcome.

Then we reach the hotel, and the next disaster strikes. At the front desk I discover the unimaginable: despite my dutiful reconfirmations, the hotel has messed up our arrival dates and has only one room reserved for us tonight—the last in the hotel. It's now 10 P.M., we're in a strange city, the manager promises there are absolutely no rooms left downtown, and Tina informs me she did not pack her "dressing gown." I wonder how things could get any worse.

Sensing my soul-crushing despair, the manager says that the room he has for us happens to be one of their very best suites, which will afford us completely separate bedrooms with—and he's very insistent on this point—our very own TVs. Tina is taking this better than I, and she smiles and says, "What else can we do?"

Upstairs, we find the final surprise. That the suite has two separate sleeping quarters is true if you count the foldout living-room couch. We call down to the desk, thinking that there has been some mistake, and the manager repeats that the whole town is booked. When I offer to go out and find myself another room, Tina says with her usual deadpan, "I know you planned this to get me alone."

I continue to apologize for what has been such a horrendous day, and in an attempt to make me feel better, Tina makes the cryptic remark, "I guess this is bridge." In the end, we decide to make do with the room. In some way, our troubles make Tina feel like she has been let off the hook. She tells me, "Any disasters I commit at the bridge table—well, I guess it's okay."

Amazingly, despite the late hour, Tina insists that we head to the tournament and "case the joint." And so after a cup of coffee from a nearby Dunkin' Donuts, we catch a cab to the Hyatt Regency, where the games are taking place. When we pull up to the hotel, the first person we see walking out is a man in a loud windbreaker covered in cards. I am gladdened by the sight, as I had promised Tina that we would spot some serious fanatics.

But as we step into the hotel, all sense of the familiar fades away. In the middle of the lobby—where I would expect to see sleepy bellhops behind desks—is an octagonal elevated dance floor rising from a pool of water and surrounded by scaffolding from which hang booming speakers and flashing lights. In the ear-splitting half-dark people with glow sticks slung around their necks are grinding to "Sweet Home Alabama" as showers of bubbles rain down on their heads—and I think Tina is going to turn tail and run. Apparently the hotel has a nightclub, and there is some sort of rowdy midweek convention in town.

Before Tina can bolt, I ascend an escalator to the front desk and learn that the bridge players are competing three and four floors below us. So we descend into the bowels of the hotel, far from the strobes and sounds of Lynyrd Skynyrd.

It's about eleven fifteen, and the evening games are getting out. Tina and I are going against the tide of players, all of whom have been cooped up for the past three and a half or so hours. They rush by, chatting, flirting, and fighting with each other. We are now two levels belowground in the middle of a madhouse. We pass down a long hall with a bar at the end, and suddenly we're outside the first playing area.

People whirl by clasping martinis and convention cards and oversized purses; they're all rushing to get home to bed or to sign up for the midnight game. Sometimes Tina and I are going with the stream, and sometimes we're against it. Meanwhile, packs of pushy players weave in and out.

The scene is crazy and claustrophobic, not unlike running with the bulls in Pamplona. But while I am used to the habitual hurry and thoughtless manners of the tournament bridge player—they're competitive, excitable people and this is their Woodstock—I am furious when someone almost knocks Tina over. Everywhere people are bumping into each other, cutting one another off, and refusing to hold any doors. So I step in front of Tina to provide some blocking, and now I'm one of the mob, barreling my way through. I pass a lot of familiar faces—Bob Hamman, Andrew Robson, caddies I know from Gatlinburg—but this is no time for hello. As Chicago's beloved native sons, the Blues Brothers, once said, "We're on a mission from God."

We find the newcomer area where we'll play our game tomorrow. After sizing it up—noting the check-in table, the start time, and the nearest restrooms—we beat a hasty retreat back through the hordes and up the escalators. When we get outside, I can tell Tina is somewhat shaken. All she says is, "That makes me groggy." Instead of hopping into a cab, she wants to walk part of the way home to shake out the cobwebs. On Michigan Avenue we pass what I take to be a gay Olympian—a buff fifty-something guy wearing rainbow-hued spandex.

As we're saying good night, I present Tina with her Team Tina shirt, which she genuinely seems to like. I think it's her first T-shirt, as she mutters something that sounds like, "Oh, cute—I'm not sure I have one," before promising she'll find a suitable matching top. Lights out is 1 A.M. I don't stay up practicing on my laptop because I don't want to make Tina nervous.

I hear Tina's TV come on around 7 A.M., earlier than she said she was getting up, but at breakfast in the hotel restaurant she says she slept well. We both have French toast, which Tina washes down with four cups of coffee. I don't have the heart to tell her that managing bathroom breaks mid-match might be a little tricky.

By the cold light of morning, the Hyatt lobby is a more sober place, the footloose conventioneers having been replaced by business travelers with cell-phone headsets clipped like darts in their ears. The center of last night's revels is calm, the dance floor filled with tables of early risers sipping orange juice while the fountains innocently burp up short shoots of water.

The tournament produces its own newspaper, called the *Daily*

Bulletin, which is like the bulletin from Gatlinburg only longer and published on real newsprint. It usually runs some twenty pages with pictures, announcements, and the odd article, such as "Older Couple Finds Bridge, Romance Online."

Copies of today's issue are strewn around the lobby. We pick one up and double-check our playing area. We have arrived a little early, so we venture downstairs and wander around. A sign posted by the registration desk announces that tonight is Polish Night, complete with dancers and sausage. Registration at the tournament is optional—one simply has to sign up for individual games—but we give our names at the desk and receive a big plastic bag of goodies before being directed to the newcomer desk, where we are to receive another bag of booty, this one designed for the low-level master point–holder in mind. Next to that desk we sign up for our game, which costs us $14.50 apiece, a price at which I feel we deserve an ethnic dance.

The room is a typical hotel ballroom, the walls and carpet an impersonal meditation on a shade of beige. The tables are of the simple foldout variety, their padded vinyl tops undraped, with blue bidding boxes affixed to the corners. We pick an unoccupied one in the corner, but soon we have company, Doris and Ray, a husband-and-wife pair from Florida. She wears a fish sweater, and he is a big, cheerfully disorganized John Candy kind of guy in a baby blue blazer, his wallet and pockets bulging with train schedules and newspapers. They got up at five this morning to be here, and they are psyched.

When we paid our money, the tournament official informed us there was a free pregame presentation, and there, in the far corner of the room, a man on a mike is standing in front of a sign that says "Celebrity Speaker" and lecturing a sizable crowd on something called "balancing doubles." Doris heads over to hear him, while Tina tries to tune him out, afraid she'll get confused. I fill out our entry slip, and Ray goes through his wife's goody bags.

The newcomer bag offers your basic bridge freebies: a plastic sleeve for holding one's convention card, a pen, a notepad that proclaims the user "Mad About Bridge!," and a sixty-page illustrated almost–comic book called *Adventures in Duplicate Bridge,* which curiously seems to be written for kids and covers such topics as keeping score and how to fit in as the newcomer in your local club game (hint: play it like "Joe Cool").

The general tournament bag contains more practical goodies: a stainless steel coffee mug with "2006 Chicago NABC" and the city skyline printed on the side, a list of the tournament events with a guide to local restaurants, a White Sox pocket schedule, coupons for fast food, a pack of peanut M&Ms, and a small quilted sticker with the tournament name on it. This last is a collector's item and apparently is best displayed on one's convention card holder to mark the nationals one has attended—or so said the woman who gave us the bag.

At the other tables, people eat bagels and bananas and sit with their coffee. Most discuss their systems or talk about hands, though one seasoned pro sits down within earshot and proclaims—as she produces from her purse a sandwich in a large plastic container—that she has found the secret to lunch: buy early, before the long lines.

We are at table #5 in Section AA in Columbus Hall A, otherwise known—in the tournament's halfhearted attempt at a baseball theme—as "the infield room" (a pinstriped sign proclaims: THE PLACE WHERE NEWCOMERS AND INTERMEDIATES PLAY). I find the name a tad demeaning, and I'm hoping that somehow by hook or by crook Tina and I will knock one out of the park.

We are sitting North-South, so we will stay put as the East-West pairs switch out between rounds. I am North, making it my job to keep score, which means after each round I have to fill out a score slip that the caddies will pick up after our opponents initial it. It's not a big deal, but it's a little extra pressure—just more clerical work for an already burdened reporter. Suddenly I'm on edge. What have I gotten us into? The room feels very small despite the rows and rows of tables—tables that are rapidly filling up with bristling, bustling bridge players. The pep, for lack of a better word, in the place is almost unbearable. It's not yet ten o'clock, and given that we are about to embark on three-plus hours of sedentary activity, this is an eerily ecstatic bunch. While our game is protected—you can have no more than fifty master points—I notice a lot of merciless-looking newcomers rubbing their hands with glee. I wonder that they didn't name this "the feeding-frenzy room" ("The Place Where Chum Comes to Play").

In an attempt to clear my head, I escape to the bathroom, but when I open the door I see a very hairy and pale shirtless man freshening up at the sink. After splashing around, he slips on what I assume to be a clean T-shirt and walks out the door. Has he been here overnight?

Back at the table, I try to imagine how Tina and I look to the competition. Do we strike fear in their hearts? There are plenty of younger players, but they tend to be playing with their peers. I wonder if anyone thinks I'm some young pro Tina has hired for the day. If only they knew that essentially the opposite was true—that I have to import my own more mature partner. I am wearing my Team Tina T-shirt underneath a button-down, and I have warned Tina that if the going gets tough I won't hesitate to reveal it.

A little before our official 10 A.M. start, the director hands us three boards and tells us to take out the cards and sort them into suits. After we have done that, she passes us some sheets diagramming the hands for each board, and we start to set them up one at a time. This already makes Tina tense, but there is no time for a pep talk because a voice over the PA announces the game is about to begin. The disembodied voice booms an Orwellian command, "Smile at your partner; treat him or her with respect," but we're too panicked to smile—we're not done making our boards. We finish in the nick of time and hand them to the next table, where by design they'll be passed on and on— but never played by us. Doris and Ray have to shift over, too, as every East-West pair moves one table up.

Suddenly the room is ready, and exactly one year, two months, and twenty-eight days after our very first bridge lesson, Tina and I are sitting down to a duplicate match at the year's biggest bridge tournament. The moment feels surreal. I am underslept, overstimulated, and nervous as hell. I try to marshal a year's worth of study—all those tricks and tips from Zia and Zeus, Hamman and Mimi, and the other lights of the game—but all I can summon are the words of Jeff, our coach and supervised-game instructor, who says every Saturday, "Bridge is a blood sport."

Things go a little hazy as I reach for the first board and pull out the cards.

On the top floor of the Hyatt, at the end of a long hall, a paper sign outside a dark wooden door announces ACBL PRESIDENTIAL SUITE: INVITED GUESTS ONLY. On the other side of the portal stretches a twenty-five-hundred-square-foot suite that can hold up to 150 people, with a living room, dining room, and long marble wet bar with bottles at the ready, plus a fireplace, pool table, and baby grand piano.

Inside, Harriette Buckman is in the middle of cleaning out her purse. She tells me, "At this time in a tournament, it usually weighs about fifteen pounds." She pulls out items at random and drops them onto the dining room table. "Here's some old paper, here somebody gave me a beanie baby for something, here's the CD of last night's musicians . . ." And so the pile grows, assorted trinkets and favors that more correctly might be called gifts of state, for at the summer NABC Harriette Buckman is something of a celebrity, the game's reigning dignitary, halfway as she is through her one-year term as president of the ACBL.

When you've spent a year worshiping at the altar of the ACBL, learning their rules, reading their publications, chasing their master points—and now you're a guest at the world's biggest bridge circus—an audience with Buckman can be a bit like meeting the great and powerful Oz. By that I mean it's a little disconcerting to learn that the wizard behind all the thunder and lightning—the commander in chief of a 160,000-member corps that operates on a $15 million budget, sells $2 million worth of merchandise, and sanctions some 2.5 million bridge tables a year in 3,200 clubs and 1,100 tournaments nationwide (not to mention another 200,000 online)—is a seventy-year-old woman with a thick Chicago accent wearing sandals, slacks, and a sweater with bright fruit on it.

The purse now neglected, we move into the living room, and Buckman introduces me to a man and woman at the bar chopping onions for a salad. With a sweep of her hand, she says, "We entertain up here every night." And with that, Madam President takes a seat in an olive chair, while I settle into a brown suede couch and try to keep from staring at the spectacular downtown views.

This tournament happens to be a homecoming of sorts for Buckman, who describes herself as "a Chicagoan born and bred." Her father was a bridge player, and as an only child she soon picked up the bug. She started caddying at the age of twelve. At fifteen, she played with her dad in her first game of duplicate. In high school, she would deal out hands by herself and try to figure out what to do with them.

She didn't play bridge in college, because she already had been introduced to duplicate, and "what those kids were playing wasn't the same game." She continued caddying, however, until the year she was married. She could make $25 or $30 a weekend at a time when her tuition at Northern Illinois University was $90 a quarter.

A member of the ACBL since 1950, she's been a caddy, a tournament director, a unit official, a district official, a board member, and now president. She laughs: "There's no place else to go, so I guess I'll retire."

But before she can do that, she must serve out her term, and the president tends to keep herself busy. The day-to-day operations of the league are carried out by an office of about eighty-five employees in Memphis. Buckman's duties include setting policy for the league, as well as chairing the board meetings held three times a year at the national tournaments. In between meetings, the president visits regional tournaments and serves as the public face of the league.

But what really gets Buckman excited is talking about her "project." She declared this year to be the Year of the Teacher. As she travels, she has been honoring local teachers at special dinners, where the price of admission is their favorite teaching tip. At the end of her year, Buckman will begin posting the tips online.

It is not surprising that Buckman is focused on teachers, her-self having taught middle school for twenty-two years. To this day she is a bridge instructor. Perhaps her favorite pupil was her first husband, Bob, whom she taught when he got out of the Army. His picture is downstairs on the Wall of Honor on the main tournament floor, a good-looking man making a toast in a gray suit and bow tie. She says, "I lost Bob in 1989 to cancer. I'll never forget the support from people in the bridge community: the cards and the expressions of sympathy—in some cases from people who only knew us as a pair at the bridge table."

I try to gently switch tacks. At long last I have come face-to-face with someone prepared to give me the definitive word on bridge—after all, isn't that the whole point of having a governing body, an ultimate authority, that the buck finally stops here?—and I have plenty of questions. In the course of our conversation we pass over many of the touchstones of my bridge odyssey: from the Gatlinburg phenomenon ("Gatlinburg is like the eight-thousand-pound gorilla. What can it do? Anything it wants!") to the little old ladies playing their weekly social foursome ("They're still playing bridge, but that's not the same game you and I are playing.") to the overwhelming spectacle of a summer NABC ("This is the largest bridge tournament anywhere in the world!") to the differences between tournament bridge at home and abroad ("We are stewards of our members' money—we are very sensitive to how we spend it—so we don't hold tournaments in the lavish European style. I mean, we think we're doing a good job when we're serving brats or hot dogs at the end of the night!") to the importance of volunteerism in the game ("Whether you're talking about the person who picks up the coffee cups at the club at the end of an evening or the people who man the booths at the tournaments—there isn't enough money in the world to pay for the things that they do.").

I even manage to bring up the complaints that Zia voiced to me and Bob Hamman writes about in his autobiography—that perhaps bridge conventions have gotten out of hand. I mention Zia's dream of a conventionless tournament and Bob's beef that with ridiculously complicated systems full and fair disclosure is never really possible. Buckman sighs and says, "That pops up every so often. Over the years, there have been contests between the Scientists and the Naturalists. But the definition of a convention is a problem-solving tool. It solves the problem of being able to ask a certain question or give a particular piece of information couched in bridge terms. And as long as the people who live on bridge Mount Olympus—the people who create this stuff—as long as they continue to see ways of solving problems, there are going to be people who will take that ball and run with it."

As she continues, the president gets a little worked up. "You know what I liken it to?" she asks. "You're too young to know, but plumbers used to walk around with big leather bags that had eighty-nine wrenches and pliers in them because they never knew what they would need when they came into your house. That's kind of what bridge conventions are. You walk around with all these things up in your head because you never know what you're going to need during the session. Does it complicate the game? Yes. Does everybody use them? No. Does it make better bridge players out of them? Well, I don't see Zia or Bob Hamman giving up their tools so easily."

I drop the subject, because what I really want to focus on is the future of the game. When I mention that Tina and I played yesterday, Buckman's face lights up. She says, "We work hard at developing and maintaining a program for the incoming interested player—like you!" She tells me that yesterday's morning game broke the record for newcomer participation—with still almost four days to go.

But what about drawing young people into the game? Typically, the ACBL junior program is run with more than a whiff of desperation. There is a Web site with the unfortunate address www.bridgeiscool.com—a title that seems marketed mainly at grandmothers. The site doth clearly protest too much. There is a blog, pictures of girls and boys in sunglasses and on cell phones, and a sixty-second animated video with a hip-hop soundtrack that flashes pictures and graphics that say "Hit it!" and "It was cold as ice until she took the hook!" There is even a section called "Be Cool," where you can download bridge wallpaper and instant-messenger icons, though that a teen would want his online image to be the word "finesse" might be a bit of a stretch. Overall, the site seems to miss the point that clever kids attracted to complex card games might have a sense of the sardonic.

Perhaps a more successful endeavor has been the ACBL's School Bridge Lesson Series program, which provides stipends and materials to educators willing to teach the game to their students. The program reaches sixty-five hundred schoolchildren a year, and in 2005 the number of sponsored classes was up 25 percent. Still, getting bridge into schools has proved something of an uphill battle. Buckman says, "Too many superintendents, too many principals are ignorant about cards. There is a built-in prejudice about playing cards at school. They don't see the benefit of it."

To illustrate the benefits, Buckman points to a recently released study funded in part by the ACBL Education Foundation that will be heralded in the August 2006 *Bridge Bulletin*. A researcher in Illinois has found a link between learning to play bridge and higher test scores. Middle school students who were taught to play bridge outperformed their schoolmates in all five subject areas covered by a standardized test: reading, math, social studies, language, and science.

The ACBL also has tried to forge alliances with educational organizations like the National Council of Teachers of Mathematics. And when Bill Gates and Warren Buffett offered their $1 million endorsement to start public school programs, the league was quick to latch on. But even for the billionaires, it hasn't been easy. Buckman says, "They are having difficulty getting into schools. They put up the money, but now they're trying to spend it. There are just so many laws."

At this point, she suggests we talk to the man chopping onions, Dick Anderson, who was the president of the ACBL in 1998. He is from Canada and wears a shirt with a moose on it. Buckman says, "In Canada, they are wildly more successful than we are with their school bridge programs." Anderson stops chopping long enough to say, "They're not going to all take the game up right away, but we think it's the future of bridge. No doubt about that. We're looking forward to a new generation of bridge players."

Buckman agrees that the aging of the bridge population is a problem. The average age of the ACBL member is sixty-eight—and rising. While a 2005 survey sponsored by the ACBL found that the average age of the 25 million bridge players in the country at large is only about fifty-one, this is still bad news. I mention these facts, and Buckman tells a parable of sorts.

"Do you know anything about the ABA—the American Bridge Association?" she asks. The ABA is an African-American bridge association founded in 1932 by a group of tennis players in Buckroe Beach, Virginia. Buckman says, "It's no surprise that in the days of segregation, African Americans made their own organization, and the ABA has always been an institution in the black community. They're structured very similarly to the way we are, and their demographic is similar to ours—though, by the way, their organization predates ours by a couple of years." Like the ACBL, the ABA's membership is aging, and, because they started as a smaller organization, Buckman says, "There is some thought that within a given number of years, they won't have enough people to sustain any sort of national organization." Thus, the ACBL has staged crossover events and nationwide "unity games," because, as Buckman says, "If it's good for bridge, it's good for all of us."

It seems an odd story to tell when asked where bridge is heading. Buckman also mentions the ACBL's new partnership with the American Association of Retired Persons, or AARP. Seventy-eight percent of ACBL members are over fifty-five, and the league has long wished to work with the 35 million-member organization. "Their demographics and ours are so similar," says Buckman. "They have just come to understand that fact." This year the league is sponsoring five special AARP games, the winners of which will receive a free trip to October's AARP "Life@50+" member event in Anaheim, which features headliners such as Elton John, Bill Cosby, and Connie Chung. Buckman says the AARP game in Chicago drew twenty-eight tables.

The ACBL is heavily promoting the partnership. Yesterday the *Daily Bulletin* ran a picture of the visiting president of the AARP board. It seems the league is poised to cash in on all those retiring baby boomers. When listing what she found attractive about bridge, Buckman made sure to mention some of the game's more boomer-centric selling points.

But does all this talk send the wrong message—has the ACBL resigned itself to the fact that the kids just want to play poker? What does the future of bridge look like—is the game in jeopardy? After a pause, Buckman replies, "I think there will always be bridge. Will the American Contract Bridge League always be one hundred sixty thousand strong—who knows? There are a lot of things vying for your leisure hours and your leisure dollars. But will there always be bridge? Yes—because the game is too great to ever die."

This leads me to my final question, the answer to which I've been chasing the entire book. Just what is it about bridge in particular that gets people so hooked? Everywhere I have seen the evidence of addiction: the eager throngs traveling to tournaments, the little old ladies meeting for a lifetime of lunches, the cutthroat competitors at big-city bridge clubs, the caddies on the road like diehard bridge bums, the brilliant and peculiar professionals young and old alike, the hot-blooded bridge couples, and all the smitten statesmen, celebrities, gamblers, and rock stars.

To me, the allure is at once understandable and inexplicable. Part of it must be the idea that the most worthwhile victories are the hardest won. Because for all the sexy publicity—the instant-messenger icons and showgirls in sarongs—bridge remains without a doubt one of the most difficult games around. As I have learned this year, even with studious application, stern concentration, and no day job, a player can only go so far so fast.

But such explanations fall short. The motivation must go deeper. Bridge is a battle between fate and chance mediated by skill. To play is to try to rationalize the irrational, to outwit chaos. From a finite deck of fifty-two, a universe opens of near-infinite permutations that—from the moment the cards are dealt—players try to reduce, by sheer mental will, into a manageable, knowable outcome. Communication falters, conventions fall apart, partners dupe and opponents dissemble, but the cards never lie. Thus the game is a mix of probability and psychology, rigorous in its uncertainties, mathematical in its mystery. Once the deal is made, the future is circumscribed—the potential for tricks becomes limited—but the play of the hand itself is a revolt against that certainty, as players try to finesse their fate through logic, imagination, and perception. To its most serious adherents, bridge offers a manageable microcosm, a fantasy of control. It is life reduced to a parlor game, able to be confronted and defeated time and time again in the antiseptic brightness of the clubhouse, its mysteries laid out on the table for careful inspection.

I ask President Buckman what she thinks, how she can explain the legions of fanatics gathered some thirty floors below. Surveying the skyline from her suite in the clouds, she says, "That's the question, isn't it? What draws us and keeps us? I believe it comes down to the snowflake theory—no two hands are identical. That's kind of it. The challenge, the beat goes on. And maybe that's the answer—that there is no answer. For people who enjoy puzzles, this is one they will never solve."

This is the sixteenth national tournament to be held in Chicago. The first, in 1927, attracted more than three hundred players. These days, the summer NABC is the most popular of the ACBL's three national events. By the end of this year's eleven-day tournament, 6,108 people from twenty-nine countries and all fifty states will have sat down to play cards, taking home a whopping 105,007.98 master points and accounting for 13,373 tables in play. You know it's an NABC by all the Polish periodicals discarded on benches, and aside from the usual international suspects—Canada, England, Italy—there are players from far-flung lands such as Egypt, Russia, Turkey, Hong Kong, India, Iran, Iceland, and Israel. From what I can tell, many people have traveled great distances to see nothing more of Chicago than the inside of the Hyatt.

They are here to play bridge. Sessions start at nine in the morning and run well past midnight in a bewildering schedule that offers something for everyone—pair games, team games, multisession events, plus something called the "Fast Open Pairs" where players have eleven minutes to finish every two boards.

Some teams are competing in the College Bridge Championships, an event that begins online with a field of thirty and finishes at the summer nationals with a round-robin tournament between the final eight. Among the contenders, majors run from the typical pocket-protector sciences (physics, math, biology, engineering) to brainy combinations of such (biochemistry, bioengineering) to a lone brave history major. In the end, the University of Michigan Wolverines will eek out a squeaker against the Princeton Tigers to win the college title and a set of $500 scholarships.

Dr. Steven D. Levitt, the University of Chicago economics professor behind the best-selling book *Freakonomics*, was at the tournament earlier in the week running experiments on participants. Apparently the study was on decision-making. Subjects played games against each other that involved betting, bluffing, and various rewards. Next, Levitt was off to Las Vegas, where he was going to run the same tests on poker players. (Of course I'm very curious to learn his results—which are to appear in a follow-up to *Freakonomics*—but e-mails sent through his editor are never returned.)

Undoubtedly the main event of the tournament is the Spingold Master Knockout Teams, in which top-level squads of four to six players compete for a trophy donated in 1934 by reporter-turned-movie-mogul Nathan B. Spingold. Along with the Vanderbilt Cup—which is contested at the spring nationals—the Spingold Trophy is the league's most coveted honor. It is a grueling seven-day slugfest in which teams are whittled down in head-to-head NCAA-tournament-style knockout competition until there is one winner. In his book, Bob Hamman says with uncharacteristic swagger, "The Spingold isn't a tea party. We play hardball there."

In his long career, Bob has won the Spingold a record thirteen times. While it is a team event, he seems to see this year as something of a grudge match. Before the tournament began, he told the *Chicago Tribune* that at some point he hopes to come up against the formidable Lorenzo Lauria—a member of the Italian team that unseated the United States in the last world championship and the man who has surpassed Hamman as the number-one ranked player in the world.

In its promotional literature, the ACBL frequently likens its national tournaments to "eleven-day-long bridge parties." In his autobiography, Zia is less restrained. He says each NABC is "an orgy—of bridge." And while the vibe might be somewhat "scruffy" and "anti-social" for his tastes, "the level of competition is the highest in the world."

The summer nationals presents an oddly cloistered carnival. There are belly dancers, mimes, and comedians, plus a peculiar insistence on nightly "ethnic entertainment"—beer barrel polkas, Klezmer music, Irish dances, Mexican ensembles, Greek choruses, and the like. Sometimes the performances complement the free late-night snack, which runs the gastronomical gamut from bratwurst to baklava, cheesecake to churros, not to mention egg rolls and fortune cookies stuffed with bridge-related forecasts. The tournament offers childcare for children three months to thirteen years, with pizza parties, music, games, "dramatic play," and, of course, bridge lessons. There are bus tours to the homes of Hemingway and Frank Lloyd Wright and the haunts of Al Capone, plus evening excursions to White Sox games and the musical *Wicked*. There is even an on-site blood drive, though at the risk of sounding like a cynic, I wonder how many players are willing to tear themselves away from the table—even for a good cause.

While bigger than Gatlinburg by more than 2,100 people, the national tournament is in some ways not as impressive a sight. Sure there are more tables in play, but they are tucked away in a catacomb of rooms on multiple levels. There is no single vast chamber, no single awesome spectacle of bridge.

Still, the people are priceless, their costumes taken to the next level. Nobody bats an eye at women wearing bright full-body bridge motley or the man whose shirt proclaims, "My wife said if I didn't stop playing bridge she's going to divorce me. God, I'm gonna miss her." The place is full of the typical jokers, like the man in a Hawaiian shirt at the water station who tells every hotel employee who passes by, "I think you ought to fill one of these with vodka or gin."

I overhear the predictable partnership squabbles, like the middle-aged man who says, "I'm just trying to tell you gently, honey, how I feel . . ." in a voice that comes out sounding something like a hiss. On the other side of the room, another couple is spoiling for a fight, as a woman says, "It never dawned on me you shifted to the jack-third of diamonds," as she shoots her hubby a dirty look and storms into the ladies' room. It seems the younger the partnership, the more open the hostility, as a teen in a T-shirt screams at his buddy, "Why would you lead that from queen-ten-four—that's so fucking hopeless!" Witnessing this last display, an elderly woman tut-tuts the youth with a word, "Language!"

The halls resound with the unmistakable accents of Canada, Texas, and New York, plus plenty of those wonderfully broad vowels native to the land of Lincoln. Everywhere I go I hear postmortem pointers ("With sixteen points you gotta double!"), breathless recaps ("I can't believe I bid six and made it!"), and vaguely serious threats ("You better play good with my wife."). A woman in a crowd makes an insincere—and roundly ignored—cry for help: "I can't believe this bridge playing has overtaken my life!" A man calls down the escalator, "Anybody want to go to the OTB?"

The color scheme of the Hyatt is a gravedigger's medley of greens, beiges, and browns, with nondescript hotel paintings placed at inoffensive intervals. It is a bland, evenly lit cocoon. It doesn't take long before one falls into the subterranean rhythms of a major bridge tournament, the curious comings and goings serving to mark time in the air-conditioned limbo. There are meal breaks, smoke breaks, and mad scrambles before a match. At one moment the halls are clogged to fire-hazard capacity; then, in an instant, they're empty—save for the players dialing missing partners shouting, "Where the hell are you?" When the game ends, the floor again comes furiously alive, if only for a few minutes, while players compare scores.

Nearby, a red LED sign flashes, "Play Bridge with Zia—$10." The ever-popular pro—unbowed after failing to win a world championship in Verona—is raffling off a chance to play with him to raise money to build a school in his earthquake-torn Pakistan.

In one out-of-the-way corner, a man in a golf shirt uncovers a piano and bangs out a jazzy rag for the benefit of two white-haired groupies, who sway with the beat. When he switches to old standards—a one-two punch of "Makin' Whoopie" and "On the Sunny Side of the Street"—the ladies join in singing. When a man in a baseball hat stops to do a funny jig, the crowd goes wild.

There are tables of buttons and flyers for upcoming cruises and tournaments in places such as Mexico, Zimbabwe, Kentucky, and Oregon. On one side of the floor, vendors sell everything under the sun that can be emblazoned with the iconography of bridge: totes, wallets, pens, address books, earrings, lipstick holders, boxers, scarves, mugs, napkins, spreaders, shot glasses, and so on. Next to the booths is a "comfort station," where for $5.00 you can get a five-minute chair massage.

This is where I run into Zeus, who seems pleased—if somewhat surprised—to learn Tina and I sat down at the table. He is having a ball, though he admits the tournament is a bit of a bubble. He says, "You get here and entirely lose the outside world. There's a war going on, New York has been in the dark for a week—and I haven't heard a word about it." I am about to give him an update on the blackouts back home, when his partner waves him over to discuss pressing business.

It turns out Team Tina is not the only squad with a uniform; there is a Dutch contingent sporting mismatched orange polos, a far cry from our snazzy limited-edition shirts. In general, I spy the same nervous neurotics in their white sneakers and ill-fitting slacks, though perhaps people are a little dressier since this is a national. That said, after surveying a room of rumpled pros on her first night here, Tina was quick to announce, "These guys are hardly clothes horses."

At night, this motley crew lets its hair down. By ten thirty, a lady in a yellow T-shirt is roaming the halls holding in her hand a quarter bottle of white wine stacked beneath an open can of Bud. Meanwhile, an oenophilic foursome is holding court on a couch laughing and swilling pinot noir from fancy oversized crystal. Down by the newcomer area, a sizable poker game breaks out. It's mainly caddies and young pros in hoodies and hats, with someone's girlfriend dealing. A few middle-aged men have sidled up to watch, and one old codger with a ponytail and dark shades sits down to play. I bump into Alex, the precocious undergraduate from Gatlinburg, who says he's having a terrible tournament. He offers to give me a "very depressing interview" about how by the end of the week he will have wasted eleven days.

It's after midnight on the playing-room floor, and the price of interviewing Jeff Meckstroth, who, with his team, just finished handily defeating a squad made up mainly of Icelanders in the quarterfinals of the Spingold and in about twelve hours will face Zia's team in the semis, is a beer. Specifically, a Miller Lite, which he carries into an empty ballroom before settling into a seat.

Meckstroth, fifty, is a big guy with a trim—but not prim—beard and short brown hair. At first glance, he looks like a good old boy from Tampa, where he lives—more like a special teams football coach than a professional bridge player, or at least someone more at home on the golf course than in the math lab. (As it turns out, Meckstroth was a scratch golfer as a teen.) I have been trading e-mails with him since I played with his son, Rob, in Gatlinburg and watched him compete in Las Vegas. When Jeff learned I was coming to Chicago, he said to find him one night after a match and we'd talk.

To nonbridge players, that kind of easygoing invitation might not seem that strange. But to the initiated, it's like saying Tiger Woods suggested you look him up after a round at the Masters. Meckstroth was a child phenom, crowned in 1974 as the "King of Bridge," the ACBL's top honor (along with the "Queen of Bridge") given to a graduating high school senior. Since then, he has won a reputation for sniffing out a successful line of play in even the most hopeless of contracts. He has the third most master points of any person, living or dead, and he currently leads the race for the player who has accumulated the most points this year. He was named the Player of the Decade by the ACBL for his dominance during the 1990s. He is one of the handful of living players who has won the three major world events, the so-called triple crown of bridge: the World Team Olympiad, the World Open Pairs, and the illustrious Bermuda Bowl (which he has won four times). He is considered one of the game's fiercest competitors. In his autobiography, Bob Hamman writes simply, "Meckstroth is a tiger."

Meckstroth and his regular partner Eric Rodwell form the deadly duo "Meckwell"—according to the *New York Times,* "considered by most to be the best pair in the world." In the bridge world, the name Meckwell can serve as shorthand for either the powerhouse partnership or their homegrown bidding scheme, "R-M Precision," a supercharged version of a strong-club system. The Meckwell system is legendary for both its brilliance and its complexity. Meckstroth and Rodwell bid early and often, exerting tremendous pressure on their opponents—making it difficult for them to bid and easy for them to make mistakes. In the *Times,* bridge columnist Phillip Alder writes, "They bid on hands that most players would pass in their sleep."

To describe a bidding system as complex isn't just saying that a bid of one club means this and one diamond means that—and on up the line, one bid for one meaning. The bids tell different stories depending on what comes before them and how the opponents have acted, so it's more like saying what a bid of two hearts means after the person in the second seat bids X after partner has bid Y at favorable vulnerability—and so on, in an ever-widening tree of possibility.

Meckstroth and Rodwell have analyzed thousands and thousands of bidding sequences from the real to the hypothetical, the likely to the astronomically rare. In Harriette Buckman's bridge-player-as-plumber analogy, Meckwell's leather bag would be the size of a Volkswagen. Better yet, they wouldn't even be plumbers—they'd be some kind of infuriating know-it-all super–Boy Scouts, always prepared to handle whatever sticky situation or freak hand they might face. It's an interesting kind of bridge player who invents systems upon systems. He knows the odds are against him—he'll never be able to tame the game, to close up all the gaps in his bidding, no matter how textured his system, but at the same time he feels a contrary impulse to try. On this point, Rob was happy to rat his father out, telling me in Gatlinburg, "They make up conventions they don't even use—for fun!"

Jeff Meckstroth grew up in Ohio. In 1971, when he was fourteen, he learned to play bridge from his father, a once-a-month duplicate player. His older brother wanted to pick up the game before going off to college, and Jeff was too competitive with his sibling to sit out. He borrowed a book from his dad—Ernest Rovere's *Contract Bridge Complete*—and after ten or so chapters and two days of kibitzing, he was ready to dive in. The third time he played, he and his brother won the club tournament.

After that, Meckstroth began playing with his dad, and in a few years he became a Life Master. But his ambition was to play serious golf, not bridge, and he was recruited by Ohio University. A week before the team tryouts, he broke his elbow and turned his attention to bridge. By his junior year, he had "the urge to prove something at bridge," and so with the blessing of his mother (and to the dismay of his father) he dropped out to become a pro player.

While Meckstroth was still in high school, a mutual friend introduced him to a young player named Eric Rodwell. Meckstroth smiles as he describes the beginning of a beautiful bridge friendship. "I met Eric in 1974," he remembers, "and the first time we played, in January 1975, we played in a two-session open pair and won the event. That was the first tournament win of any kind Eric had ever had. I was—quote, unquote—the 'King of Bridge,' and so in his view a big star. But the day I met

Eric, the summer before, when we played on a team together, I said, 'This is the guy.' We've been playing together thirty-one years now, which makes us, I believe, the longest-standing partnership in the world."

Seven years after the two met, they won a world championship, the 1981 Bermuda Bowl. What's kept them together, according to Jeff, is "a lot of work." He says, "We've learned so much from each other because we see the game so differently at times. At the beginning we were like night and day. I'm more of a natural player, and he's more . . . analytical."

At this I have to laugh, because Rodwell, who lives outside Tampa in nearby Clearwater Beach, is acknowledged to be the brains behind the vaunted Meckwell system. Meckstroth admits, "Well, yes, Mr. Rodwell is a bit obsessive-compulsive when it comes to bidding. Obviously I've been very involved in the development of our system, but he's probably done eighty percent of the work."

I have read that the Fibonacci numbers—a particular mathematical sequence in which each number is the sum of the two preceding it—somehow figure into their system. When I mention this, Meckstroth admits, "Yes, we employ them in several of our more complex auctions. We have Fibonacci relays to show various support permutations. You see, Rodwell is sort of a mad scientist—and a genius."

As proof of that, there are a number of online sites dedicated to cataloging the Meckwell system, and there are Internet rumors that the pair's full system notes run well over eight hundred pages. When I ask for a page count for Meckwell, I receive a surprising answer. Meckstroth says, "We used to have pages and pages, but now we pretty much have it all committed to memory."

Another rumor is that Meckwell can be bought—if you can afford it and are willing to swear an oath of secrecy. That turns out to be bunk, too. Meckstroth says, "We don't give out our notes—bridge is tough enough as it is—but we've shared our stuff with many players over the years. Lots of our ideas are out there." He goes on to point out a few common upper-level conventions that have sprung from the Meckwell partnership.

In a larger sense there is no monolithic Meckwell system—Meckwell just means whatever the two men are playing that day. I ask Meckstroth if he ever imagines a day will come when they will decide enough is enough and leave their system alone. He says, "I sure hope so," then laughs. "But we're not there yet."

Few pairs have pushed the envelope of the bidding science as they have. In essence, they are linguists, dreaming up a mother tongue and then trying to expand the vocabulary to encompass the world—or at least the 635,013,559,600 hands they might hold (and how they might relate to partner's—and the opponents'—cards). But in the end all systems must fall short, even ones that use words like "Fibonacci." To me, that would seem frustrating, like spending thirty-one years and only coming up with pig Latin, but Meckstroth claims the failure is what keeps him interested.

He then says something that would warm the heart of any "naturalist" bridge player in the world. "You don't need that much in the way of conventions," he tells me in all earnestness. "The most important thing in bridge is that you and your partner are on the same page—that you know what the bids mean. What methods you play, exactly, aren't really that critical."

This finally leads Meckstroth to let slip what he truly feels to be the key to his brilliant long-running partnership. He says, "What we do is allow judgment to rule supreme. You are never forced to do this or that. You can judge. And that's what bridge is—it's a game of judgment."

Thus the heart of the Meckwell system: it's not the pursuit of the perfect science, scope, or synchronization, but the allowance for nuance, for action outside of the system. For any critics who might think of Meckwell as ruthless killjoys taking all the mystery out of the game, human computers crunching

numbers and crushing opponents with complicated conventions—there clearly is more than a little magic in what they do
at the table.

As Meckstroth puts down his empty beer, he says, "I relish
these times. I love playing in a national event. For me, it's the
World Series of baseball or the NBA Finals. Tomorrow we're in
the semifinals of the Spingold, a place I've been maybe twelve
or thirteen times before. See, I just love it. I'm exactly where I
want to be."

Even late in the afternoon on the eleventh—and final—day of
the tournament, the platoons of players are refusing to rest.
Instead, they shuffle around the lobby asking each other, "Are
you all packed?" and shout down long hallways, "See you at the
next tournament!" There are hugs in the carport ("Okay, call
me when you want to play.") and encouragement for those still
competing ("Go get 'em, guys."). The last open games started at
two, and by now they are over. Only the most serious of players are still in the hunt. Two multisession top-level competitions will conclude early this evening, one of which is the main
event—the much-heralded Spingold. It is an hour before the
final session of the Spingold, and a few pros, some still in it,
some not, trickle into the hotel. They are eyed with approval by
the laymen in the lobby with early evening flights, who sip coffee among the potted plants while waiting for significant others
to wheel over their luggage.

Downstairs many tables are put away, their chairs stacked
in neat rows. Tournament directors walk around wearing leis,
and there are macadamia nuts on hand to remind everyone that
the next NABC will take place this fall in Honolulu. According to the bulletin, the itinerant caddies are heading next to
Omaha for a regional. In general, the playing floors have the
look of a high school gym after the prom, but the energy is
high, and nearly an hour and a half before the match I hear
players asking for directions to the Vugraph theater, where

the Spingold finals will be broadcast live onto screens. Thirty minutes before the start, women with wine begin to gravitate toward the room.

The Spingold started on Monday with a field of seventy-eight teams. All the big shots were playing, though now only two teams remain. Last year's winners, the number-one seed, have already been knocked out in the sweet sixteen by a squad that went on to defeat a team with young Justin Lall (playing with his father, Hemant) in the quarterfinals. Lall was having a good tournament, having won—with his father and Bob Hamman, among others—an earlier event called the Grand National Teams, which is considered a national title. In a week, Lall would head to Bangkok with his junior team to successfully defend their world championship.

Officemate Bart Bramley also hit his stride early in Chicago, winning the Life Master pair event—though in the Spingold his squad was defeated by Zia's team. Zia and his merry men advanced to the semifinals, where they lost to the fearsome Nick Nickell team.

The Nickell crew is a highly successful hit squad put together by Frank T. Nickell, the fifty-something president and CEO of Kelso & Company, a well-known New York private equity firm. The team is anchored by the famed Meckwell, and includes world-class heavyweights Bob Hamman and his partner Paul Soloway, as well as Nickell and a Hall of Famer named Richard Freeman. The team holds multiple national and international titles; they are all business, to the point of employing a first-class coach, successful writer and Canadian player Eric Kokish, who accompanies them to tournaments and briefs them on their opponents. The Nickell squad represented the United States in the most recent world championship; they have won the Spingold seven times, most recently in 2004 after a huge semifinal comeback. Asked the secret to the success of the Nick Nickell team, Jeff Meckstroth says simply, "Team chemistry—we've got the right mix."

Facing Nickell in the finals is a lineup organized by James E. Cayne, national bridge champ and chairman and CEO of the investment banking firm Bear Stearns. The Cayne team is anchored by two pairs from the reigning world champion Italian side—who won the title by defeating the Nickell team in the finals of the most recent Bermuda Bowl. The squad is rounded out by Cayne, Michael Seamon, and nonplaying captain Charles Weed. The summer nationals is the first outing for the brand-new team Cayne, and they pretty much have cruised into the finals—giving Bob Hamman his grudge match against the Italians and his world-ranking nemesis, Lorenzo Lauria.

For the past two days, the final rounds of the Spingold have taken place in an upper-level room away from the mayhem of the playing-room floor. Two pairs from each team face off behind screens, both tables playing the same hands, à la duplicate. For the first time at a national tournament, the events are being monitored and recorded with real-time cameras. Floors below, in the ballroom that has become the Vugraph theater, some 350 seats sit in the dim light before three large screens. In front of each screen stands a laptop hooked up to a projector. At an elevated table on one side of the room sit the commentators, a revolving cast of professionals and personalities, many of whom have been knocked out of the contest. Already they are cracking jokes with each other, as the rest of us sit in the quiet drone of the AC. The mood is giddy and worshipful—like at the beginning of a rock concert, when everyone knows the band is waiting in the wings. This is a room ready to be bowled over.

It is the last session of the Spingold final. The score is close. The teams played thirty-two boards this morning, and at the half, Nickell leads Cayne by seven international matchpoints (or IMPs), sixty to fifty-three. As six o'clock approaches, seats quickly fill up. People stand in the aisles until they are yelled at by those whose view they've obstructed. At the very back of the room, a gaggle of teens and twenty-somethings play cards, trying to look somewhat unimpressed—I hear the clatter of poker chips hitting the table. When the match starts, they'll scramble for seats.

Suddenly, the outer two screens come alive. Identical sets of hands appear in the colorful Vugraph format: four white boxes, arranged North, South, East, and West, showing each player's cards organized by suit. Each box is headed by a name, beside which a little flag indicates that person's nationality. Both screens make it clear that despite being a so-called national tournament, this is a showdown between the Italians and the Americans. Immediately upon the appearance of the cards, the "bidding" commences in a chart in the upper-right corner. With the auction over, cards start appearing in little blue boxes in the middle of the "table." Once a card has been played, it is dimmed to a ghostly gray in the hand. The dummy hand is indicated by a darker background. A tally in the lower right keeps track of the number of tricks for each side, while a box in the upper left keeps a running score of the match.

Despite the widespread anticipation, the start seems to have taken the commentators by surprise, and there is minor confusion while microphones are located. In this round, Meckstroth and Rodwell are playing North-South on the left screen against Alfredo Versace and Lorenzo Lauria, while Hamman and Solo-way are sitting East-West on the right screen (and in reality in a different room) against Fulvio Fantoni and Claudio Nunes. I wonder if Bob is saddened not to be going head-on against Lauria. In a match this close, the sponsors won't play anymore, and in fact there is a rumor that Cayne has already flown home.

The play occurs simultaneously at both tables, and in their play-by-play, the commentators jump back and forth. "Hamman has unblocked the queen," says one, while another chimes in, "And of course Meckstroth bids three no-trump." The announcers are certainly not above a little editorializing. In fact, other than explaining the bids, that seems to be what they enjoy most, sometimes sneering ("Now we wouldn't have done that, would we?"), sometimes shouting ("Where's the double?").

They bicker among themselves about the "correct" bid to make. Of course they freely admit they are at great advantage being able to see all four hands. They also have at their disposal a computer to analyze what contracts will succeed.

As for the audience, they get a little rowdy themselves, muttering with their seatmates and yelling back at the commentators if they don't agree with their learned assessment. I join in to boo their bad puns ("I played that convention as a kid—we called it Brooklyn bridge!"). Scattered among the room are some of the top players in the world, many of whom are surrounded by groupies hanging on their every word. Everyone is having a ball, even exhausted bridge reporters. Sure, there is some dorky bridge humor, but the Vugraph makes for good theater. You might have to be something of a buff to understand the thrill of the phrase—"Here's some excitement: Is Rodwell going to overcall three no-trump over three spades?"—but even to the outsider, this would be a surprisingly dramatic show. With the commentators on hand to clear up the bidding (and judge which side can make what contract), it is exciting to watch the same hands being battled over side by side at different tables—with any difference resulting in a swing of points.

In general, it seems to be a pro-Nickell (or pro-American) room. There is an outburst of applause when Hamman plays the heart that will set the Italians' three no-trump contract and a huge groan when Soloway passes and misses a slam in spades.

Sometimes the play grinds to a halt while a pro stops to think for eight minutes or so, but in general the match goes pretty fast. On those quiet occasions, the commentators fill the dead air by recognizing notables in the audience, like the champion University of Michigan team or an American squad that did well in Verona. Occasionally their arguments wander far off track, leading to curious commentary like, "He sounds like a mashed potato salesman with a mouthful of samples."

The play is of the highest caliber and makes me think of Harriette Buckman's bridge Mount Olympus. Halfway through, in a dramatic reversal, the score stands ninety-one to eighty-five for Cayne and his Italians. On the commentators' table now stands the seventy-two-year-old Spingold trophy, a slender and shiny tall silver cup. The crowd is excited as the match is going down to the wire. On the other end of my row, I spy a very attentive Rob Meckstroth sitting with his brother.

The score remains tight. In general, Hamman and Soloway have been bidding very well, rightly ending their auctions one level below their Italian counterparts at the other table, Versace and Lauria.

Then five boards from the end comes what the announcers claim might be the fatal error. Rodwell is declaring a three no-trump contract that—in the other room—Hamman and Soloway have set by two tricks. When Versace, the Italian defender, plays the king of hearts on his partner's opening lead, the Vugraph room goes nuts. They can tell that Versace could have won the trick with the nine—as the highest heart declarer has is the eight—and now Versace has thrown in his king unnecessarily. He has missed a chance to make a crucial cheap trick. How Versace is supposed to know this, I can't imagine, but immediately the commentators are all over him, saying the nine is an obvious percentage play. This so-called mistake—on the very first trick—ends up allowing Rodwell to make the contract, giving Nickell a big thirteen-point swing.

Hamman and Soloway (or Hamway, as a woman tells me they are now known) are first to reach the final board, and every mouth in the room drops when it becomes clear that there is a slam possible in spades but Hamman doesn't bid it—perhaps leaving the door open for the lagging Italian pair. Now Versace and Lauria have to bid and make six clubs and six spades on the final two hands against Meckwell—to steal the win. On the second to last board, the Italians stop in three no-trump—like Hamway before them—missing a good six-club contract. That makes it a lock for Nickell, and the room exhales, even though the Italians do find the spade slam on the last board and get the swing—it just isn't enough. With the dust cleared, team Nickell is victorious by a mere six IMPs.

While it is incredibly unfair to single out one hand in a match of sixty-four, I wonder how long it will be until the Italians begin bemoaning that ill-fated king of hearts. To do everything right but lose a championship on one card must be cold comfort indeed. I am reminded of a bit of philosophy from Meckstroth's book: "You have to accept that bridge is not a perfect game—it's a game of mistakes."

There is thunderous applause when team Nickell walks into the room and Meckstroth hoists the Spingold trophy, gathering the group for a picture. Soloway is absent, as is Nick Nickell. The players smile and clasp each other and their family and friends, who cluster around the now almost-empty ballroom. It's eleven. The tournament is over, the fans having quickly slipped away, back to their beds, their homes, their less-exciting less-bridge-full lives, leaving the reigning national champions to ride the escalator up, one by one, and disappear into the hotel.

Back at table #5 in Section AA in Columbus Hall A—still in the early days of the tournament and far from the eyes of Hamman and Meckstroth and the Vugraph audience—Team Tina makes its gutsy run for the title.

Our first opponents are a pair of local women in their fifties, who start things off with what seems to me to be an aggressively hearty, "Welcome to Chicago." I realize that all the cool kids are going to be showing off hellacious Northern cities vowel shifts, but there's no time to worry about that, because I have live cards in my hands. To this day I cannot picture what the women look like, partly due no doubt to post-traumatic stress syndrome and partly because I hardly looked them in the face. When my eyes aren't boring holes into the backs of my cards, I'm grinning like an idiot at Tina, trying to buoy her spirits. No doubt the fact that her partner seems to have undergone some sort of psychic break does little to make her feel better. The first three boards pass in a flash. We defend all of them, twice successfully, once not, so we're off to a pretty calm start, considering. The room is silent, like we're miles underwater. Tina's hand shakes when she picks up her glass.

It turns out that was just a warm-up for round two, when we come up against a team I'll call The Terminators, two joyless women in business suits who hunch over the table, never look up, speak in monosyllables, and beat the ever-living crap out of us. They play fast, without breaks in tempo, and always seem to make the right choice. We give them overtricks on the first two boards, and then they set me three on my first chance to play a hand—a four-heart contract that, once all is said and done, seems like it should have been doable. When the carnage is over, the women rise in unison and say, "Thank you." In the end, they will have given us our worst round of the day.

But bridge is nothing if not a study in contrasts, and now we draw a pair of silly, giggling forty-something gals in name tags that I'm sure would have certain vowels dotted with hearts if they afforded the space. Unfortunately, Tina and I help out Tweedle-Dum and Tweedle-Ditzy by having our first true bidding disaster.

Dum opens a heart, Tina passes, Ditzy passes, and I double, a signal to Tina that I have a good hand and want her to bid something, anything—just to give me a clue what she is holding. She bids two diamonds, which makes my heart flutter—I have a great hand in diamonds. But then, because we're at nationals, because the auction seems to be going our way, because I've probably had too much coffee, because we've been bidding in sync so far, because of our opponents' vacant stares, I decide to get a little fancy—and make a truly rookie mistake. I'm not sure how high we should be. And instead of just settling on diamonds, I coyly bid two spades in an effort to tell her a little more about my cards (I have some spades), though I know we likely won't want to play in spades (if Tina had them, she would have bid them). In my mind, I'm just artificially keeping the auction alive so I can learn more about Tina's hand. Unfortunately, that's not how Tina—or any other bridge player on the planet—sees it. She doesn't read my two-spade bid as one that forces her to act, and she passes. Suddenly I'm playing in two spades. When the dummy comes down, I see that not only have we missed a big score in diamonds, but we only have five trumping spades between us! Luckily the opponents didn't double. I try not to clue Tina in to my trouble, but I think she realizes something's up. Mine was a dumb, entirely inappropriate, beyond inexcusable, too clever by half, what-kind-of-fancy-pants-numbskull-partner-are-you bid. I had relaxed my vigilance, let go of my fear for an instant, and my mind betrayed me. I might as well have been back in our beginner class. I don't dare to apologize or clear up the confusion at the table—not only is that a partnership faux pas, but it could shatter what little confidence we have. Best to soldier on and go down two tricks.

I end up declaring the next two hands, too, making a no-trump contract and then getting set in diamonds. At least we're not having any problems feeling rushed. We finish this round early and have a moment to catch our breath. I'm worried how the match is going, though to be honest it's almost impossible to tell. Last round's wretched spade slip-up has been our only obvious misstep—there's no way to know how our other results stack up. Maybe our one-sided bloodbath with The Terminators was replicated around the room. And in games past, tentative bidding has kept us from game contracts that, from time to time, don't have a chance to make. So hope springs eternal. I finally can recall a piece of bridge wisdom, something uplifting from Bob Hamman on why the game is so great. He writes in his autobiography, "In bridge, there's no way to lie down on the ball and play it cozy. The greatest single danger in a match when you're ahead is that you'll get robbed on a series of hands. To keep this from happening, you've got to get into the pot and take risks. You've got to bid as aggressively as you would if the match was tied. . . . You can't run out the clock in bridge."

Our next opponents are two nice ladies toting multicolored handbags. On the first auction, after passing twice, Tina—much to my surprise—doubles. Her left-hand opponent and I pass, and the women end up in three diamonds doubled. I casually repeat the contract as I write it on the score slip, and Tina asks, "Who doubled?" We look at her, surprised. The bids are still on the table, and when we point to the red X on top of the pile before her, Tina takes a sharp breath. Apparently she meant to pass, but the double card—which is of similar shape and size—was mixed in with her passes. She reached for it without noticing, dropped it, and never looked down. While Tina and I are resigned to playing in three diamonds doubled—a great boon for our opponents and seemingly the honorable thing to do—the women favor calling the director, just to see what she does. So up shoots a hand, and the director glides over.

Apparently, it's a sticky question. After hearing what happened, the director calls over a more senior official, and the two have a joint discussion. In the end, they rule it was a "mechanical error," so Tina can take back her pass. But, after examining the cards of Tina's left-hand opponent, the second director says if she wants to bid on, she may. She declines, and the auction ends with three diamonds—undoubled—and one shaken Tina. She is mortified by the attention. I imagine that will be her last double in Chicago.

As luck will have it, on the next hand Tina winds up the declarer—for the first time that morning. I worry she's still flustered, but she carries the day, playing confidently and craftily, and making overtricks to boot. I should have known better than to doubt. Tina is a tiger. The last hand goes well for us, when we appear to scare the opponents away from bidding an easy no-trump game. The handbag maidens, it seems, have handed us three decent results.

Next up is a pair of older British caricatures. He's a genial henpecked twit in a rumpled blue-checked shirt, and she an ice queen in a navy suit with proper white piping and a back as straight as a board. They don't do us any favors, though the round hardly seems a disaster. She spends most of her energy fussing at him for his questionable bids, such as when he raises her in hearts with only two of them in hand. Still, he keeps a stiff upper lip and bids well enough to allow his wife to make an all-business three no-trump contract. On the last board, they again misbid their hearts, which should end up helping us.

Round six deals us a jokey man and his wife who both are too chicken to bid. They have the lion's share of the cards, but they underbid their hands and miss what I believe could have been a slam. When they get up, I'm pretty pleased. This could be a good round for us—a bit of a sprint down the homestretch.

Unfortunately, the couple played interminably slow, and Tina and I miss a short break everyone else gets to take. Our next opponents arrive freshly restored. Me, I'm feeling like a marathoner. I'm sweating, I'm tired, and my back is beginning to ache. The table feels cramped—there doesn't seem room under it for eight legs—and I'm constantly stretching and shifting my weight around while trying not to look like I'm peeping.

We face a friendly twosome from Georgia. On the first hand Tina picks up a whopper. She bids two no-trump, showing twenty to twenty-one points, and I with a few measly cards raise her to three. Tina tries valiantly, but she goes down one. On the next board, I rustle up our requisite eight tricks in spades thanks in part to the fact that I started with seven of them. On the last hand, it's their turn to make it in spades.

For the eighth and final round, we face two tan matter-of-fact married baby-boomers. They give us what I fear is a bad run, though there's a chance they aren't wildly outperforming other tables. The man plays twice, making his contracts, while Tina plays once, making hers. I'm impressed by my gal. This is the longest and most serious bridge game both of us have ever played, but on the last board Tina is still in there swinging, despite—as she tells the man afterward—she felt he "knew" every card she had. It turns out the couple was yesterday's winner, though they say today isn't going as well.

And then suddenly it is over. The caddy picks up the last slip, the baby-boomers shuffle off, and Tina lets out a sigh of relief. I'm exhausted but excited. When we stand and stretch—at 1:30, after twenty-four boards and more than three and a half hours of deadly serious cards—Tina announces, "I'm paralyzed in my behind."

That said, we feel pretty good as we crowd around stanchion AA waiting for the results. Now that the trial is over, Tina is loosening up. She will have a ball for the rest of her time in Chicago, or so she will tell me, saying over and over, "I can't believe I'm here." I think she might even regret her initial decision to stay only a few nights; I will be there through the end of the week. That afternoon she will buy a gift for Jeff, our coach: a pack of white tube socks embroidered with cards, because, as she'll say, "I'm a practical person." She will be delayed again on her flight going home, though on the phone from New York the first thing she'll report is that she got carded buying a drink at the airport.

So in some ways how we did at the tournament is beside the point. Then again, I'd be lying to say we didn't care. We traveled some eight hundred miles for this very moment. This morning, despite our ups and downs, we made only one truly disastrous mistake—my bidding blunder. We could come out anywhere. In bridge, as in many things, the final results can be something of a mystery.

Then the scores are posted.

I would like to say we won the match, nay, went on to great glory, our pictures on the wall, our names in the bulletin, perhaps even earning a spot on team Nickell. Maybe I should embellish our finish, ratchet up the drama and take you, dear reader, off for some serious wish fulfillment. But, alas, this is not a book about poker. It's a book about bridge, where skill almost always trumps luck, pluck, and outsized ambition. The good players win out, underdogs be damned, and there are no fairy-tale endings for a guy in a Team Tina T-shirt and his lovable eighty-three-year-old partner.

We are dead last. Bottom of the heap, and by a pretty good margin. It turns out those Terminators and twits alike really cleaned our clocks. The winners receive trophies and smile for photographs. Tomorrow we'll read their names in the bulletin.

But as we watch the other pairs celebrate, Tina looks at me and says those three little words that warm a partner's heart.

"I'd play again."

NOTES

The Introduction I Am Not Qualified to Write: A Brief Bridge Tutorial
xviii Odds of receiving a full suit from a shuffled deck (one in 158,753,389,900):
"Player Says Everything Turned Up Trumps," *Calgary Herald* (Canada), January 27, 1998.

xx History of the Stayman Convention:
Truscott and Truscott, *New York Times Bridge Book,* 115–16.

Chapter One—A Clean, Well-Caffeinated Place
3 Number of possible hands in bridge (635,013,559,600):
"Bridge Players Bid for Ego, Fame, Pride," *Los Angeles Times,* November 28, 1987.

3 Alan Sontag quoting Marshal Smith—"the conceit of a peacock, night habits of an owl, rapacity of a crocodile . . .":
Sontag, *Bridge Bum,* 88.

7 Average lifespan of bridge champions and results of players in their eighties:
Truscott and Truscott, *New York Times Bridge Book,* 243.

7 Bridge reducing the risk of Alzheimer's and dementia:
"Mind Games May Trump Alzheimer's," *Washington Post,* June 19, 2003.

7 1999 University of California-Berkeley study:
Truscott and Truscott, *New York Times Bridge Book,* 247.

10 Poker shows, magazines, and vitamins:
"Poker Periodicals: How to Hold 'Em," *Washington Post,* May 10, 2005.

10 2006 worldwide buy-in for live poker tournaments:
PokerPages.com Industry Index: PPII (www.pokerpages.come/ppii).

10 2005 traffic on partypoker.com:
"Is Poker Losing Its First Flush?," *New York Times,* April 16, 2006.

10 Congress cracks down on online gambling:
"Online-Gambling Shares Plunge on Passage of U.S. Crackdown Law," *New York Times,* October 3, 2006.
"Neteller Arrests Bode Ill for Online Gambling," *BusinessWeek Online,* January 18, 2007.

10 "Poker" as most popular search term in 2006 on lycos.com:
"On Poker," *San Antonio Express-News,* December 28, 2006.

10 Churchill quote—"The king cannot fall unworthily if it falls to the sword of the ace":
Truscott and Truscott, *New York Times Bridge Book,* 102.

10 Bridge enthusiasts—George Burns, Deng Xiaoping, and Mahatma Gandhi:
Ibid., 110.

10 Bridge enthusiasts—Marx Brothers:
Sontag, *Bridge Bum,* 87.

10 Bridge enthusiast—George S. Kaufman:
"Unheard of in Bridge: Cavendish Club Folds," *New York Times,* June 2, 1991.

10 Bridge enthusiast—Wilt Chamberlain:
"A War of the Minds," *Courier-Post* (Cherry Hill, New Jersey), March 11, 2003.

10 Bridge enthusiast—Charles Schulz:
"Snoopy's Finest Card Game (Trump That, Red Baron!)," *New York Times,* July 10, 2000.

10 Bridge on Mount Everest and atop the Eiffel Tower:
"Bridge: Games at Highest Level (Measured in Altitude)," *New York Times,* October 25, 1992.

10 Bridge at the South Pole:
"Very Cold Contract," *Bridge Bulletin,* April 2006.

11 Maugham on bridge—"I would have children taught bridge . . .":
"Bridge: A Top Score Was One Way to Celebrate 88th Birthday," *New York Times,* December 31, 1987.

11 WWII Dutch duplicate in West Java:
Truscott and Truscott, *New York Times Bridge Book,* 105.

11 John McCain's bridge grudge:
"McCain's Party," *The New Yorker,* May 30, 2005.

11 Abu Ghraib bridge club:
"Bridge in the Desert," *Bridge Bulletin,* December 2005.

11 Buffett on bridge: "Bridge is such a sensational game that I wouldn't mind
    being in jail . . ."
ACBL promotional pamphlet, *"American Contract Bridge League: Your Best
    Partner in Bridge,"* copyright 2005.

11 Bridge in Alcatraz:
"Killing Time," *The Spectator* (U.K.), May 28, 2005.

11 Bridge in Leavenworth:
"Bridge: Prisoners in Leavenworth Show Their Card Skills," *New York
    Times,* June 18, 1971.
"Bridge: The Liberating Side Effects of Having Cards in Prison," *New York
    Times,* October 16, 1997.

11 San Quentin serial killers and bridge:
"San Quentin's Killer Bridge Parties," *Los Angeles Times,* October 16,
    1990.

12 U.S. bridge statistics:
2005 ACBL Nationwide Bridge Survey.

12 Figures on the ACBL (budget, membership, etc.) provided by the ACBL.

19 Number of Vanderbilt Cup teams with sponsors at the Pittsburgh NABC
    and what the professionals can earn:
"Bridge Aficionados Play for Keeps," *Pittsburgh Tribune Review,* March 6,
    2005.

20 Study comparing a session of tournament bridge to surgery:
Sontag, *Bridge Bum,* 54.

21 Objectivist bridge players:
"Ayn Rand, in Spades," *New York Times,* June 29, 2003.

Chapter Two—The Miseducation of a Bridge Player

25 The bridge club as an "upmarket dating agency":
"How to Play Bridge," *Washington Post*, February 29, 2004.

32 Online bridge statistics—4.1 million Americans playing over the
    Internet, with more than 12 percent playing daily:
2005 ACBL Nationwide Bridge Survey.

32 Bridge Base traffic during the 2005 world championship:
"Sometimes, a Trick Lost Early Can Pay Dividends in the End," *New York
    Times*, November 10, 2005.

35 My information on the advanced state of computer chess comes from
    Tom Mueller's fascinating article: "Your Move," *The New Yorker*,
    December 12, 2005.

35 Why computers can't play bridge:
"Bring Bridge Back to the Table," *New York Times*, November 27, 2005.
"Older Players Have an Edge," *New York Times*, April 23, 2005.

36 Deep Finesse:
Truscott and Truscott, *New York Times Bridge Book*, 242.

36 Results of the 2005 World Computer Bridge Championship:
"Knockout Punch," *Bridge Bulletin*, January 2006.

37 The history of the Rule of Eleven:
"Rule of Eleven," *The Official Encyclopedia of Bridge*, 393.

38 The second earl of Yarborough and his hand:
"Your Questions Answered," *The Express* (U.K.), April 29, 2006.
"Good Yarboroughs and Bad," *New York Times*, May 29, 2004.
"Bridge: Betting with the Odds," *New York Times*, January 18, 1987.

39 Definition of backwash squeeze—"A unique type of trump squeeze in
    which both menaces are in the same hand . . .":
"Backwash Squeeze," *The Official Encyclopedia of Bridge*, 23–24.

39 Chance for a backwash squeeze in the 1994 Vanderbilt Cup finals:
"Bridge," *New York Times*, March 21, 1994.

39 Omar Sharif column on the 2006 backwash squeeze: "Caught in the
    backwash of the high trump."
"Puzzles: Bridge," *The Observer* (U.K.), August 6, 2006.

42 The country's youngest Life Master:
"The Prodigy," *Bridge Bulletin*, May 2006.

42 Barry Crane murder:
"Barry Crane, Bridge Expert, Found Slain in Los Angeles," *New York Times*,
        July 7, 1985.
"'Dallas' Director Found Murdered," *The Times* (London), July 8, 1985.
"Detectives Hunt for Killer of TV Director," United Press International,
        July 6, 1985.

43 Previous McKenney Trophy winner paying the pros not to play:
"The Bridge Game," *Washington Post*, March 3, 1981.

43 The 2005 Barry Crane winner:
"Alan Stout Sets His Sights on the Record," *Daily Bulletin,* Summer North
        American Bridge Championships, July 27, 2005.
"Stout's Odyssey," *Bridge Bulletin*, March 2006.

Chapter Three—Kibitzing in Cowtown

51 The Bennett bridge table murder:
"Slaps Wife in Bridge Game; She Kills Him," *Chicago Daily Tribune,*
        October 1, 1929.
"Hand at Bridge Murder Cause," *Los Angeles Times*, October 1, 1929.
"Wife Kills Husband in Bridge Game Spat," *New York Times*, October 1,
        1929.
"Photo Standalone: Kills Husband After Row over Bridge Whist," *Chicago
        Daily Tribune*, October 2, 1929.
"Killed by Wife," *Chicago Daily Tribune*, October 2, 1929.
"Try Woman for Killing Husband at Bridge Game," *Chicago Daily Tribune,*
        February 24, 1931.
"Seek Married Man Jury to Try Husband Slayer," *Chicago Daily Tribune,*
        February 25, 1931.
"'Jim' Reed Re-enacts Bridge Game Killing," *Chicago Daily Tribune,*
        February 28, 1931.
"Bridge Slaying Victim Called Bad Tempered," *Chicago Daily Tribune,*
        March 1, 1931.
"Bridge Slayer's Sobs Interrupt Mother's Story," *Chicago Daily Tribune,*
        March 3, 1931.
"State Attacks Bridge Murder Case Testimony," *Chicago Daily Tribune,*
        March 4, 1931.
"'Accident,' Sobs Bridge Widow in Her Defense," *Chicago Daily Tribune,*
        March 5, 1931.
"Bridge Murder Jury Is Locked Up for Night," *Chicago Daily Tribune,*
        March 6, 1931.

"Jury Acquits Wife of Slaying Husband in Bridge Game Row," *Chicago Daily Tribune*, March 7, 1931.

"Wife Is Acquitted in Bridge Slaying," *New York Times*, March 7, 1931.

"It's Not Just a Game, It's a Subculture," *Miami New Times*, January 19, 1994.

"Mystery and Savagery," *Kansas City Star*, May 21, 2000.

Truscott and Truscott, *New York Times Bridge Book*, 37–38.

Daniels, *Golden Age of Contract Bridge*, 179–84.

Woollcott, *While Rome Burns*, 191–96.

Chapter Four—A Short History of Bridge: From Hoyle to Halloween

59 Hugh Latimer Advent sermon:
Daniels, *Golden Age of Contract Bridge*, 7.

59 Derivation of the word "whist":
Ibid., 10.

59 Edmond Hoyle and his pamphlet on whist:
Truscott and Truscott, *New York Times Bridge Book*, 1–2.
Daniels, *Golden Age of Contract Bridge*, 12–13.

60 Fourth earl of Sandwich:
"Sandwich with a Side of Gambling Chips," *Los Angeles Times*, July 6, 2005.
Truscott and Truscott, *New York Times Bridge Book*, 2.

60 Washington, Talleyrand, Hornblower, devotees of whist:
Truscott and Truscott, *New York Times Bridge Book*, 2–3.

60 Sherlock Holmes and whist:
"For Holmes, a Hard Contract Is Elementary, My Dear Etc.," *New York Times*, September 24, 1974.

60 Napoleon played whist:
Daniels, *Golden Age of Contract Bridge*, 26.

60 Kalamazoo tray:
Ibid., 33.

60 Poe on whist: "The best chess-player in Christendom may be little more than the best player of chess . . ."
Stern (ed.), *Portable Poe*, 334.

60 Poe on table presence: "He examines the countenance of his partner, comparing it carefully with that of each of his opponents."
Ibid., 335–36.

61 The rules of the early bridge:
Daniels, *Golden Age of Contract Bridge*, 39.

61 Origin of the name "bridge":
Truscott and Truscott, *New York Times Bridge Book*, 7.
Daniels, *Golden Age of Contract Bridge*, 36–38.

62 Henry Barbey and the introduction of bridge in the United States:
Daniels, *Golden Age of Contract Bridge*, 43.

62 King Edward VII and the first duplicate bridge game in 1904:
Ibid., 48–49.

62 1908 rules of auction bridge:
Ibid., 52.

62 Women bridge instructors:
Ibid., 83.

62 Life and murder of Joseph Elwell:
Ibid., 84–85.

63 Milton Work, Wilbur C. Whitehead, and Sidney Lenz:
Ibid., 85–87, 89, 94.

63 Contract bridge, plafond, and S.A.C.C.:
Ibid., 76–77.

63 Vanderbilt's historic Halloween game:
"The Opening Bid: 40 Years Ago," *New York Times*, December 26, 1965.

63 Vanderbilt, the America's Cup, and his social clout:
Truscott and Truscott, *New York Times Bridge Book*, 23.
Daniels, *Golden Age of Contract Bridge*, 107.

Chapter Five—Gamblers and Grannies

64 Bob Hamman and the history of SCA:
"Making It in Big-Time Bridge," *New York Times*, July 26, 1987.
"Bridge," *New York Times*, March 8, 1992.
"Risky Business," *Cigar Aficionado*, July/August 1998.
"A Trump Card for Unusual Risks," *New York Times*, February 13, 2000.
"The Oddsmaker," *D Magazine*, November 1, 2000.
"A Tribute to Joe Musumeci," *ACBL District 16 Scorecard*, March/April
    2004.

"High Profile: Bob Hamman," *Dallas Morning News*, April 25, 2004.
"A Risky Biz," *San Diego Union-Tribune*, February 12, 2005.
Truscott and Truscott, *New York Times Bridge Book*, 175, 178.
Sontag, *Bridge Bum*, 28–30.
Hamman and Manley, *At the Table*, 11–13, 15–16, 74–75, 79, 88–89, 91, 117, 126, 230, 258.

69 Buffett on Hamman—"I could have started playing bridge when I was a three-year-old . . .":
"High Profile: Bob Hamman," *Dallas Morning News*, April 25, 2004.

69 Origins of Texas Hold'em:
"Show of Hands," *Anchorage Daily News*, March 3, 2006.
"Texas Hold'em in Legal Limbo," *Corpus Christi Caller-Times*, February 13, 2005.

72 Hamman's hand against the Italians at the 2005 world championships reprinted in the article "What Might Have Been," *Bridge Bulletin*, January 2006.

80 Justin Lall and the 2005 World Youth Team Championship:
"Well done, Mates!" *Bridge Bulletin*, November 2005.

84 Ely Culbertson's double entendres:
"Winsome & Loathsome," *Bridge Bulletin*, November 2005.

Chapter Six—A Short History of Bridge: From Ballyhoo to Mr. Bridge

96 1926 notice in *Los Angeles Times* about bridge-table divorce:
"Even Murder Justifiable," *Los Angeles Times*, April 9, 1926.

96 History of the Vanderbilt Knockout Team Championship and the Vanderbilt Cup:
Truscott and Truscott, *New York Times Bridge Book*, 25.

96 1931, best-selling books:
Ibid., 49.

96 Remarkable early history of Ely Culbertson:
Daniels, *Golden Age of Contract Bridge*, 108–18.
Truscott and Truscott, *New York Times Bridge Book*, 36–37.

96 Bertrand Russell on Culbertson—"The most remarkable, or at any rate psychologically interesting, man . . .":
Truscott and Truscott, *New York Times Bridge Book*, 36.

97 Culbertson and Jo take on the American bridge world:
Daniels, *Golden Age of Contract Bridge*, 96, 119, 122, 126, 139.
Truscott and Truscott, *New York Times Bridge Book*, 37.

98 Waldemar von Zedtwitz:
Truscott and Truscott, *New York Times Bridge Book*, 27.
Daniels, *Golden Age of Contract Bridge*, 123.

98 The Anglo-American bridge match of 1930 and the birth of *The Blue Book:*
Truscott and Truscott, *New York Times Bridge Book*, 38.
Daniels, *Golden Age of Contract Bridge*, 142–43, 150.

99 The success of Culbertson provokes a backlash:
Truscott and Truscott, *New York Times Bridge Book*, 43–44.
Daniels, *Golden Age of Contract Bridge*, 152, 154–55.

99 The Culbertson-Lenz bridge match and its aftermath and analysis:
"World Barred by Bridge Duel," *Los Angeles Times*, December 7, 1931.
"Rival Bridge Stars Compete Tonight," *New York Times*, December 7, 1931.
"Lardner Finds City Agog Over Match," *New York Times*, December 8, 1931.
"Culbertson Lead Jumps 2,950 Points," *New York Times*, December 19, 1931.
"Good Luck Tokens Given to Players," *Los Angeles Times*, December 20, 1931.
"Lenz Naps as He Waits for Culbertson to Play," *Los Angeles Times*, December 24, 1931.
"Jacoby Resigns as Lenz's Bridge Partner in Row," *Los Angeles Times*, December 29, 1931.
"Culbertsons' Lead Passes 20,000 Mark," *New York Times*, December 31, 1931.
"Fists Trumps for a While in Bridge Match," *Chicago Daily Tribune*, December 31, 1931.
"A Line o' Type or Two," *Chicago Daily Tribune*, January 1, 1932.
"Culbertson Victor in Bridge Test Play," *New York Times*, January 9, 1932.
"Bridge Victory to Culbertson, and That's That," *Chicago Daily Tribune*, January 9, 1932.
"Distribution Seen as Crux of Bridge," *New York Times*, January 10, 1932.
"Vanderbilt's Card Game," *Washington Post,* March 1, 1981.
Truscott and Truscott, *New York Times Bridge Book*, 44–51.
Daniels, *Golden Age of Contract Bridge*, 156, 158–76, 184, 195.

102 Bridge as Hollywood's second favorite "indoor sport":
Keaton and Samuels, *My Wonderful World of Slapstick*, 185.

102 Bridge-playing moguls:
Ibid., 185–87.

102 The film *Grand Slam:*
"An Opening Grand Slam Bid," *New York Times,* July 31, 2004.

103 Bridge in 44 percent of American homes in the 1940s:
ACBL press release: "Bridge Trumps Food and Fire," PR Newswire, June 13, 2005.

103 The great Charles Goren:
Truscott and Truscott, *New York Times Bridge Book,* 87, 90–91, 94–95.
"King of Aces," *Time,* September 29, 1958.
"Vanderbilt's Card Game," *Washington Post,* March 1, 1981.
"Does Bridge Need a Hand?" *Chicago Tribune,* July 26, 1989.
"Bridge Columnist Charles Goren, 90," *Chicago Tribune,* April 12, 1991.
"World-Renowned Bridge Player Dies of Heart Attack," Associated Press, April 12, 1991.
"Charles Goren, 90, Bridge Expert, Dies," *New York Times,* April 12, 1991.
"Bridge," *New York Times,* April 21, 1991.
"Obituary: Charles Goren," *The Independent* (U.K.), April 25, 1991.

105 Bob Hamman on the development of the game—"My level of play with the Aces when they were at their peak wouldn't be good enough to win as often as I win today . . .":
Hamman and Manley, *At the Table,* 303.

Chapter Eight—The Kids Are Alright in Gatlinburg

110 Gatlinburg facts:
Gatlinburg Department of Tourism, press releases: "What Is It About Gatlinburg?" "Great Smoky Mountains National Park," and "Convention Center."

110 Gatlinburg population:
"36 Hours: Gatlinburg, Tenn.," *New York Times,* April 28, 2006.

110 Great Smoky Mountains National Park:
National Park Service Web site, "Great Smoky Mountains National Park," http://www.nps.gov/grsm/index.htm.
National Park Service leaflet, "Safety in Bear Country."

113 Gatlinburg census data:
U.S. Census Bureau, *Census 2000,* "Fact Sheet: Gatlinburg, Tennessee."

138 Hamman quote on Ryman and Wolpert—"It shows the face of bridge is changing . . .":
"Bridge: He Played a Three, and the Shift Was On," *New York Times,* November 28, 2005.

Chapter Nine—Social Studies
145 History of the Regency Whist Club:
"Regency Whist Club," *The Official Encyclopedia of Bridge,* 370.
"Bridge: New Club to Open," *New York Times,* September 6, 1936.
"Bridge Club Backers Sued by Culbertson," *New York Times,* November 13, 1937.
"Culbertsons Start Suit," *New York Times,* November 13, 1937.
"Bridge: Crockford's Passes," *New York Times,* May 1, 1938.
"Bridge: A Suit and a Countersuit Are Settled," *New York Times,* July 17, 1938.
"Contract Bridge," *New York Times,* October 28, 1961.
"Bridge," *New York Times,* June 13, 1964.
"A Little Bit of History," excerpted from the upcoming Regency club book.

146 Corporate America's Six Honchos (C.A.S.H.):
"Gatecrasher," *Daily News* (New York), April 23, 2005.
"Careful Player Moves Closer to the Top at Bear Stearns," *New York Times,* July 14, 1993.

146 Regency regulars:
"Bridge," *New York Times,* March 13, 1999.
"Where the Ace Is King," *New York Times,* June 11, 1989.

155 Bridge celebrities:
Truscott and Truscott, *New York Times Bridge Book,* 110.
"Bridge," *New York Times,* June 17, 1996.
"In the Gallery With: Isaac Mizrahi," *New York Times,* November 30, 1997.
"Players: Bridge Wins—Hands Down," *The Patriot Ledger* (Quincy, Massachusetts), November 18, 1999.
"Building a Bridge for a New Generation," *Oregonian* (Portland, Oregon), March 21, 2006.

156 Omar Sharif, bridge star and now no "slave to any passion":
"Sharif Bridge Circus," *The Official Encyclopedia of Bridge,* 410–11.
"The Rake's Progress," *salon.com,* December 8, 2003.

156 Peter Lynch on bridge: "Play bridge, poker, or hearts."
"From Lowly Caddy to Fidelity Champion," *The Times* (U.K.), October 18, 2002.

157 Michael Becker—"There is a relationship between playing bridge and
       trading options":
"Hall-of-Fame Bridge Player Finds Deck Stacked in His Favor," *Palm Beach
       Post*, March 29, 2006.

157 Michael Becker's AMEX disciples:
"'Secret Society' of Traders," *San Francisco Chronicle*, January 23, 1990.

157 Bill Gates, Warren Buffett, Sharon Osberg, and bridge:
"Bridge," *New York Times*, May 13, 1989.
"All in the Game," *Washington Times*, July 21, 1993.
"Bridge," *New York Times*, July 24, 1993.
"Corporate Clout," *Chattanooga Free Press*, August 20, 1996.
"Gates and Buffett Consider Bridge a Rich Experience," *Daily Bulletin*, Fall
       North American Bridge Championships, November 25, 1999.
"How to Trump Bill Gates and Warren Buffett," *Business 2.0*, December 1,
       2003.
"Billionaires Bank on Bridge to Trump Poker," *USA Today*, December 20,
       2005.
"The Bridge Club," *San Francisco Chronicle*, January 22, 2006.
"The World's Billionaires," *forbes.com*, March 9, 2006.
"Buffett Finds Business Success in Timeless Formula," *NPR: Morning
       Edition*, June 27, 2006.
"A $31 Billion Gift Between Friends," *New York Times*, June 27, 2006.
"Buffett's Bridge Bash Mirrors Ryder Cup," *Sunday Times* (U.K.), August
       20, 2006.
"The Forbes 400," *Forbes*, October 9, 2006.

161 Osberg's Op-Ed and the Buffett-Gates bridge program:
"Bring Bridge Back to the Table," *New York Times*, November 27, 2005.
"Billionaire and Trump of a Different Ilk," *Hawkeye* (Burlington, Iowa),
       August 3, 2006.
"Billionaires Build Bridges with Youth," *Hawkeye* (Burlington, Iowa),
       August 6, 2006.
"Fans of Bridge Get Major Helping Hand," *Omaha World-Herald*, August 6,
       2006.
"What I Did Over the Summer," *Bridge Bulletin*, October 2006.

Chapter Ten—Fear and Loafing in Las Vegas

163 The Cavendish Club in New York:
"In Bridge Circles, the Cavendish Is a Big Deal," *New York Times*, November
       21, 1980.
"Unheard of in Bridge: Cavendish Club Folds," *New York Times*, June 2, 1991.
Sontag, *Bridge Bum*, 53.

163 History of the tournament:
The Cavendish Invitational Web site, www.thecavendish.com.

165 History of the Tropicana and facts about the intersection of Tropicana
     Avenue and Las Vegas Boulevard:
Tropicana Resort and Casino press releases: "Tropicana Resort and Casino
     Fact Sheet," "Tropicana Chronology of Events," "Folies Bergere—
     History," "Tropicana Opens New Poker Room."
"Tropicana's Closing Shuts Door on History," *Las Vegas Sun*, April 2,
     2006.

167 Intersection of Tropicana Avenue and Las Vegas Boulevard:
MGM Grand Las Vegas press release: "MGM Grand Fact Sheet," "MGM
     Grand Opens New Poker Room."
New York-New York Hotel and Casino press release: "New York-New York
     Fact Sheet."
Excalibur Hotel Casino press release: "Fact Sheet," "Excalibur Expands
     Poker Room."

169 Bridge players are "widely rumored not to have mothers, having
     devoured them at birth":
From the 2006 Cavendish Invitational Pairs program.

171 John Roberts:
"John P. Roberts, 56, a Producer of Woodstock and Its Revivals," *New York
     Times*, November 2, 2001.

173 Zia on bridge players—"that rare animal, something between an artist
     and a hustler . . .":
Mahmood, *Bridge My Way*, 14.

173 Tasmanian women traveling to see Zia:
"'Let's Go to an American Tournament,'" *Daily Bulletin*, Spring North
     American Bridge Championships, April 4, 2006.

173 Zia plays last hand at Cavendish:
"Unheard of in Bridge: Cavendish Club Folds," *New York Times*, June 2,
     1991.

175 The kinds of people bidding at the Cavendish:
Sontag, *Bridge Bum*, 42, 53–54.

178 Ethical use of information in bridge:
Truscott and Truscott, *New York Times Bridge Book*, 137.

179 Lanzarotti and Buratti cheating scandal:
"A Cheating Charge Is Upheld at European Championships," *New York Times*, June 30, 2005.
"How to Undermine Opponents, Even with Good Intentions," *New York Times*, July 2, 2005.
"Sometimes, Down One Is Actually a Victory," *New York Times*, November 24, 2005.

179 International bridge scandals:
Truscott and Truscott, *New York Times Bridge Book*, 138–39, 141, 150–51, 161, 165–67.

180 Anticheating measures—and their success:
Ibid., 156, 160, 169.

184 Zia going to bed early:
"Changed Days, Indeed," Cavendish Invitational bulletin, May 12, 2006.

189 Zia's sleeping habits at tournaments:
Mahmood, *Bridge My Way*, 49.

Chapter Eleven—London Bridge Isn't Falling Down, But It Might Come Second to Fishing, Part I

200 Wodehouse on London—"A city like New York makes the new arrival feel at home in half an hour...":
Wodehouse, *Psmith in the City*, 25–26.

200 London as the world's third-most expensive city:
"A Family Vacation in London, Guided by Scrooge," *New York Times*, April 23, 2006.

201 Zia:
"New Zone Appears Certain for '81 World Tournament," *New York Times*, May 1, 1981.
"U.S. Wins Bermuda Bowl, But Women's Team Loses," *New York Times*, October 31, 1981.
"Pakistan's Team is Called World Play's Top Surprise," *New York Times*, November 2, 1981.
"Larger Than Life," *Bridge Bulletin*, February 2006.
"The China Syndrome," *Bridge Bulletin*, June 2006.

201 Zia and President Musharraf:
"Night of the Generals," *Daily Bulletin*, Summer North American Bridge Championships, July 20, 2006.

202 Hamman on rubber bridge:
Hamman and Manley, *At the Table*, 19.

203 Woman on the Côte d'Azur was like "picking up a ten-card suit for the
      first time . . .":
Mahmood, *Bridge My Way*, 72.

203 Zia on bridge players—"Cricketers and footballers might need a
      bodyguard to keep girls out of their rooms . . .":
Ibid., 191–92.

204 Pessimistic Pakistani player has to buy new return ticket:
Ibid., 168.

209 Zia against the computers:
"Bridge," *The Independent*, April 9, 2000.
Mahmood, *Bridge My Way*, 11.

211 The sale of Forward:
"The Donor List," *The Guardian*, June 2, 2006.

211 History of the Garrick Club and the founding idea that "it would be
      better that ten unobjectionable men should be excluded . . .":
From history of the club posted on the club's Web site: www.garrickclub.
      co.uk/aboutus.asp.

212 The Portland Club:
"Bridge: When Bidding Six Is Less Costly Than Five," *New York Times*,
      September 27, 1987.
"Bridge," *New York Times*, September 5, 1994.
"Portland Club of London," *The Official Encyclopedia of Bridge*, 350.
Daniels, *Golden Age of Contract Bridge*, 37–40.
"The Portland Club," *Bridge Plus*, January 1994.

213 The Anglo-American bridge match of 1930:
Daniels, *Golden Age of Contract Bridge*, 140–41.
"Bridge: Ghosts and a Phantom," *New York Times*, June 8, 1986.

214 Zia says, "The biggest insult you can pay someone is to call him a
      professional":
Mahmood, *Bridge My Way*, 112.

214 On not admitting a pro at the Portland—"I don't mind subsidizing his
      racehorses, but I won't pay his rent":
Sheehan, *Big Game*, 2.

Chapter Twelve—London Bridge Isn't Falling Down, But It Might Come Second to Fishing, Part II

222 Who's playing bridge in the U.K.:
"Play Bridge," *Washington Post,* February 29, 2004.
"Bridge the Latest Big Deal," *The Scotsman,* June 20, 2000.
"Sex, Bridge, and Swapping," *The Times* (U.K.), June 19, 2000.
"Lonely Hearts Let Bridge Do the Trick," *The Independent* (U.K.), May 23, 1999.

222 Colin Greenwood on bridge—"There's more pressure playing a four diamond contract than playing in front of 2,000 people":
"Anyone Can Play Cards," *The Island Ear* (Long Island, New York), August 16–29, 1993.

229 Susanna Gross's column on Bob Hamman's bridge memory:
"Total Recall," *The Spectator,* July 30, 2005.

231 Susanna's column on Neil Mendoza's bad hand:
"Freak Conditions," *The Spectator,* June 3, 2006.

232 "Ponies," "monkeys," and "sticks" and the rules and trips of TGR's:
Sheehan, *Big Game,* iv, 17, 28, 73, 99.

233 The Great Irving Rose:
"Bridge," *New York Times,* February 19, 1998.
Sheehan, *Big Game,* iv.

235 The average winnings at rubber bridge:
Sheehan, *Big Game,* 2.

Chapter Thirteen—East Side Story

242 Honors' record attendance in 1999:
"Bridge," *New York Times,* June 29, 2000.

242 Beverly-Honors bridge club feud:
"Playing Dirty Tricks," *Crain's New York Business,* September 30, 1996.
"Bridge," *New York Times,* June 1, 1998.
"Bridge," *New York Times,* September 30, 2000.

Chapter Fourteen—The Battles of Gettysburg

253 Battle reenactment versus Bike Week:
"Hotel Managers Furious About Postponement," *Gettysburg Times,* June 29, 2006.
"Reenactment Crowds Sparse," *Gettysburg Times,* July 10, 2006.

254 The proposed casino in Gettysburg:
"Gettysburg Casino Plan Starts Whole New Battle," *New York Times*, June 23, 2005.
"In Gettysburg Casino Fight, Two Visions of Tourism Collide," *Washington Post*, April 6, 2006.
"Neighbors Not Divided by Casino Signs," *York Daily Record*, June 18, 2006.
"Gambling with Gettysburg," *Civil War Times*, July 2006.
"Boro Alters Casino Financial Agreement," *Gettysburg Times*, July 11, 2006.

254 Slot machine statistics:
"Sit and Spin," *Atlantic Monthly*, December 2005.

263 Eisenhower and bridge:
Sontag, *Bridge Bum*, 87.
Truscott and Truscott, *New York Times Bridge Book*, 106, 110.
"Bridge: Another Reason to Like Ike," *New York Times*, September 27, 1992.
"Declaring a Passion," *The Times* (U.K.), October 1, 2005.

264 Eisenhower—"At the moment the Thomasville battle rages, with inconclusive results":
Eisenhower, Dwight D. to Alfred Maximilian Gruenther, February 20, 1956. In *The Papers of Dwight David Eisenhower*, eds. L. Galambos and D. van Ee, doc. 1756. World Wide Web facsimile by The Dwight D. Eisenhower Memorial Commission of the print edition; Baltimore, Maryland: The Johns Hopkins University Press, 1996, http://www.eisenhower memorial.org/presidential-papers/first-term/documents/1756.cfm.

264 Eisenhower—"I am annoyed. I am looking for revenge. I expect help":
Eisenhower, Dwight D. to Alfred Maximilian Gruenther, February 25, 1956. In *The Papers of Dwight David Eisenhower*, eds. L. Galambos and D. van Ee, doc. 1758. World Wide Web facsimile by The Dwight D. Eisenhower Memorial Commission of the print edition; Baltimore, Maryland: The Johns Hopkins University Press, 1996, http://www.eisenhower memorial.org/presidential-papers/first-term/documents/1758.cfm.

264 Eisenhower decrees a friend, "Professor and Instructor in the Laws, Rules, Techniques, and Skullduggery of Bridge":
Eisenhower, Dwight D. to Alfred Maximilian Gruenther, April 30, 1958. In *The Papers of Dwight David Eisenhower*, eds. L. Galambos and D. van Ee, doc. 670. World Wide Web facsimile by The Dwight D. Eisenhower Memorial Commission of the print edition; Baltimore, Maryland: The Johns Hopkins University Press, 1996, http://www.eisenhowermemo rial.org/presidential-papers/second-term/documents/670.cfm.

264 Eisenhower—"Life gets more difficult by the minute . . .":
Eisenhower, Dwight D. Personal to Alfred Maximilian Gruenther,
    November 2, 1956. In *The Papers of Dwight David Eisenhower*, eds.
    L. Galambos and D. van Ee, doc. 2064. World Wide Web facsimile by
    The Dwight D. Eisenhower Memorial Commission of the print edition;
    Baltimore, Maryland: The Johns Hopkins University Press, 1996, http://
    www.eisenhowermemorial.org/presidential-papers/first-term/documents
    /2064.cfm.

265 The horn on the runabout at the Eisenhower farm:
"Plowing and Politics," *Time*, December 12, 1955.

Chapter Fifteen–Oh, the Sunny Saturdays I Have Missed

274 Results for the Worldwide Bridge Contest:
"It's a Wonderful Worldwide Event," *Bridge Bulletin*, August 2006.

Chapter Sixteen–Wild Times in the Windy City, *or* My Travels with Tina

286 Example article from the *Daily Bulletin:*
"Older Couple Finds Bridge, Romance Online," *Daily Bulletin*, Summer
    North American Bridge Championships, July 23, 2006.

290 Harriette Buckman an ACBL member since 1950:
"On a Mission," *Bridge Bulletin*, January 2006.

292 Bob Hamman on full disclosure:
Hamman and Manley, *At the Table*, 303.

293 ACBL's School Bridge Lesson Series program reaching sixty-five
    hundred students:
"What I Did Over the Summer," *Bridge Bulletin*, October 2006.

293 2005 report on the ACBL's School Bridge Lesson Series program:
"From the CEO," *Bridge Bulletin*, February 2006.

293 Illinois study of bridge and standardized test scores:
"Statistically Speaking," *Bridge Bulletin*, August 2006.

295 ACBL and AARP:
"A Partnership Game: ACBL and AARP," *Bridge Bulletin*, June 2006.

297 History of NABCs in Chicago:
"Chicago NABCs: A Rich History," *Daily Bulletin*, Summer North
    American Bridge Championships, July 15, 2006.

297 Statistics for the 2006 Chicago NABC were provided to me by the
ACBL, though I also found some here:
Daily Bulletin, Summer North American Bridge Championships, July 24,
2006.

297 Details of College Bridge Championships players and event:
"Beavers and Tigers and Bears, Oh My!" *Bridge Bulletin*, June 2006.
"Michigan Wins Collegiate Crown," *Daily Bulletin*, Summer North
American Bridge Championships, July 17, 2006.
"A Collegiate Title for Michigan, with Princeton Close Behind," *New York
Times*, July 29, 2006.

298 History of the Spingold:
"Spingold Knockout Teams," *Daily Bulletin*, Summer North American
Bridge Championships, July 17, 2006.

298 Hamman on the Spingold—"The Spingold isn't a tea party. We play
hardball there":
Hamman and Manley, *At the Table*, 24.

298 Hamman hoping to compete against Lorenzo Lauria:
"For 6,000 Players, It's More Than Just a Game," *Chicago Tribune*, July 14,
2006.

298 Hamman's record number of Spingold wins:
"No Letup for Nickell, 2004 Spingold Champs," *Daily Bulletin*, Summer
North American Bridge Championships, July 19, 2004.

298 One instance of the ACBL's "eleven-day-long bridge parties" line:
"Big-Time Bridge Fun in Chi-Town," *Bridge Bulletin*, July 2006.

299 Zia on the NABCs—"an orgy—of bridge," "scruffy," "anti-social,"
etc.:
Mahmood, *Bridge My Way*, 235.

300 Details of "Play Bridge with Zia" fund-raiser:
"A Chance to Play with Zia," *Bridge Bulletin*, July 2006.

303 Meckstroth as Player of the Decade for the 1990s:
"Unofficial But Hard-Won Title," *New York Times*, February 7, 2000.

303 Meckwell "considered by most to be the best pair in the world":
"The Dealing Begins, Championships on the Line," *New York Times*,
October 24, 2005.

303 Hamman on Meckstroth—"Meckstroth is a tiger":
Hamman and Manley, *At the Table*, 3.

303 Alder on Meckwell—"They bid on hands that most players would pass
     in their sleep":
"The Daring Meckwell, Unafraid to Overreach," *New York Times,* December
     1, 2005.

307 Caddies heading to Omaha:
"Trio's Motto: Have Mini-Van, Will Caddy," *Daily Bulletin,* Summer North
     American Bridge Championships, July 23, 2006.

308 Nickell team record in the Spingold:
"No Letup for Nickell, 2004 Spingold Champs," *Daily Bulletin,* Summer
     North American Bridge Championships, July 19, 2004.
"Close Finish Concludes Bridge Tournament," *New York Times,* July 25,
     2006.

312 Fatal play of the king of hearts and the final boards of the Spingold final:
"The First Trick Proves Pivotal in a Decisive Spingold Deal," *New York
     Times,* July 27, 2006.
"Nickell Wins Another Spingold," *Daily Bulletin,* Summer North American
     Bridge Championship, July 24, 2006.

313 Meckstroth wisdom—"You have to accept that bridge is not a perfect
     game—it's a game of mistakes":
Meckstroth and Smith, *Win the Bermuda Bowl with Me*, 55.

315 Bob Hamman on why the game is great—"In bridge, there's no way to
     lie down on the ball and play it cozy . . .":
Hamman and Manley, *At the Table*, 298.

BIBLIOGRAPHY

Bayone, Jeff, and Amanda Beesley. *It's Bridge, Baby: How to Be a Player in Ten Easy Lessons.* New York: Riverhead Books, 1998.

Daniels, David. *The Golden Age of Contract Bridge.* New York: Stein & Day, 1980.

Frey, Richard L., Alan F. Truscott, and Amalya L. Kearse, eds. *The Official Encyclopedia of Bridge* (Third Edition). New York: Crown Publishers, 1976.

Hamman, Bob, and Brent Manley. *At the Table: The Autobiography of the World's #1-Rated Bridge Player.* 1994. Reprint, Memphis: DBM Publications, 1996.

Keaton, Buster, and Charles Samuels. *My Wonderful World of Slapstick.* 1960. Reprint, New York: Da Capo Press, 1982.

Mahmood, Zia. *Bridge My Way.* Little Falls, N.J.: Natco Press, 1994.

Meckstroth, Jeff, and Marc Smith. *Win the Bermuda Bowl with Me.* Toronto: Master Point Press, 2001.

Sheehan, Robert. *The Big Game: Rubber Bridge in a London Club.* Buckinghamshire, England: Five Aces Books, 1999.

Sontag, Alan. *The Bridge Bum: My Life and Play.* 1977. Reprint, Toronto: Master Point Press, 2003.

Stern, Philip Van Doren, ed. *The Portable Poe.* 1945. Reprint, New York: Penguin Books, 1977.

Truscott, Alan, and Dorothy Truscott. *The New York Times Bridge Book: An Anecdotal History of the Development, Personalities, and Strategies of the World's Most Popular Card Game.* New York: St. Martin's Griffin, 2002.

Wodehouse, P. G. *Psmith in the City.* 1910. Reprint, New York: Overlook Press, 2003.

Woollcott, Alexander. *While Rome Burns.* 1934. Reprint, New York: Grosset & Dunlap, 1936.